International Relations

1914-1995

TONY REA

AND

JOHN WRIGHT

OXFORD UNIVERSITY PRESS

Oxford University Press, Great Clarendon Street, Oxford
OX2 6DP

Oxford New York
Athens Auckland Bangkok Bogota Bombay
Buenos Aires Calcutta Cape Town Dar es Salaam
Delhi Florence Hong Kong Istanbul Karachi
Kuala Lumpur Madras Madrid Melbourne
Mexico City Nairobi Paris Singapore
Taipei Tokyo Toronto

and associated companies in
Berlin Ibadan

Oxford is a trade mark of Oxford University Press

© Oxford University Press 1997

ISBN 0 19 917167 X

Printed in Spain

Author's Acknowledgements
The authors would like to thank John Liardet and Matthew
Rea for reading the script at an early stage, and Emily Burn
for providing some of the sources for Chapter 11.

In memory of Bob Bland

Publisher's Acknowledgements

The publishers would like to thank the following for their
permission to reproduce the following photographs:
Brian Aris/Camera Press: 183
Associated Press/ Topham Picture Source: Cover, 164,
    165r, 167, /L.Cironneau 186, 189t, /D. Paquin 192bl,
    /E. Warshavsky 192br
Barnaby's Picture Library: 28c.
Fritz Behrendt/ Courtesy the Centre for the Study of
    Cartoons & Caricature, University of Kent: 188b
Belgian Tourist Office: 14t.
Camera Press: 119, 160, 176, 182,
Camera Press/Imperial War Museum: 52, 56, 180b,
Corbis-Bettmann/UPI: 84, 89, 90bl, 91t, 110b,
European Commission: 138
Mary Evans Picture Library: 27b
Express Newspapers/ Courtesy Centre for the Study of
    Cartoons & Caricature, University of Kent: 50b, 135l,
    136t
John Frost Historical Newspaper Service: 71t, 150
Philip J. Griffiths/ Magnum: 161
J.V. Hasselt/Sygma: 83b
Hulton Getty: 9t, 29t, 35br, 46, 53, 58, 82, 97bl, 112cr,
    114t, 125t, 140, 150b, 156, 181t, 195b, 202bl, 202tr,
    204, 205l, 211r,
Illustrated London News Picture Library: 32, 198
Imperial War Museum: 14b, 20t, 21t & b, 22br, 23t, 30b,
    35bl, 64t, 72,74, 76, 81t, 144tl, 197, 199, 200, 201,
    206, 207, 208t, 210, 211, 212t
David King: 8t, 10t, 95t
Joseph Koudelka/ Magnum: 117t
Eric Lessing/Magnum: 114b
Mansell Collection: 17t & b,
Don McCullin/Magnum: 166l
Mirror Syndication International: 117b
Museum of London: 205r
Nasm/Sygma: 83t
National Portrait Gallery: 59tr
Popperfoto: 79r, 86t & b, 95bl, 101, 103, 111b, 134, 147,
    172, 173, /Reuter 191b, /Reuter/Haim Azoulay 193l,
    193r, 208b,
Punch: 37b, 42t & tr, 59tl, 92t, 125b, 128, 135tr,
Marc Riboud/Camera Press: 160r
Joel Robine/Popperfoto: 177
School of Slavonic Studies Library: 95br, 97tr, 105, 129
Simplicissimus: 98b, 112
Solo Syndication and Literary Agency/Courtesy Centre for
    the Study of Cartoons & Caricature University of Kent:
    38tr, 45b, 50t, 67, 212b
Sport and General: 209
Topham Picture Source: 29b, 33t, 57t, 61, 70, 75, 85, 92b,
    98t, 100t, 116, 120, 121, 144tr, 151, 153, 155, 158,
    163t & b, 170t,
United Nations: 170 bl, bc & br, 174, /Y. Nagata 175,
Admiral Sandy Woodward/Harper Collins: 154

The publisher's have made every effort to trace the
copyright holders of all photographers, but in some cases
have been unable to do so. They would welcome ant
information which would enable them to rectify this.
Designed by Peter Tucker, Holbrook Design Oxford Ltd.

All illustrations are by Jeff Edwards and Peter Tucker

Contents

Preface

The authors of *International Relations 1914–1995* are both Chief Examiners for the new GCSE examinations in Modern World History, and they have written this book specifically to meet the demands of these new syllabuses.

There are many different ways of using the book, but the first chapter is seen as an essential starting point for all users. There is some deliberate duplication of subject matter in order to preserve the integrity of the topics covered, and where this has been necessary the authors have tried to present similar material in different ways, using different sources.

To make it easier to understand new material there is a comprehensive glossary and an index, which allows cross-referencing between the chapters.

The sources, questions and exercises which have been built into each chapter will make a sound preparation for GCSE history examinations.

1 *I*ntroduction to international relations in the 20th century

The best way to use this book

International relations is really the history of how the world has been divided between those countries which have the most power at any particular time. This is sometimes called the World Order. This book is arranged into four sections which reflect how the World Order has changed in the twentieth century, and what particular problems have influenced international relations. These sections are:

A   The Old Order, 1914–1920
B   Challenges to the Old Order, 1919–1945
C   Towards a New World Order, 1945–1995
D   Case Studies in International Relations, 1914–1995

Look at the flow diagram below. This shows the main events in international relations in the twentieth century which are on the English GCSE syllabuses. It also shows which chapters cover these topics. There is some overlap between chapters, and you should be prepared to look around

the book for extra background material if you wish to do well at GCSE. The diagram will help you to do this and the text contains references to other chapters that are helpful. You can also use the index, of course. As you can see from the diagram, international relations in the twentieth century really stem from what happened in Europe at the end of the First World War; this is explained in this Chapter and Chapters 2 and 3. It may be that these three topics are part of your GCSE syllabus and you will study them in depth. If they are not, we suggest that you look at these chapters anyway, and work through the exercises in them, in order to get to grips with the topic as a whole.

1   Find out which GCSE syllabus you are following and which topics you will be studying. Make a list of these topics.
2   Which chapters of this book do you think will be essential to your study?
3   Which chapters might be useful as background material?

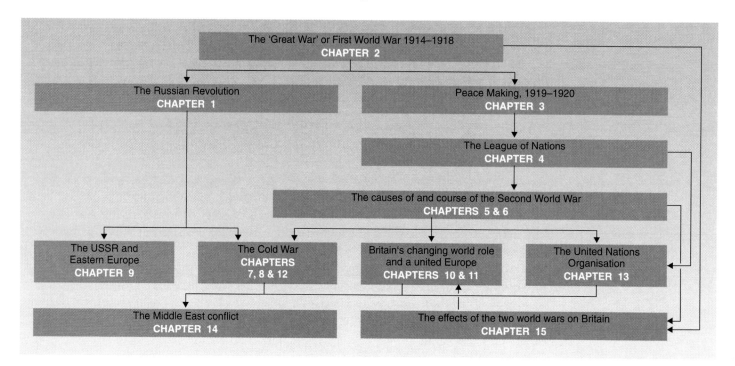

What are international relations?

A

The Observer 21 April 1996   **WORLD NEWS | 21**

Nato leaders are ready to embrace only the Czech Republic, Hungary and Poland as new members of the alliance before the end of the century

West carves up Europe in a new Yalta

To help Boris Yeltsin win Russia's presidential election in June, the West is soft-pedalling on plans to extend Nato and the EU east. **John Palmer** in Strasbourg explains the background to the post-Cold War settlement

B

Middle East Crisis

'Making peace is not a military operation'

The celebrated Israeli author **Amos Oz** is sharply critical of his country's policy of fighting fire with fire.

As envoys seek a ceasefire, **Shyam Bhatia** in Beirut and **Derek Brown** in Qiryat Shmona report on the agony on both sides.

One wet Sunday afternoon in April 1996 we were putting the final touches to this book when we saw the newspaper headlines you can see above. They seemed strange. As you can see for yourself, they were about fighting between Israel and the Lebanese and a new carve up of eastern Europe between Russia and the west. The strange thing was that we had just written a history book which covered the Middle East conflict, the break up of the Soviet Union, the European Union, and NATO. It had even covered the Yalta Conference. Now all these things were in the news again, and just when we thought we had finished!

But that is what history is like, especially the history of international relations in the twentieth century. It never really finishes. Yet it does show how useful this book is. The background to everything mentioned in these headlines is in this book.

The headlines also help us to understand what international relations are. Look at these phrases taken from the headlines. What are they about?

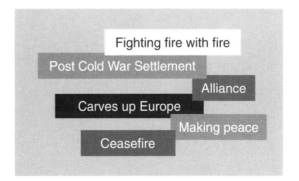

Put simply, international relations are the way countries relate to each other. What things do countries do in their relations with each other? What kind of agreements do they make? What do they do to try to keep the peace? These are the kinds of questions you will find the answers to. Of course, you will also be able to find out about the main events in the international relations of the twentieth century.

The Russian Revolution, 1917

Why is the Russian Revolution so important?

There are three events which took place early in the twentieth century which affected international relations in such an important way that you will not understand the topic without knowing about them. Look at the flow diagram on page 4. These three events are highlighted on the diagram.

The first event is the First World War, look what it led to and how it influenced other events. Both of the others happened as a result of the First World War. One was the Peace Treaties of 1919 and 1920 which ended the war, especially the Treaty of Versailles. You can see from the diagram why these were important. As you can see, there is a full chapter on this.

The third great event is the Russian Revolution of 1917. This Revolution brought the Communist Party into power in Russia and caused great tension between Russia and the Capitalist countries, especially Britain and the USA. This affected British foreign policy in the late 1930s and also explains The Cold War which dominated international relations between 1945 and 1989. The Russian Revolution and the Soviet Union 1917-1945 is an optional study in many GCSE syllabuses, and so you might study it in lots of depth using other books. For this reason it is not covered in great detail here. We have just provided you with enough information about the Revolution to enable you to understand international relations properly.

The causes of the Russian Revolution.

The Revolution had been brewing for a long time. Russia was ruled over by the Romanov family. They were tsars of Russia. (A tsar was like a king or an emperor.) In 1881 Tsar Alexander II was killed in a bomb attack. Then in 1905 there were strikes, riots and other protests in St. Petersburg, the Russian capital city. Why was there so much unrest in Russia?

a   The Russian tsars were absolute rulers. This means they had total power over the people. Many people in Russia began to resent this and wanted a more democratic system of government. In 1905 there was a small scale revolution which did bring some changes. There was then a State Duma, or parliament, which was elected to advise the Tsar. However, the Tsar did not have to follow its advice and he could dismiss the Duma when he wanted to.

b   Russia was undergoing an industrial revolution, rather like the one which had happened in Britain in the late eighteenth century (think back to your Key Stage 3 history). This brought about many pressures. There was now a working class living in poor quality housing in the Russian cities and working long hours for little wages in dirty and dangerous factories. Many of these people wanted change.

There was also a middle class who wanted change. Factory owners, and professional people like doctors, teachers, and lawyers, realised that they had little freedom and few rights. They saw that people like themselves living in other countries (such as Britain, France and Germany) had many more democratic rights. They began to demand the same. They wanted the Tsar to introduce a parliament in which they could become representatives and elections in which they could all vote.

c There was a Communist Party which wanted to go further and replace the Tsar's Government and the Duma with a Communist Government which would support the ordinary people. They also wanted the factories and farms to be controlled and organised by the Government.

d The Russian system of agriculture was very old fashioned. It was like Britain's had been before the Tudors! Russia had lots of land and much of it was very good farming land. Most of this land was owned by the Tsar, the Church or the nobility. The land was farmed by millions of peasants, poor farmers who did not own land of their own. The way they farmed was also old fashioned. They used man power and horses. There was no modern machinery, little use of fertilizers, and no selective breeding of livestock. For centuries this had not mattered. But when the Industrial Revolution occurred, more food was needed to feed the town and city dwellers. The system could not cope. To add to these problems, Russia was so big that it was very difficult to collect the food from the farms and distribute it to the towns and cities.

e Then, in 1914, the war against Germany began. Peasants were drafted into the army. More workers were needed in the factories to make weapons. More food was needed for city dwellers, soldiers, and millions of horses at the front. But there were not as many peasants to do the work. Soon there were food shortages. The price of food went up dramatically. This is called inflation. The war went very badly and there were many defeats for the Russian army. In 1915 the Tsar took over command of the army himself, but this made no difference. In fact it made matters worse. He left his wife, the Tsarina, in charge of the Government. She was influenced by a religious man called Rasputin, who many people regarded as strange or even evil. This made the Russian royal family unpopular.

The causes of the Revolutions of 1917

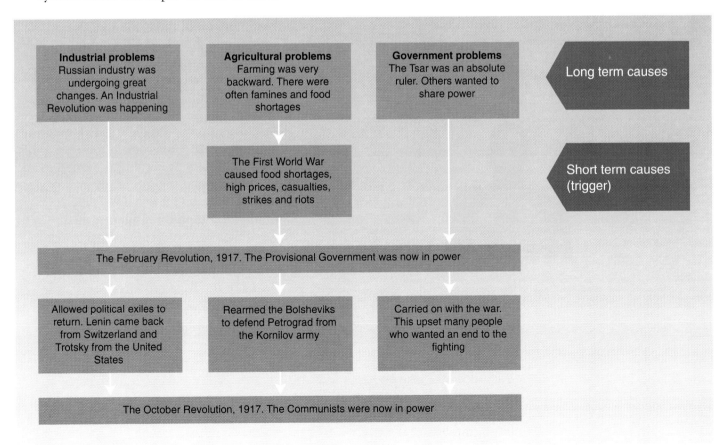

The Revolution of February 1917

The October Revolution of 1917

There were strikes and riots in Petrograd and the soldiers and sailors joined in on the side of the workers. The strikes were organised by the Petrograd Soviet. Some Communists were very active in this Soviet. (Soviet means council of workers.) The Duma members and some army officers persuaded the Tsar to abdicate, and he eventually did so. His brother was invited to become the next Tsar, but he chose not to. Instead, the Duma took over the Government. It called itself the Provisional Government and Kerensky became the Prime Minister of Russia.

Kerensky's government decided to carry on with the war against Germany and did nothing to give the people what they wanted: cheaper food in the cities and land for the peasants.

▲ Lenin giving a speech on a poster from 1920

In April 1917 Lenin, one of the Communist leaders, came back to Russia. He had been in Switzerland because the Tsar's police force wanted to arrest him. He made a famous speech in which he promised the people 'Peace, land and bread.' For five months there was a struggle between the Communists and the Provisional Government. In July the Communists tried to take over but failed. Many of their leaders were arrested or had to flee. Lenin fled to Finland. Then in September, a supporter of the Tsar, called General Kornilov, attacked Petrograd with an army. The Provisional Government gave weapons to the Communists because it needed them to help to defend the capital. Kornilov was defeated and, in October 1917, the Communists used force against the Provisional Government and overthrew them. Lenin then set up a Communist Government.

In 1918 the Russians ended their war with Germany at the Treaty of Brest-Litovsk. This angered the British and French.

Pressures on the Tsar, 1917

From the people

Demonstrators were demanding the Tsar should go

The war was going badly and the people held him responsible

Rumours about the Tsarina and Rasputin

Strikes and riots in the cities. Mutiny in the army

Should I abdicate?

From his advisers

Many thought a change of person at the top (e.g. the Tsar's brother) would calm the country down

Many nobles saw the opportunity to gain more power for themselves

Many believed Nicholas to be a weak leader. Someone stronger was needed

The Civil War, 1918-1921

The Communists did not control all of Russia at first. They had to fight 'white' armies made up of supporters of the Tsar, supporters of the Provisional Government, and groups who wanted independence from Russia, such as the Poles. There were also soldiers from Britain, France, Japan, and the USA sent to fight against the Communists

These are Russian soldiers captured by the British in 1918. They are being held prisoner in an Allied prisoner of war camp inside Russia.

The Civil War campaigns in Russia, 1918-21. This shows how the 'western' allies intervened against the Communists in Russia. Communist leaders, especially Stalin, never forgave, or trusted, the west after this.

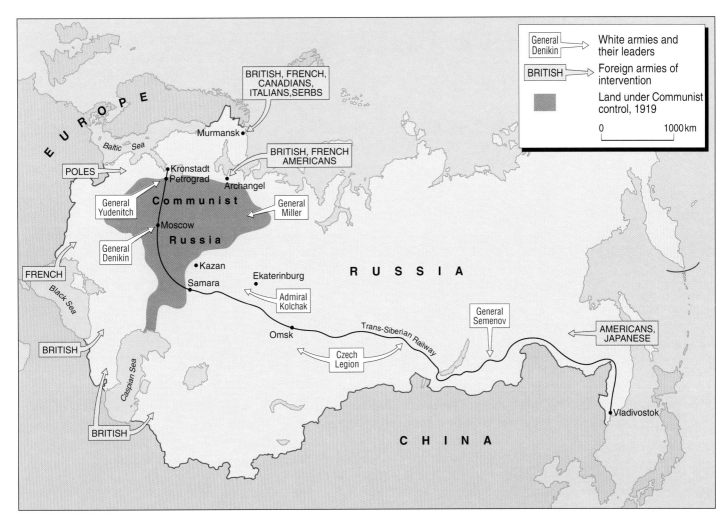

Eventually the Communists were successful, and, by 1921, were in control of the whole country. In 1923 Russia became known as the Union of Soviet Socialist Republics (USSR), also called the Soviet Union.

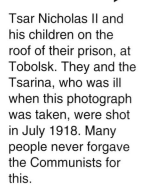

Tsar Nicholas II and his children on the roof of their prison, at Tobolsk. They and the Tsarina, who was ill when this photograph was taken, were shot in July 1918. Many people never forgave the Communists for this.

Between 1917 and 1930 the Communists developed a particular kind of country and society in the USSR.

- **Government.** The Communist Government was based on a one party system. The election held in November 1917 did not give the Communists very many seats in the National Assembly, but it did not matter because Lenin abolished the Assembly. He replaced it with a Congress of Soviets and a Council of Peoples Commissars. All the members of these were members of the Communist Party.
- **The Economy.** Soviet industry and agriculture was controlled by the Government. The State owned all the land and factories. Managers were Government employees and the workers worked directly for the state. The Government decided what had to be manufactured and what should be grown.
- **Society.** There was very little freedom for individual people. There were no free elections. The newspapers and radio, and later the television, were controlled by the Government which also controlled education and had its own propaganda agency. The police were controlled by the State and were very severe on anybody who dared to speak out against the Government. After the death of Lenin, Stalin became the leader of the USSR. Stalin became a figure almost worshipped by the people. His pictures were to be found everywhere. He was like a father figure to the whole country and there was a deliberate attempt to develop a 'cult of personality' around Stalin.

The effects of the Russian Revolution on international relations

The whole point of finding out something about these events in Russia is to see how they affected international relations later in the twentieth century.

a The success of the Soviet State under a Communist Government was seen as a threat by the western Capitalist countries, like Britain and the USA. They were in very many ways the total opposite of the Soviet Union. Their Governments were democratic and their economies were run along Capitalist, free enterprise lines.

b This threat was made worse by the fact that Communist ideas were all about world revolution. Slogans like 'workers of the world unite' made the western democracies very frightened. In 1919, the Comintern, an international Communist movement, was formed and there was an attempted Communist revolution in Germany.

c The Soviet Union also felt threatened by the western countries. There was already a Russian fear of the west, which had attacked Russia in 1854 and 1914. The British, French, and the Americans had also sent soldiers to try to defeat the Communists in the Civil War.

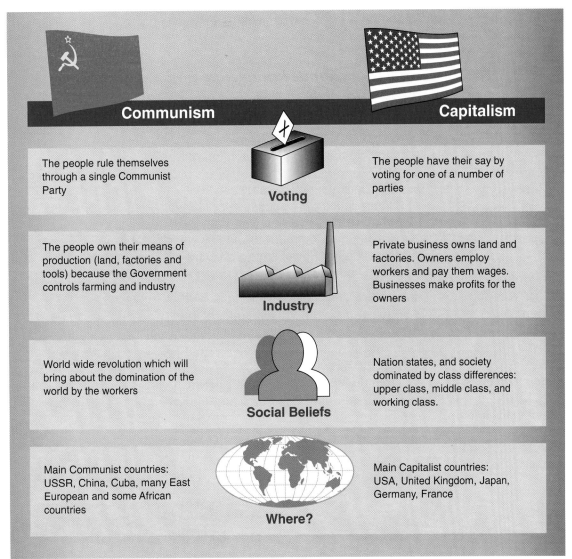

The differences between Communism and Capitalism

Communism		Capitalism
The people rule themselves through a single Communist Party	**Voting**	The people have their say by voting for one of a number of parties
The people own their means of production (land, factories and tools) because the Government controls farming and industry	**Industry**	Private business owns land and factories. Owners employ workers and pay them wages. Businesses make profits for the owners
World wide revolution which will bring about the domination of the world by the workers	**Social Beliefs**	Nation states, and society dominated by class differences: upper class, middle class, and working class.
Main Communist countries: USSR, China, Cuba, many East European and some African countries	**Where?**	Main Capitalist countries: USA, United Kingdom, Japan, Germany, France

So it seems that the Russian Revolution, and the establishment of a Soviet State, caused a great deal of mistrust between the Soviet Union on the one hand and the western, Capitalist democracies on the other. This can be seen in many ways during the following years.

i Communist Russia was not at first recognised as a state by the west. This resulted in Russia not being allowed to join the League of Nations which was set up after the First World War. In fact, it was not until 1934 that the Soviet Union was admitted to the League.

ii Britain was very distant towards the USSR during the 1920s and 1930s; and in the late 1930s, when the USSR wanted to make a pact with Britain against Nazi Germany, Britain refused. This was because of distrust.

iii Britain, the USA, and the USSR did become allies against Germany from 1941 to 1945. But as soon as the war was over, relations between them again deteriorated because of mutual distrust. The west believed the USSR was trying to spread Communism when it dominated the east European countries (see Chapter 9.) The Soviet Union believed the west was trying to spread Capitalism when the USA announced the Truman Doctrine and Marshall Plan in 1947; and were convinced of the USA's bullying tactics when the Americans announced their possession of the atom bomb in 1945. The tense relationship between the USA and the Soviet Union after 1945 is called the Cold War (see Chapters 7 and 8)

4 Why was the Soviet Union frightened by the west?

5 Why did the western democracies feel threatened by the USSR?

6 Explain how the Russian Revolution has affected international relations in the twentieth century.

GCSE questions

You are going to take a GCSE examination at some time and it will help you if you are familiar with the type of questions you are likely to come across. All of the questions may use sources to help you, but the questions can be broken down into three main types:

A Questions which focus on testing your knowledge and understanding of history.

B Questions which ask you about interpretations of history.

C Questions which concentrate on the skills you need to use sources well.

Here are some examples of GCSE type questions. They are all about the Russian Revolution. Try to identify the target of each question before you answer it as this will help you to see what you have to do to gain high marks.

Questions about knowledge and understanding

7 Describe Russia before the Revolutions of 1917.

8 Why did the Tsar abdicate in February 1917?

9 Explain in your own words why the Communists were successful in 1917?

10 What was the Russian Civil War and why did the Communists win this war?

11 Describe the Soviet state set up by Lenin and Stalin.

Sometimes, especially with longer, essay type questions, you will get some help in forming an answer. For example, the questions of one Examinations Group often begin like this -

Use the words in the boxes below to help you to explain why the Communists were successful in 1917:

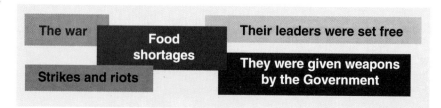

The war   Food shortages   Their leaders were set free

Strikes and riots   They were given weapons by the Government

Questions about interpretations

12 Many historians have argued that the First World War brought about the Russian Revolution in 1917. Others say that the war delayed a revolution which might have happened earlier. Explain how it is possible for historians to hold such different interpretations of the causes of the Russian Revolution.

13 Many people in Russia were pleased when the Communists won the Civil War in 1921, but others were very angry. Explain why Russian people held such different views.

Questions about sources

Study the following sources and then answer the questions which follow.

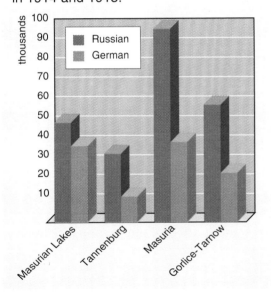

Deaths in major battles in 1914 and 1915.

- Russian
- German

(Masurian Lakes, Tannenburg, Masuria, Gorlice-Tarnow)

If we have three days of serious fighting, we may run out of ammunition altogether. If we had a rest from fighting for a month our condition would greatly improve. What I say is strictly to you. Please do not say a word of this to anyone.

From a letter from the Tsar to his wife, the Tsarina, in September 1915.

Now, before I forget, I must give you a message from our friend [Rasputin]. It comes from what he saw in the night. He begs you to order an advance towards Riga. He says it is necessary or the Germans will dig in firmly for the winter.

From a letter from the Tsarina to the Tsar in October 1915.

The Tsar was even more absent-minded than at the last meeting. He was constantly yawning and took no part in the discussion. It came out that the problems of supplies for the soldiers were caused by frequent changes of Minister. Most were appointed to offices of which they had no knowledge. They were then moved before they could bring any organisation into being.

From the memoirs of a Russian General, Brusilov, describing a meeting with the Tsar in 1916.

14 What does Source C tell you about how Russia was progressing in the war up to 1915?

15 What can you learn from Source F about the problems facing the Russian army in 1916?

16 Sources D and E are both private letters. Explain how this might affect the reliability of these sources.

17 Which of the Sources, C, D, E, or F, is the most useful for understanding why the War was going badly for Russia? Explain your answer.

18 Source E mentions 'our friend [Rasputin].' Did Rasputin play an important part in either the War or the Revolution. Explain your answer.

You should notice that GCSE questions often ask you to explain your answers. In GCSE History the marks are awarded for the quality of your explanation. It often will not matter whether you agree or disagree with something, for it will be the strength of your explanation that will earn you marks. In GCSE examinations you will be told how many marks each question is worth and you should use this as a guide to how much time to spend on a question and how much to write.

2 *The war to end all wars 1914–1918*

A

A recent photograph of the Menin Gate at Ypres

A photograph of Ypres during the First World War

B

The Menin Gate was built after the First World War as a memorial to those British and Commonwealth soldiers who died near the Belgian town of Ypres (also known as Ieper) between 1914 and 1918. It only contains the names of those British and Commonwealth soldiers who died there but have no known graves, and yet there are 54,896 names engraved on the stones. This should give you some idea of the scale of the First World War.

Every evening the Ypres police arrive to stop traffic driving through the Gate. Then buglers step forward and stand in the middle of the road. At precisely 8 o'clock they sound the 'last post', a bugle call which is always sounded at the burial of a British soldier.

This simple service has taken place every evening since 1923, except for the period 1940-45 when Ieper was occupied by German soldiers.

After four years of fighting, approximately 20,000,000 soldiers and civilians had been killed during the First World War.

The First World War was one of the most important events in the twentieth century. It changed the world in many ways and it affected international relations in major ways.

This chapter will enable you to understand the reasons why the War began in 1914, how each of the countries involved was affected by the type of fighting, and how the people and the policy makers in those countries were influenced by the War.

The causes of the War

The long term causes of the War

The long term causes can be divided into five.

a **The growth of Germany.** Germany's was the fastest growing economy in Europe by 1914. By 1900 its industrial output had overtaken Britain's and was second only to the USA's. This meant that Germany could afford to spend money on its army and navy. This worried Britain. Britain was an industrial and trading country. Would she now lose out to Germany?

b **Colonial rivalry.** German industrialists and the ruler of Germany, Kaiser Wilhelm II, wanted to gain an overseas Empire like those of Britain and France. The industrialists wanted more markets to sell their goods into and the Kaiser was jealous of Britain and France.

Also he was worried by the Entente Cordiale between Britain and France. He decided to test this alliance to see how strong it was. In 1905 he offered to help the Sultan of Morocco to get the French out of his land. The Kaiser hoped this would split the Entente as Britain might like the French out of Morocco. However, Britain and France stuck together and a conference at Algeciras in 1906 settled the issue. The Kaiser had to back down. In 1911 the Kaiser sent a German gunboat called *The Panther* to Agadir in Morocco. He hoped to force France and Britain into allowing him to expand his territories in central Africa. Again he had to back down. These two crises in Morocco show:
a that Germany was becoming increasingly bold in its attempts to expand, and
b the Entente Cordiale of 1904 was strong enough to resist Germany.

These two incidents did not result in war, but they made a definite contribution to the raising of tension between the European powers.

c **The growth of the armed forces.** The size of the armies and navies of the main countries were growing year by year. The German army had become very large and this worried Britain, France, and Russia. They became frightened of Germany. Britain was also worried by the growth of the German navy, because this threatened Britain's position as a great sea power. An 'arms race' developed with each country trying to out do the others. In 1906 Britain began to build many new, faster, and more powerful battleships called 'Dreadnoughts' and the Germans did so too. In 1913 Germany widened the Kiel Canal which let her ships into the North Sea much more easily.

d **The system of alliances.** In order to protect themselves, the larger countries formed alliances with other friendly countries. In 1879 Austria-Hungary and Germany formed the Dual Alliance, and this became a Triple Alliance in 1882 when Italy joined them. In 1892 the French and Russians allied together. In 1904 the 'Entente Cordiale' between Britain and France was signed, and in 1907 this became a Triple Entente when Britain and Russia allied. Germany had most to fear from this system of alliances. As you can see from the map on page 16, an alliance between Britain and France in the west with Russia in the east trapped Germany between its enemies. If there was to be war for Germany, it would be a war on two fronts.

e **Problems in the Austrian Empire.** At the time that Germany was developing, its ally, Austria, was in decline. Austria controlled a large empire called the Austro-Hungarian Empire which included part of the Balkans. Austria was still trying to keep control of this land, but the people of this part of Europe were trying to become independent.

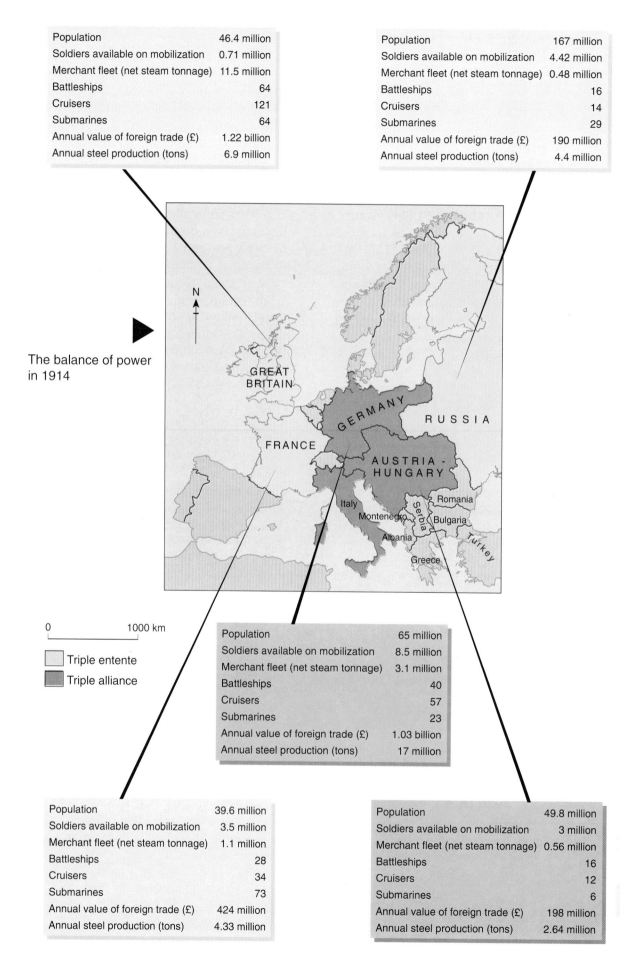

Population	46.4 million
Soldiers available on mobilization	0.71 million
Merchant fleet (net steam tonnage)	11.5 million
Battleships	64
Cruisers	121
Submarines	64
Annual value of foreign trade (£)	1.22 billion
Annual steel production (tons)	6.9 million

Population	167 million
Soldiers available on mobilization	4.42 million
Merchant fleet (net steam tonnage)	0.48 million
Battleships	16
Cruisers	14
Submarines	29
Annual value of foreign trade (£)	190 million
Annual steel production (tons)	4.4 million

The balance of power in 1914

N

GREAT BRITAIN

GERMANY

RUSSIA

FRANCE

AUSTRIA - HUNGARY

Italy
Montenegro
Serbia
Romania
Bulgaria
Albania
Greece
Turkey

0 — 1000 km

Triple entente

Triple alliance

Population	65 million
Soldiers available on mobilization	8.5 million
Merchant fleet (net steam tonnage)	3.1 million
Battleships	40
Cruisers	57
Submarines	23
Annual value of foreign trade (£)	1.03 billion
Annual steel production (tons)	17 million

Population	39.6 million
Soldiers available on mobilization	3.5 million
Merchant fleet (net steam tonnage)	1.1 million
Battleships	28
Cruisers	34
Submarines	73
Annual value of foreign trade (£)	424 million
Annual steel production (tons)	4.33 million

Population	49.8 million
Soldiers available on mobilization	3 million
Merchant fleet (net steam tonnage)	0.56 million
Battleships	16
Cruisers	12
Submarines	6
Annual value of foreign trade (£)	198 million
Annual steel production (tons)	2.64 million

The Turkish Empire had once covered all of the Balkans. However, by 1900 it had been pushed back and a number of Balkan countries had won their independence. Bulgaria, Greece, Romania, and Serbia were all now independent. The independence of these 'slavonic' countries bordering its Empire worried Austria. The Austrians thought that this independence movement would spread to slavs inside their Empire. To stop the spread of this nationalism, and to prevent the expansion of Serbia, the Austrians took over Bosnia in 1908. This angered the Serbs and slavs inside the Austro-Hungarian Empire. Many secret societies were formed with the intention of removing Austria from Bosnia. One of these was called the 'Black Hand'.

In 1912 Bulgaria, Greece, Serbia, and Montenegro joined together to force the Turks out of most of the Balkans. At the end of this Balkan War, Serbia became bigger. This added to Austria's worries.

The short term causes of the War

In 1914 the ruler of Austria, the Emperor Franz Joseph, sent his heir, Archduke Franz Ferdinand, to the Bosnian capital, Sarajevo. On 28th June the Archduke and his wife were assassinated by a Bosnian Serb gunman from the 'Black Hand'.

 The Archduke Franz Ferdinand and his wife just before their assassination

Within weeks Europe was at war. The diagram on page 18 shows the chain reaction that this assassination set off. As you can see it took less than forty days before all the major European powers were at war. After the war Germany was blamed for having started it, but historians now question this. What do you think? Look at the sources which follow and then answer the questions.

 The assassin, Gavrilo Princip, being captured by police

C

The alliance system caught Germany between two enemies; France and Russia. In the late nineteenth century a German General called von Schlieffen devised a plan to solve this problem. A plan to get soldiers to the right place, ready to fight is called a mobilisation plan.

It was always thought that the Russian army would take a long time to get into action. So the plan was to attack France with almost the whole German army, take it by surprise and quickly capture the capital city, Paris. This would mean passing through Belgium, but that was not thought to be a problem. Once victory in France had been achieved, most of the army would move to the east to fight the Russians. To make this plan possible Germany had been building vast amounts of railway line which concentrated on the Belgian border. Railway timetables had been constructed to move thousands of soldiers into Belgium. There was one problem. When all the plans had been put in to action there was to be no turning back. Mobilisation, for most countries, meant just that; preparing for a war. For Germany it meant war itself.

A description of the Schlieffen Plan.

1

On 28th June 1914

Archduke Franz Ferdinand was shot in Sarajevo, Bosnia.

2

Germany promised to back-up Austria against Serbia. This is called the 'blank cheque'.

4

Russia mobilised her entire army on 31st July. This was to defend the Serbs but it also threatened Germany.

3

Austria sent an ultimatum to Serbia on 23rd July, to give up the assassins. She invaded Serbia on 28th July. Russia stood by Serbia.

Austria   Serbia   Russia

5

Germany declared war on Russia on 1st August. Frightened by thoughts of a war on two fronts, Germany put into operation the Schlieffen Plan. She declared war on France on 3rd August and invaded via Belgium on 4th August.

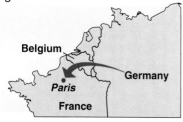

Belgium

Germany

Paris

France

6

On 4th August, Britain declared war on Germany. This was because of a treaty of 1839 in which Britain agreed to protect Belgium. There is no doubt, though, that Britain was also very keen to stop German power.

D

Germany's diplomacy was based on her desire for economic growth. Sometimes it was friendly and based on conciliation; at others it was aggressive, but the ultimate objective was always the expansion of German power.

Adapted from Fritz Fischer, a German historian writing in 1967.

E

The war of 1914 was due to the unbearable tensions inside the Austrian Empire. But the Austrian crisis could not have grown into a general war without tensions between the Great Powers. These tensions were the result of colonial rivalry and usually concerned regions far from Europe.

From a British historian writing in 1965.

The disaster of 1914 had its roots in 1870 when Prussia (Germany) defeated France and captured some of its land. Germany then wanted more conquests. This made Germany the object of alarm to every other leading nation except her Austrian ally.

A British historian writing in 1936.

1 Look at Source C. Explain in your own words how the Schlieffen Plan was supposed to work? What was the purpose of this plan?

2 It has been argued that the existence of the Schlieffen Plan places the blame for the war upon Germany. Others have argued that Germany had to develop a plan which would avoid a war on two fronts. What do you think? Does the Schlieffen Plan put the blame upon Germany?

3 Read Sources D, E, and F. Give each Source a mark out of 5 on whether it seems to be a good explanation of the causes of the War. Good explanation = 5 marks, weak explanation = 0. Which do you think is the best explanation for the War? Explain why.

4 The authors of Sources D, E, and F have different opinions about the causes of the war. Explain how it is possible for historians to have such different opinions.

The Western Front, 1914–1917

Why do we need to find out about weapons, fighting, and casualties in a book about international relations? It is because they each affected the attitudes of many people, some of whom made important decisions years later. The fighting in the First World War was very different to fighting in just about any war before it. The type of fighting led to enormous casualties. For example, Britain lost 750,000 soldiers killed, France 1.4 million, and Germany 2 million. Losses such as these had a great effect upon the public and politicians in many countries. First we shall find out what the fighting was like. Then we shall see what effect this had on those countries who were to shape international affairs over the following twenty years.

In the first months of 1914 there was a great deal of movement of soldiers. In Belgium and France, the Schlieffen Plan was put into operation. In the east, Russia invaded Germany. But this 'war of movement' soon ground to a halt.

The Schlieffen Plan failed. Germany had expected to be able to move quickly through Belgium. This did not happen. The Belgians resisted and their small army fought bravely. Britain declared war on Germany and sent a small force, called the British Expeditionary Force (or BEF) to Belgium where it attacked the advancing German army. This delayed the German attack. It also had the effect of diverting the attack away from Paris, which was its main target. In late August 1914 the French army halted the Germans north of Paris at the Battle of the Marne. On the Russian Front, Germany was more successful, but here too the war soon settled down. As each side concentrated upon defence a system of trenches was built which eventually stretched from the coast of Belgium, through France to the Swiss border. The trenches were protected by barbed wire fences and sand bags. Some had concrete reinforcements. The soldiers in the trenches had machine guns and

Machine guns, modern rifles and barbed wire halt a German infantry charge

rifles. The defenders had a clear advantage in this kind of warfare. All along this line of trenches the British and French (allied), and German armies faced each other for more than three years. There was not much movement at all and the line of trenches stayed more or less fixed throughout the war.

The sources on these pages show some of the main weapons of the war and what effects they had. Machine guns were extensively used in all armies. As you can see, these guns were reasonably small, light, and manoeuvrable. They only needed a crew of two or three soldiers to work them. Yet they were devastating in action. A machine gun like the one in Source G could shoot hundreds of bullets each minute and could kill a soldier two kilometres away. Try to imagine the effect of lots of these guns firing at lines of advancing soldiers walking towards them. Also many heavy guns were used. Before any attack a barrage of artillery fire would rain down on the enemy trenches with the aim of destroying defences and weakening morale.

A British howitzer being pulled through the mud towards the front line, 1917

Newer and yet more destructive weapons were developed, such as gas, flame throwers, and tanks. Gas was first used at Ypres in 1915. It was such a shock that soldiers dropped their weapons and ran. Gas and gasmasks soon became part of the regular war scene. There were two types of gas, chlorine and mustard gas. Altogether 91,000 soldiers died from gas and many more were seriously injured.

Tanks were first used in 1916 by the British, and at first they took the enemy by surprise. But they were unreliable and too few in number to make a great impact. Even in the air new weapons became the norm. Balloons and aeroplanes were used to provide information about the enemy and to bomb them.

In Britain, France, Germany, Russia, and the USA, the whole country became involved with the war effort. Men and women worked in the factories. In 1914 Britain made 287 machine guns; in 1916 it made over 33,000. In May 1915 British industry produced 70,000 shells per week for the army; by 1916 it was 238,000 per week. Horses and London buses were conscripted into war service! Men volunteered or were conscripted to fight. Women served as nurses, in factories and on farms. In most countries food was rationed to overcome shortages. The First World War has been described as 'total war' because it affected almost everybody in the countries involved and affected most aspects of their lives. This was to leave a great impression on everybody involved (also see Chapter 15).

British tanks and infantry move up to the front line. The cribs attached to the tanks were dropped into enemy trenches to allow them to be crossed.

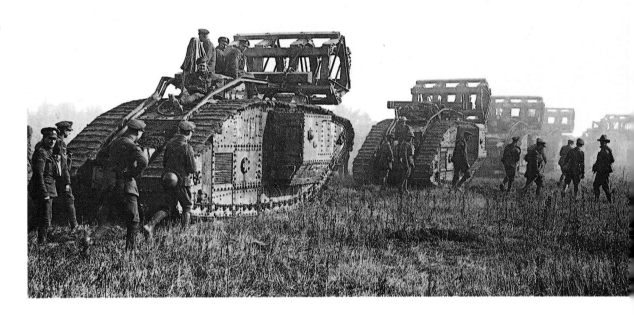

The Battle of the Somme, 1916

Sometimes there were great attacks. A study of one of these attacks will help you to understand why the First World War was so important. In 1916 the British and French generals decided to attack the Germans north of the River Somme in France.

This attack was partly aimed at making a breakthrough into German held territory, but mainly it was to help the French army. The French were being attacked by the Germans at Verdun and an attack on the Somme area would help them by diverting German soldiers.

On 1st July 1916, when the British attacked the German trenches in northern France, 60,000 of them were killed or wounded by German machine guns. Most of these were in the first hour of the attack. This method of fighting, massed infantry against well protected machine guns, was common during the War. It accounts for the enormous casualties of the War. There was a great sense of futility at the pointless destruction caused by these massed attacks.

The attack itself came after a whole week of shelling by the British. Big guns like those in Source J were used. The noise could be heard in England! However, at 7.00 am on 1st July 1916 the noise stopped. It was time for the attack. The following sources describe what it was like.

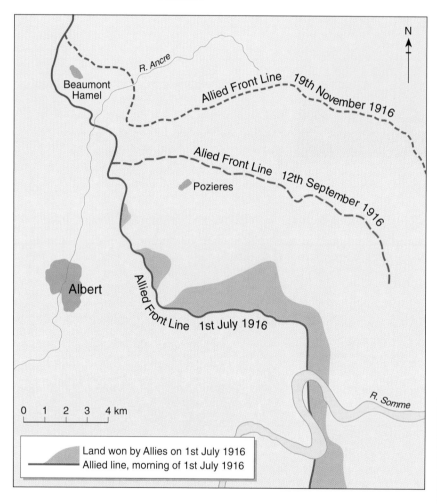

Land won by Allies on 1st July 1916
Allied line, morning of 1st July 1916

J A British 12 inch howitzer being used to bombard the enemy trenches

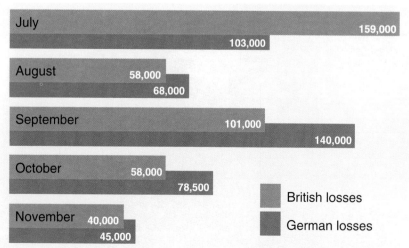

	British losses	German losses
July	159,000	103,000
August	58,000	68,000
September	101,000	140,000
October	58,000	78,500
November	40,000	45,000

This photograph of Pozieres on the Somme shows the devastating effect of an artillery bombardment on one town. This photograph was taken in July 1916.

Again and again we had to dig ourselves and our comrades out of masses of blackened earth and splintered wooden beams. No food or water reached us. Down below, men became hysterical and we had to knock them out so as to prevent them from running away and exposing themselves to the deadly shell splinters. Even the rats panicked and found refuge in our shelter where they ran up the walls. We had to kill them with our spades.

From the memoirs of Kurt Westmann, a German soldier who served as a medical officer during the war. He was not a doctor, but a medical student who had volunteered for the army. In July 1916 he was with the German army at Beaumont Hamel, opposite the British and Commonwealth soldiers. The first aid post Westmann worked in was more than 7 metres underground so that it would not be destroyed by shelling. Here he describes the artillery bombardment.

As soon as the signal was given, the regiment left the trenches and moved steadily forward. Machine gun fire at once opened on us and artillery fire also. The men were mown down in heaps. In spite of the losses the survivors steadily advanced to the enemy wire, by which time few remained.

Part of a report by a British officer describing the opening of the Battle of the Somme.

It was like no sound on earth. 'Jesus', said Stephen, 'Jesus, Jesus'...
It was for a moment completely quiet as the bombardment ended and the German guns also stopped. Skylarks wheeled and sang in the cloudless sky. Then the German guns resumed. To his left Stephen saw men trying to emerge from the trench but being smashed by bullets before they could stand. The gaps in the wire became jammed with bodies...He walked hesitantly forward, his skin tensed for the feeling of metal tearing flesh. He turned his body sideways, tenderly, trying to protect his eyes. He was like an old woman in the cocoon of tearing noise... he could see a long, wavering line of men, primitive dolls progressing in tense deliberate steps, going down with a silent flap of arms, replaced, falling, continuing as though walking into a gale.

From *Birdsong*, a novel written in 1993.

German machine gunners and rifle men crawled out of their holes, with inflamed and sunken eyes, their faces blackened by fire and their uniforms splashed with the blood of their wounded comrades. They started firing furiously, and the British had frightful losses. It has been estimated that their dead amounted, within the first ten minutes, to at least fourteen thousand men.

Kurt Westmann describes what happened once the shelling stopped.

5 What can you learn from Source M about problems facing soldiers on the Western Front during the First World War?

6 In what ways do Sources M and N support the evidence of Source O?

7 Source N is a novel written in 1993. It is a piece of fiction. How reliable is Source N likely to be? Explain your answer.

8 Which of Sources L, M, N, or O gives you the most vivid picture of the fighting? Which is the most factual? How would you explain the differences between these sources?

9 Explain the value of Sources L, M, N, and O in helping you to understand why progress during the Battle of the Somme was so slow.

The role of the generals, especially Sir Douglas Haig

The deadly accuracy of the modern machine gun means that 'no man's land' must be crossed in the shortest possible time. If men are held up by mud, attacks like this become impossible because of the losses which they suffer.

Part of a report by Field Marshal Sir John French, Commander-in-Chief of the British Forces in France until 1915. This was written in February 1915.

The generals responsible for the great massed attacks of 1915-1917 came in for a great deal of criticism. The generals of both sides were bad at inventing ways of avoiding heavy casualties. They could not make a breakthrough until 1918, which we will see later. Sir Douglas Haig was Commander-in-Chief of the British forces in France from 1915 until 1918. He was responsible for launching attacks which cost hundreds of thousands of lives. Haig was convinced that victory in the war would come, and that it would happen on the Western Front. This belief often brought him into conflict with Prime Minister Lloyd George, who was in favour of attempting a victory in South Eastern Europe. Haig was sure that the artillery bombardment would have destroyed the German defences and broken the barbed wire. The soldiers were ordered to walk not run. In fact they could not run. The men were fully equipped. They had their normal packs, plus a rifle, a bayonet, two gas helmets, 220 rounds of ammunition, two grenades, two sandbags, a spade, a pair of wire cutters, a flare and other smaller items. Most men carried a pack which weighed about 38 kilograms. Haig was guilty of being over optimistic in his plans for the Battle of the Somme. Yet he was able to claim a partial victory as six or seven miles of land along a 30 mile front had been captured by October 1916. The generals consistently got things wrong. Their plans failed again and again.

"Good morning; good morning!" the General said.
When we met him last week on our way to the line.
Now the soldiers he smiled at are most of 'em dead
And we're cursing his staff for incompetent swine.

"He's a cheery old card", grunted Harry to Jack
As they slogged up to Arras with rifle and pack.

But he did for them both by his plan of attack.

This is a poem written by Siegfried Sassoon, a British officer who fought in the war. It is criticising the generals for their planning at the Battle of Arras.

In the autumn of 1917, General Haig ordered an attack north of Ypres, near the village of Passchendaele. This battle was called the Third Battle of Ypres. Hundreds of thousands again lost their lives, many swallowed by the deep mud in that part of the battlefields. Haig was often out of touch with the conditions at the Front because his headquarters were far from the fighting and communications were sometimes poor. Lloyd George tried to demand a new approach from Haig, but the general was very confident of a victory and of his own way of winning it. Mass attacks! After the failure of the Third Battle of Ypres in 1917, Lloyd George reduced Haig's fighting strength to save casualties. 760,000 men were deliberately kept away from France and 300,000 front line troops were kept in Britain.

It is easy to criticise Haig, but we must remember the circumstances which he was operating under. He was not the only general to rely on mass attacks. General French had been dismissed in 1915 following 300,000 British casualties in that year. Haig was not in fact in overall command, because the French generals always commanded the allied armies. Haig was not always given all the details he needed. For example, in 1917, he had not seen the map which showed that the area near Ypres where he intended to use tanks was far too marshy for them. His Chief-of-Intelligence, General Charteris had never sent it to him because he did not wish to depress Haig. And the fact that he was never at the front line should not surprise you. It would be stupid to send a field marshal so close to the enemy.

10 Source P is dated 1915, more than a year before the other sources in this section. Why were attacks like the one described in Sources M and N still being carried out in 1916?
11 Many historians have criticised the British generals for their handling of battles like the Somme. Use the sources and your own knowledge to explain why the generals have been criticised.
12 Are these criticisms fair? Use the sources and your own knowledge to explain your answer to this question.

The Gallipoli Plan

The stalemate on the Western Front forced both sides to consider alternative ways to break the deadlock. Turkey had joined the war on Germany's side. Winston Churchill was a senior British politician in 1915. He had a plan to attack the Turks at Gallipoli in the Dardenelles. If successful, this would allow the Allies to attack Germany from the South East and possibly link up with the Russians. In April 1915 Allied soldiers, mainly from the Australian and New Zealand Army Corps, the ANZACs, were landed on the beaches near Gallipoli. The landings themselves were successful, but the troops were unable to break out from the beaches. This was because the Turkish soldiers, under the command of German officers, had been well prepared. Over 200,000 casualties were suffered before the decision was made to evacuate them in December 1915.

The war at sea

It seems a little odd that there were no decisive sea battles during the War. This is especially true when you recall that the naval arms race had been one of the causes. In May 1916 the British and German fleets had clashed at Jutland in the North Sea. Each side suffered losses, the British more than the Germans. The German fleet went back to its base and so did the British. This battle can be considered more of a British victory. If the German fleet had managed to get into the Atlantic Ocean it could have done enormous damage to Britain's supply of food and materials.

German submarines were always a threat to British shipping. In 1915 the German Government declared the Western Approaches to the British Isles a war zone. This meant that the ships of any country, even those not at war, were liable to be sunk. This angered the neutral countries, including the USA, and after the sinking of the *Lusitania* in 1915, warnings from the US President forced Germany to abandon unrestricted submarine warfare. At the same time, however, the British fleet was able to impose an almost totally effective blockade of German ports. Food was not getting through to Germany and eventually the country began to starve.

In 1917, in a last attempt to bring Britain into submission, Germany resumed unrestricted submarine warfare. This was very successful. In April 1917, 875,000 tons of shipping were sunk by German U-Boats and Britain had just six weeks food left. By the end of the War, German U-Boats had sunk 15 million tons of shipping. But unrestricted submarine warfare also contributed to the involvement of the USA in the War.

Changing circumstances in 1917 and 1918

1917 was the year of change. Firstly, there was the Revolution in Russia (see Chapter 1) which led to the Russians making a peace treaty with Germany. In 1917 the Tsar of Russia, Nicholas II, was forced to abdicate. The War was not the only reason for this; Russia had many other problems. But the War certainly made conditions much worse and led to a situation in which the Tsar could not carry on. He was replaced by a more liberal government. This new government decided to carry on fighting against the Germans, but did not do very well. It only lasted six months before it was overthrown by the Communists led by Lenin. The Communists ended the war in March 1918 when they signed the Treaty of Brest-Litovsk with Germany. This Treaty gave Germany two big advantages. First Germany gained land, including the grain growing land of the Ukraine, which helped to provide food. Second, it meant that all the German soldiers who had been fighting against Russia on the Eastern Front could now be used in the West. So in March 1918, Germany was able to launch a major attack against the Allies in France. This was the Spring Offensive which was successful at first. Storm troopers had been specially trained to burst through at particular points. The British troops were battle weary and were pushed back by the greater numbers of Germans for up to 40 miles. However, after 10 days the attack ran out of steam. The Germans could not supply their advancing soldiers who began to stop to find food. The attack was repeated in the following four months against both the British and the French; at one point it even looked as though Paris might again be threatened, but again the Germans were held. And then the Americans began to arrive.

The USA enters the War

The second reason for 1917 being a year of change is that this was when the USA joined the fighting on the side of the Allies. For many years the USA had wished to keep out of European affairs. Public opinion there was strongly in favour of isolation, keeping out. This wish was clearly stated in the nineteenth century by President Monroe. He said that the USA would not become involved in the affairs of any European nation as long as the European powers stayed out of the USA's area (the Caribbean, the Pacific basin and South America.) But the USA had been supplying the Allies with materials for the war effort. Much of this trade was transported in US ships. In 1915 the Cunard liner, the *Lusitania*, was sunk by a German submarine. 128 US citizens were killed. Events such as this, and the effect of the German submarine campaign on trade, began to change opinion in America. In April 1917, Congress declared war on Germany 'to protect democracy, the rights and freedom of small nations, to bring peace and safety and to make the world itself free at last.' It took many months before the US soldiers arrived in France in large numbers, but by June 1918 they were pouring into France at the rate of over 200,000 per month. These were fresh and idealistic men in the peak of condition and made a great impact upon the course of the War.

A postcard commemorating the sinking of the liner *Lusitania* by a German U-Boat

Why did Germany lose the War?

In August 1918 General Ludendorff told the Kaiser that the War was lost. Yet in a way Germany didn't lose the War. The German army was not defeated, in fact it marched back to Germany with its weapons in 1918. There had been no fighting in Germany itself during the War. But in 1918 Germany asked for the fighting to stop and for a peace treaty to be negotiated. This is called an armistice. It happened on 11th November 1918 and is why we still have Remembrance Day in November.

The German army marching home in 1918

Once the Schlieffen Plan had failed, in 1914, Germany was fighting a war on two fronts and this proved too much for German resources. Germany simply could not keep the war effort going. Germany had gained land from Russia in early 1918 at the Treaty of Brest-Litovsk; and had made advances against the Allies in France in 1918. But it couldn't last. The British naval blockade of German ports stopped food coming into the country. There was real starvation in Germany and the politicians were afraid of a revolution. By the summer of 1918, superior allied numbers and the use of more modern weapons, such as tanks, were beginning to push the Germans back.

So in November 1918 an armistice was arranged and the fighting stopped. French soldiers went into Germany and stayed there until the peace treaty was signed in 1919.

13 Why was 1917 a year of change in the First World War?
14 Explain why Germany asked for an armistice in 1918.

How did the War affect each country?

Britain

At first there was a feeling of victory and of punishing Germany for the horror of the War. But this did not last. People soon began to consider if the war had been worthwhile. The politicians had promised this would be 'the war to end all wars' and said that Britain afterwards would be 'a land fit for heroes.' Yet Britain was bankrupted by the War and was heavily in debt to the USA. The Government began to disarm. This means to reduce the armed forces. Ships were broken up for scrap. Aeroplanes were sold off to flying clubs, and the army was greatly reduced. This meant many men were now looking for

jobs. By the mid 1920s, Britain's armed forces were very weak indeed. But it did not seem to matter. Nobody wanted another war and nobody thought there would be one. In 1919 the League of Nations had been formed and people thought this would prevent future wars. And people now had more say. In 1918 many more men, and for the first time women, were allowed to vote. This gave ordinary people more sense of involvement and control. It also helped the growth of the Labour Party, which some people thought would be more pacifist.

Most important of all, the ruling class in Britain had been personally affected by the war. Every senior politician in the years just after the war had lost a son or a nephew in the fighting. Thirty years later, during the 1951 General Election, the two main parties, Conservative and Labour, were led by men who had seen active service during the First World War.

France

France had suffered even more than Britain; most of the fighting had been inside France.

French losses in the war.

1,400,000	soldiers killed
2,500,000	soldiers wounded
23,000	factories destroyed
5,600km	of railway line wrecked
300,000	houses destroyed
2,000,000	people forced to flee from their homes
90%	of the coal and iron industries destroyed
£5,400	million spent on defence.

First World War cemetary at La Targette, France

Damage done to the French town of Albert, which was close to the front line for four years

How would you feel if so much damage had been done to your country in a war? What would you want to do to the enemy once it had been defeated? Not surprisingly, after the War the French wanted to punish Germany for the War and the French Government made heavy claims on Germany at the Treaty of Versailles (see Chapter 3). The French also wanted to weaken Germany in order to protect France from any future attack.

We are always invaded, we are always the ones to suffer. Fifteen invasions in less than six centuries give us the right to insist upon a victor's treaty that will offer us something more realistic than temporary solutions and uncertain hopes.

A French politician speaking in 1919.

Later the French Government built a large and expensive system of forts along the border with Germany. This was called the Maginot Line.

Germany

A new liberal government was set up in 1919, called the Weimar Government. There were lots of unemployed soldiers following the War, and food was still scarce. In 1919 there was a revolution in the German capital, Berlin, led by the Communists. This was put down by the Government. The Weimar Government kept control but there were often riots, attempted revolutions and unrest, especially in 1921, 1923 and 1930-33. But the most important effect of the War upon Germany was the way it affected how people thought. Whereas in Britain people now wished to avoid war, in Germany the people felt cheated and many wanted revenge for the way Germany had been treated in the peace treaty (see Chapter 3). This was one of the reasons why the Nazi Party, led by Adolf Hitler, grew in popularity during the 1930s.

Italy

Italy had changed sides during the War. Italy ended up on the winning side, but was not rewarded in the Treaty of Versailles, although she became a member of the League of Nations. This, together with unemployment and a fear of Communism, led to Mussolini coming to power in Italy. Mussolini had seen some military service during the War, and wished to make Italy a great power with an Empire. As we shall see, this caused problems later (see Chapters 4 and 5).

Russia

In many ways Russia was affected more than any other country. From October 1917 Russia was a Communist country and became known as the USSR. The Communists ended the war in early 1918, when they signed the Treaty of Brest-Litovsk with Germany. This broke the alliance with Britain and France, who found it difficult to forgive Russia. They sent soldiers to Russia to fight against the Communists and try to put the Tsar back on to the throne. They did not allow Russia to join the League of Nations. The Communists never forgave them. So, the main effect on future international relations was the great distrust between the USSR and the British and French. This would surface many times in the 50 years after the end of the War.

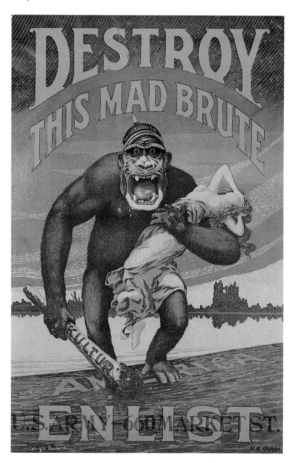

An American recruitment poster accusing the Germans of inhuman brutality

The United States of America

The USA did not join the fighting until 1917, but had been supplying the allies before this. Most Americans did not want their country involved in any European war. They believed that the loss of American lives in the War was a waste. Joining in the fighting had meant a change in US foreign policy. After the War the USA wished to go back to its policy of isolation. This means keeping out of European affairs. For this reason the USA refused to join the League of Nations. But it was not entirely successful. Britain and France owed the USA billions of dollars. So, whether the Americans wanted it or not, the USA did have an interest in Europe. This became very real in 1925, when the USA had to come to the aid of Germany. The USA made loans to Germany so that Germany could pay reparations to Britain and France, who could then pay off their debts to the USA. So after the War the USA had more influence over the main European countries than before, even though it did not really want to get involved.

How did the First World War affect international relations?

a The League of Nations Organisation was formed. It was an international organisation which aimed to keep the peace by allowing countries to talk and sort out their problems without fighting (see Chapter 4).

b There were changes to the balance of power. In Europe the Austrian Empire was broken up and Germany was weakened. Many new countries were created or gained their independence. For example, Poland and Hungary became independent countries and Czechoslovakia and Yugoslavia were created. Russia had lost land at Brest-Litovsk and was devastated by years of war and revolution. Russia was not invited to become a member of the League of Nations.

c In the Middle East, the Ottoman (Turkish) Empire was broken up. The Turks had fought with Germany and paid the price for this in 1919. Much of the Turkish Empire was now controlled by Britain and France. For example, Palestine was looked after by Britain. On a world wide scale, the power of Britain was shown to be declining. Britain had relied very heavily on its Empire for troops, and was heavily in debt to the USA by the end of the War. The USA, on the other hand, was now a great power, even though it seemed reluctant to accept that responsibility.

d The War altered the alliance system in Europe. The Triple alliance of Austria, Germany, and Italy was broken. The Treaty of Versailles would prevent any future alliance between Austria and Germany (see Chapter 3). The Triple Entente was also broken. Russia had left this alliance in 1917. Britain and France had remained allies throughout the War. But now that the War was over, Britain became concerned at the power held by France.

e The USA had shown that it was prepared to join in European affairs if the situation demanded it. The USA had helped the allies to win the War and was to play an important part in the negotiations of the peace treaties. But the USA then decided to follow its previous policy of isolationism and refused to join the League of Nations (see Chapter 4).

15 Describe the effects of the First World War on Germany and Italy.

16 What were the immediate effects of the First World War on international relations?

17 Source T shows how the American government tried to get men to join the army in 1917. After the War, the USA returned to 'isolation' from European affairs. Explain why this change came about.

3 *Peace making 1919–1920*

1919 was the year after the Armistice. The First World War had ended. People were thankful that the fighting had stopped, but many people in Britain and France now wanted to punish Germany for the War.

 A The front cover of the British magazine *The Sphere*, November 1918. It shows the crowds in London celebrating the Armistice.

 B

> In November [1918] came the Armistice. The news sent me out walking alone...cursing and sobbing and thinking of the dead. Siegfried Sassoon's famous poem celebrating the Armistice began:
>
> > Everybody suddenly burst out singing,
> > And I was filled with such delight...
> > But 'everybody' did not include me.

From the autobiography of Robert Graves, who was an officer in the British army during the War.

 C

> Last night, for the first time since August in the first year of the war, there was no light of gunfire in the sky, no sudden stabs of flame through darkness, no spreading glow above black trees where for four years of nights human beings were smashed to death. The Fires of Hell had been put out.

From Philip Gibbs, an American newspaper reporter writing from France in November 1918.

1. Look at Source A. How would you describe the mood of the crowd? How might this mood have influenced the politicians who went to Paris to decide the settlement?
2. Do Sources B and C support or contradict the evidence of Source A? Explain your answer.
3. How might you explain the different attitudes shown in these sources?
4. How reliable are sources A, B, and C for deciding how people felt at the end of the War in 1919?

The aims of the peace makers

Lloyd George   Clemenceau   Wilson

The leaders of all the countries that had been fighting met in Paris to decide on a peace settlement to end the War. Britain was represented by the Prime Minister, Lloyd George. He had just won a General Election in Britain. The people had voted for Lloyd George believing that he would 'make Germany pay' for the War. But it was France who really wanted to punish and weaken Germany. They were represented by their Prime Minister, Clemenceau. Most of the fighting had been in France. Many French towns and villages had been destroyed and hundreds of thousands of French people were homeless. France's northern coal mines and farm land had been badly damaged. Clemenceau went to Paris for revenge. He also wanted to protect France in the future by ensuring that Germany was kept weak. Woodrow Wilson was in Paris representing the USA. He was the US President, although his party had lost the majority in the US Senate. He went to Versailles with a Fourteen Point Plan, which was to form the basis of the peace settlement and the prevention of further wars. Wilson's position was not strong because he knew the American people did not want to become involved in Europe again. Lloyd George and Clemenceau had accepted the Fourteen Points, but they also aimed for a harsh peace settlement in order to satisfy the people at home. These three had by far

the biggest say as they were the victorious powers.

Russia was not at the meetings because of the Revolution of 1917 and the change of government there (see Chapter 1). Italy and Japan were there as part of the victorious Allied delegation, but did not have such a big say. The defeated powers were all there but they were given very little say in the debates. They were there simply to sign the treaties. Germany hoped for a reasonable settlement. The Kaiser had abdicated and there was now a more liberal government in Germany. But the Paris treaties were not negotiated. The treaties were forced upon the Germans and also on the Austrians, Bulgarians, Hungarians, and the Turks.

From: President Wilson, US
To: President Clemenceau, France
Prime Minister Lloyd George, United Kingdon
Date: January 1918

The Fourteen Point Plan

1. Open agreements and alliances, no secret agreements in future.
2. Freedom of navigation of the seas.
3. Removal of economic barriers to free trade.
4. Reduction of armaments to the lowest possible level.
5. Colonial claims to be dealt with in the interests of the populations concerned.
6. All Russian territory to be evacuated.
7. Belgium to be restored in full and free sovereignty.
8. All French territory to be freed. Alsace-Lorraine should be returned to France, righting the wrong done by Germany to France in 1871.
9. Italy's frontiers should be adjusted according to nationality.
10. The people of Austria-Hungary should be given the opportunity of self-government.
11. Montenegro, Romania, and Serbia to be given independence. Serbia to be given a coastline.
12. Turkey to be a separate state. Other parts of the Ottoman Empire to be given independence. The Dardenelles to be permanently free to all shipping.
13. An independent Polish state to be set up and given access to the sea.
14. An Association of Nations to be set up to preserve future peace.

From President Woodrow Wilson's Fourteen Points, 1918.

5 Look at Source D. Make a table with four columns. Write out the Fourteen Points under the following headings. (Some points may go into more than one column, one or two may not fit.)

Keeping peace or avoiding war.	Solving issues of independence or nationality.	Punishing or weakening the defeated or rewarding the victors.	Encouraging freedom of trade in the World.

6 Does your table help you to understand what Wilson was aiming for with his Fourteen Points? Do you think that any of Wilson's aims were likely to work against the others? Explain your answers.

The terms of the treaties

Separate treaties were made with each of the defeated countries:

- At Versailles the Allies made a treaty with Germany
- At St. Germain the Allies made a treaty with Austria.
- At Trianon the Allies made a treaty with Hungary.
- At Neuilly the Allies made a treaty with Bulgaria.
- And at Sevres the Allies made a treaty with Turkey.

These treaties altered borders, reduced the size of their armed forces and agreed reparations. These were payments from one country to another for the damage done in the War. Many new countries were created as a result of these treaties. For example, Czechoslovakia, Hungary, Poland, and Yugoslavia. In the case of Turkey, most of her Empire was lost. In each case the defeated country had little alternative but to accept the Treaty.

Treaty of St Germain September 1919
Austria paid reparations. Austrian army limited to 30,000 soldiers. Bohemia and Moravia given to the new state of Czechoslovakia. Bosnia and Herzegovina went to Yugoslavia. Galicia was given to Poland. South Tyrol and Istria went to Italy.

Treaty of Neuilly November 1919
Bulgaria paid reparations. Bulgarian army limited to 20,000. Bulgaria lost land to Yugoslavia, and lost Western Thrace which went to Greece.

Treaty of Trianon June 1920
Hungary paid reparations. Army limited to 35,000. Handed over war criminals. Transylvania given to Romania, Rutheria and Slovakia to Czechoslovakia; Croatia and Slovenia to Yugoslavia

Treaty of Sevres August 1920
Turkey lost Eastern Thrace and Smyrna to Greece. This was disputed and led to a war. In 1922 the **Treaty of Lausanne** returned Smyrna to Turkey. Turkey gave up all claims to territory in the Middle East.

Territory lost by Austria-Hungary
Territory lost by Bulgaria
Territory lost by Turkey

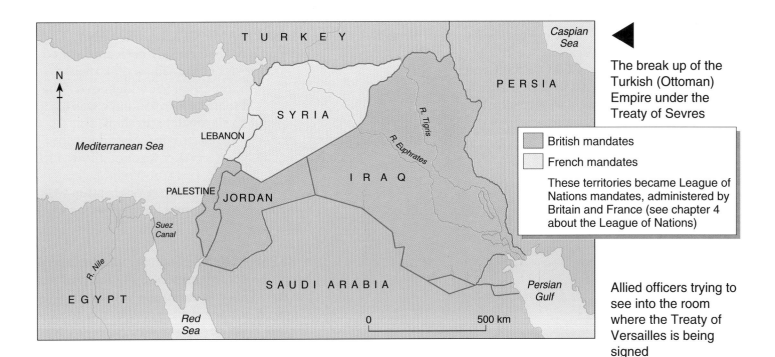

The break up of the Turkish (Ottoman) Empire under the Treaty of Sevres

British mandates

French mandates

These territories became League of Nations mandates, administered by Britain and France (see chapter 4 about the League of Nations)

Allied officers trying to see into the room where the Treaty of Versailles is being signed

The Treaty of Versailles, June 1919

Sir William Orpen's painting of the signing of the Treaty of Versailles on 28th June 1919 in the Hall of Mirrors at Versailles

At Versailles the Allies made a treaty with Germany. Germany had to accept the Treaty of Versailles because the Allies still blockaded German ports and thirty-nine divisions of Allied soldiers were on the Rhine ready to invade Germany if necessary. The Treaty of Versailles gave Clemenceau the opportunity to seek revenge for the war. Wilson's aim of an international association was also met. The League of Nations was to be established (see Chapter 4).

The German colonies which became League of Nations Mandates

This is what the Treaty of Versailles decided:

• **COLONIES.** German colonies in South, East and West Africa, and in the Far East, were to become Mandates of the League of Nations.

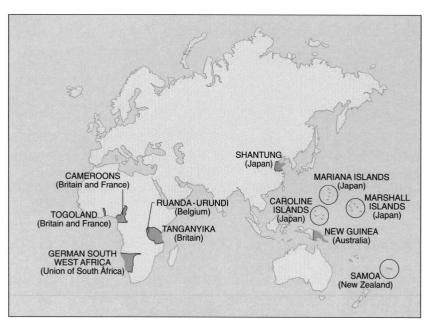

This meant that Germany lost her colonies and the League of Nations would look after them until the people were ready to rule themselves. In practice other countries looked after them on behalf of the League (see map above).

• **GERMANY'S BORDERS.**

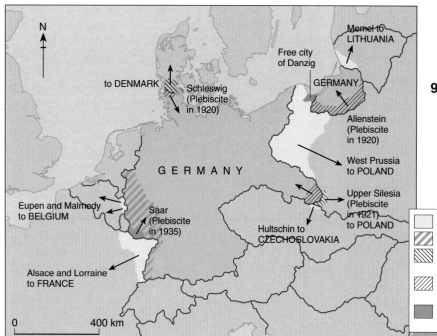

• **DISARMAMENT OF GERMANY.** The German navy had already been confiscated by the British but the sailors sank their own ships rather than hand them over. The Treaty said that the German navy was to be limited to six small battleships, six cruisers and 12 destroyers. No submarines were allowed. Germany was not allowed to have an airforce. The army could be no more than 100,000 men. Conscription was not allowed. Tanks and heavy guns were banned.

• **REPARATIONS.** Germany and her allies had to accept full responsibility for causing the war. This was called the War Guilt Clause. Germany then agreed to pay for damage done during the war. No figure for this could be fixed in 1919. Instead a Reparations Commission was set up to decide the amount. This figure was eventually fixed at £6,600 million plus interest. Much of this was to be paid in goods, such as coal, and the German merchant fleet was handed over to the Allies.

7   Look at Source E. Describe exactly what the men in the photograph are doing. What does this tell you about the importance of the Treaty of Versailles?

8   Look at the map of Germany (Source G) and at President Wilson's Fourteen Points. Work out which of the Fourteen Points had affected Germany's boundaries. What else had affected Germany's borders? Explain your answer.

9   One of Wilson's aims was to prevent further wars. Do you think that treating Germany and the other defeated countries this way would help to do this? Give your reasons.

How fairly was Germany treated at Versailles?

This really depends on whether or not you think Germany started the War. If you believe Germany started the War, as Clemenceau did, then it does not seem unreasonable to expect Germany to pay something towards the costs of the damage. Even so, the reparations payments were fixed at such a high level that it was unreasonable for Germany to pay, especially as her economy was ruined, her colonies lost, and much of her industrial capacity confiscated. Alsace and Lorraine had been French, so it could be argued that they were now being returned. But the loss of territory to Poland and Czechoslovakia, land containing many German speaking people, was resented by most Germans. German colonies were now administered by the victorious nations, which looks very much like an unfair gain from the War.

If you believe that Germany was not entirely to blame for the War and that it was more of a shared blame, then the Treaty begins to look very unfair indeed.

10 Make two lists. The first should contain all those parts of the Treaty of Versailles which a French person, in 1919, would think fair and reasonable. The second list should contain everything that a German would think unfair.

11 Is there anything on both lists? Why?

Today in the Hall of Mirrors of Versailles the disgraceful Treaty of Versailles is being signed. Do not forget it! The German people will press forward to reconquer the place among nations to which it is entitled. Then will come revenge for the shame of 1919.

From a German newspaper on the day of the signing of the Treaty.

A German cartoon, 1919. The Allies are shown as devils preparing to make Germany sign the Treaty.

A cartoon from the British magazine *Punch*, 1919

THE RECKONING.

PAN-GERMAN. "MONSTROUS, I CALL IT. WHY, IT'S FULLY A QUARTER OF WHAT *WE* SHOULD HAVE MADE *THEM* PAY, IF *WE'D* WON."

" PERHAPS IT WOULD GEE-UP BETTER IF WE LET IT TOUCH EARTH "

Briand   Lloyd George

A cartoon by left wing artist David Low. This was published in January 1921 and is criticising the high level of reparations payments which Germany had to make.

'Clemenceau: "Curious! I seem to hear a child weeping!"'
A British cartoon published in 1920. The Allies have just signed the Treaty. A German child who will be an adult in 1940 can be heard crying.

12 Look at the Sources H,I,J,K, and L. How do these sources help you to understand how Versailles appeared to different people in different countries at the time?

13 Which of these sources are the most useful for telling you how people felt about the Treaty in 1919? Explain your answer.

The consequences of Versailles

The loss of her colonies might have helped Germany. These colonies had not been very important to her. She was now no longer distracted by having to look after an overseas empire. This may have helped her to concentrate on rebuilding her position in Europe.

The new countries around Germany were supposed to act as a safeguard against future German expansion. But these countries were not strong enough to resist Germany once she became strong again. Many Germans resented having land taken away. It became a matter of pride for Germany to get back the lands taken away at Versailles. In 1935 the people living in the Saar area voted to be returned to Germany.

German soldiers and sailors also deeply resented the treatment given out at Versailles. They did not believe that they had lost the War but anyway, ways were found to beat the restrictions. For example, Germany built up an army which, although small, was well trained and professional. Small, yet fast and powerful, ships were built. It was very difficult to check on the number and size of tanks and guns.

The German people bitterly resented the way they were forced to accept the blame for the War. The Treaty was called the Diktat, in other words it was dictated, they had no say.

We are under no illusions as to the extent of our defeat and the degree of our powerlessness. We know that the strength of the German army is broken. We know the intensity of the hatred which meets us, and we have heard the victors' passionate demand that as the vanquished we shall be made to pay, and as the guilty we shall be punished.

The demand is made that we shall acknowledge that we alone are guilty of having caused the War. Such a confession would be a lie. We deny that the people of Germany, who were convinced that they were waging a war of defence, should be burdened with the sole guilt of that war.

From the speech made by Count Rantzau, the head of the German delegation at Versailles.

This resentment became focussed on the German politicians who had authorised the signing of the Armistice and the Treaty. They were called the 'November criminals' by Hitler who said they had 'stabbed Germany in the back'. The reparations payments were unrealistic. They were too high even for a strong economy. Germany found it impossible to pay. The USA had to lend massive amounts of money to Germany to help her pay off these reparations and eventually the payments had to be reduced. On the other hand, Germany was still a strong country even after Versailles, as British historian A.J.P. Taylor explained in 1969.

Germany remained by far the greatest power on the continent of Europe. It was greatest in population – 65 million against 40 million in France, the only other major power. German superiority was greater still in the economic resources of coal and steel which [equal] power. Nothing could prevent the Germans from overshadowing Europe, even if they did not plan to do so.

From *The Origins of the Second World War* by A.J.P.Taylor, 1969.

Some people have argued that the Treaty of Versailles caused the Second World War, while others, such as Taylor, say that Germany was almost bound to present future problems because it was still such a strong country. Certainly, Hitler overturned many of the Versailles decisions (see Chapter 5), and when German soldiers invaded Poland in 1939 this led to war. Though this is not the same as saying Versailles caused the War.

Hitler could have chosen peaceful methods to get back German land. Hitler may have been set on war anyway. However, in two important ways the harshness of the Treaty did help to bring about the Second World War. The harshness of the War Guilt Clause and the reparations demands made it easier for Hitler to gain power in Germany. And the severe military restrictions and territorial adjustments meant that some politicians in Britain were sympathetic to Hitler's foreign policy between 1933 and 1938.

14 Read Source M. What was Rantzau's attitude to the War Guilt Clause of the Treaty of Versailles?

15 Why did the German delegation sign the Treaty if they believed it was unfair? Use Source M and the knowledge you have gained from this chapter to explain your answer.

16 You are a German politician in 1923. You know that many Germans resent the Treaty of Versailles and those politicians who signed it. Write a short speech saying what was wrong with Versailles and what you will do about it if the people vote for you.

Essays:
i What were the peace makers trying to achieve at Versailles? Were they successful?
ii Was the Treaty of Versailles a fair settlement?

4. *The League years, 1919–1936*

A

> We must seek by the creation of some international organisation to limit the burden of armaments and diminish the probability of war.

Lloyd George, 5th January 1918.

B

> Point 14: A general association of nations must be formed to give guarantees of political independence and territorial integrity to great and small states alike.

President Woodrow Wilson, 8th January 1918.

Several months before the First World War ended, the Allies began to make clear their war aims. Lloyd George and Woodrow Wilson saw the need to establish an international association to maintain world peace. By the time that the two leaders met at Versailles, the massive death toll and huge destruction of property had convinced them that future international conflicts had to be avoided.

The body that was formed out of Wilson's 14th Point was called the League of Nations. The League's aims and objectives were set out in 26 articles known as the Covenant. Each of the peace treaties contained the 26 Articles and, therefore, those countries which signed the treaties were agreeing in principle with the philosophy of the League. President Wilson hoped that the Covenant would bind together the signatories and that this would lead to the removal of future international wars. So, for many countries the League offered the idea of collective security. This meant that all members would act together if any member were threatened by an aggressive nation.

OUR WATCH DOG.

An optimistic view of the future power of the League of Nations, published in the *Daily Graphic* in June 1920

So, the League began its life at a time of great optimism, and, during the 1920s, it did have some successes. However, in the 1930s there was a series of failures over Manchuria, Abyssinia, and German infringements of the Treaty of Versailles. By the late 1930s, the League was so discredited that it was unable to prevent war breaking out again in Europe – only 20 years after the end of the 'Great War'.

The aims and organisation of the League

Aims

The main aim of the League was, of course, to keep peace in the world and it was, therefore, committed to reducing armaments. If there were any disputes between nations then peaceful means would be used. But the League had other important aims – it was to look after the new mandated territories, improve world working and health conditions, abolish slavery, and help refugees.

The organisation of the League would help to achieve its aims and the diagram below shows how the League worked.

The structure of the League of Nations

The Assembly

The Assembly met once a year, and each member country regardless of size had one vote. The Assembly fixed the League's budget and would elect non-permanent members to the Council. Any resolutions that the Assembly made could be ignored by members.

The Council

The Council was made up of the four Great Powers – Britain, France, Italy, and Japan. These were the permanent members and the non-permanent members were chosen in rotation by other members in the Assembly. The Council was designed to cope with emergencies and could be called together at short notice. Any decisions it made had to be unanimous.

The International Court of Justice

This was set up to deal with any legal disputes that members might have. There were 15 judges from 15 different member states and its headquarters was at The Hague in the Netherlands.

The Secretariat

To ensure that the administrative work of the League was carried out effectively and efficiently, there was a Secretariat. This consisted of a Secretary-General and civil servants (chosen from member states). The headquarters of the League was in Geneva, Switzerland.

Agencies and Commissions

There was a wide range of other bodies which were created to fulfil the League's aims – the International Labour Organisation, Mandates Commission, and the Minorities Commission were among the more important.

The view of *Punch* in December 1919 on America's decision not to join the League of Nations

But, despite the high hopes that nations had for the League, there were initial problems which showed up its many weaknesses. The League did not contain all nations. The United States of America decided not to join – Congress voted against American membership and this left out the world's strongest power. Russia was not allowed to join because her leaders were keen to promote world revolution, and this was contrary to the ideals of the League. The Central Powers (Germany, Austria, Bulgaria, and Turkey) were not allowed to join, initially, as a punishment for having caused the War. It was, therefore, difficult to see the League as a body which spoke for the world. The map opposite shows the development of the membership of the League during the 1920s and 1930s.

Perhaps the most important weakness of the League was its inability to stop any state ignoring its decisions. The League could apply diplomatic pressure, economic sanctions, and even military measures to enforce a member to toe the line. However, the League was never able to call on its members to create an international peace-keeping force. This lack of any real

military power meant that in a crisis the League would be unable to combat any nation which used force. It soon became clear that if the stronger nations of the world wished to settle issues without using the League then it was powerless. Military measures were never applied and sanctions were used only once (against Italy, and then rather halfheartedly).

MORAL SUASION.

The Rabbit. "MY OFFENSIVE EQUIPMENT BEING PRACTICALLY *NIL*, IT REMAINS FOR ME TO FASCINATE HIM WITH THE POWER OF MY EYE."

 This *Punch* cartoon from 1936 shows the weakness of the League in combating aggression

1   Why were world leaders optimistic in 1920 that future wars could be avoided?
2   What were the main aims of the League of Nations?
3   Describe how the most important bodies of the League operated.
4   To what extent could critics of the League say that it did not speak for the whole world? You may need to refer to the map to answer this question.
5   What measures could the League take to ensure that members followed its decisions?

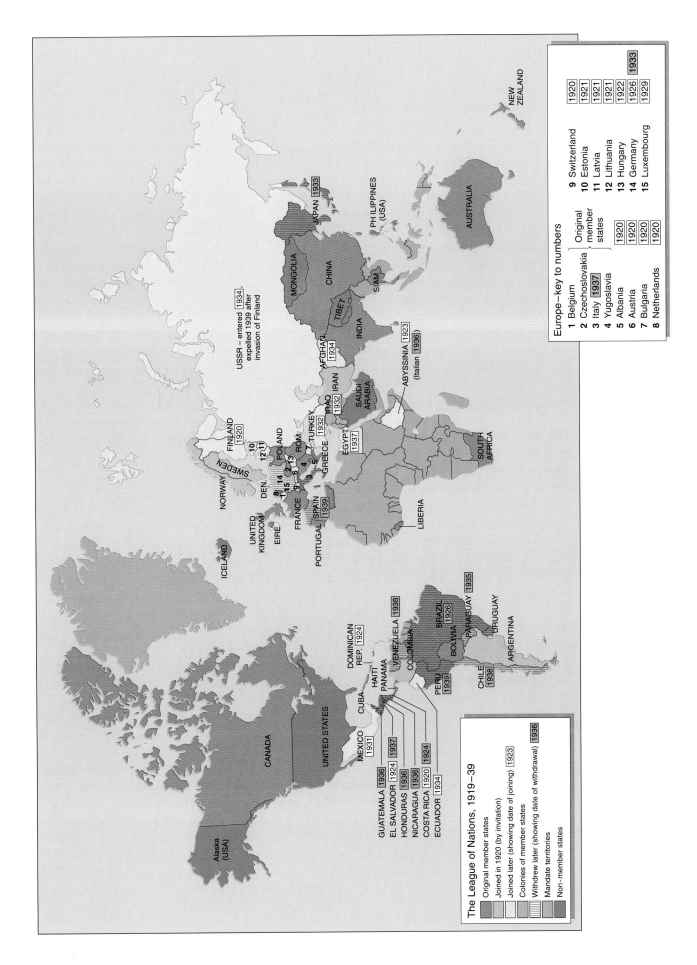

The League of Nations, 1919–39

Original member states
Joined in 1920 (by invitation)
Joined later (showing date of joining) 1923
Colonies of member states
Withdrew later (showing date of withdrawal) 1936
Mandate territories
Non-member states

Europe–key to numbers

1	Belgium	Original member states	
2	Czechoslovakia		
3	Italy 1937		
4	Yugoslavia		
5	Albania	1920	
6	Austria	1920	
7	Bulgaria	1920	
8	Netherlands	1920	
9	Switzerland	1920	
10	Estonia	1921	
11	Latvia	1921	
12	Lithuania	1921	
13	Hungary	1922	
14	Germany	1926	
15	Luxembourg	1929	

NEW ZEALAND

AUSTRALIA

JAPAN 1933

MONGOLIA

CHINA

SIAM

TIBET

INDIA

PHILIPPINES (USA)

AFGHAN. 1934

IRAQ 1932

IRAN

SAUDI ARABIA

ABYSSINIA 1923 (Italian 1936)

EGYPT 1937

SOUTH AFRICA

USSR – entered 1934, expelled 1939 after invasion of Finland

FINLAND 1920

SWEDEN

NORWAY

DEN.

POLAND

TURKEY 1932

ROM.

GREECE

UNITED KINGDOM

EIRE

FRANCE

SPAIN 1939

PORTUGAL

ICELAND

LIBERIA

Alaska (USA)

CANADA

UNITED STATES

MEXICO 1931

CUBA

HAITI

DOMINICAN REP. 1924

PANAMA

VENEZUELA 1938

COLOMBIA

PERU 1939

BOLIVIA

BRAZIL 1926

PARAGUAY 1935

URUGUAY

CHILE 1938

ARGENTINA

GUATEMALA 1936
EL SALVADOR 1924 1937
HONDURAS 1936
NICARAGUA 1936
COSTA RICA 1920 1924
ECUADOR 1934

The work of the League in the 1920s

The League was able to show the world its potential for doing good works directly after the war, when it repatriated thousands of soldiers and refugees. However, there was some irony here, because the League was unable to stop the war between Greece and Turkey, yet it was able to help the 1.5 million refugees escaping the conflict.

There were distinct areas of success for the League in the 1920s, e.g. against slavery, prostitution, and drug trafficking. There were even economic packages created which helped the economies of some European countries – Austria, Bulgaria, Hungary, Greece, and Estonia were all recipients of such economic help.

Territorial disputes

The two wars which were fought at the beginning of the 1920s did foretell future problems for the League. The conflicts between Greece and Turkey, and Poland and Russia saw aggressive member states go to war by attacking non-member states. The League was not obliged to interfere and it seemed as if there was a degree of hypocrisy involved when the League did nothing to end the fighting.

However the League could point to successes in several areas by the end of the 1920s, e.g. Aaland Islands, Silesia, Iraq, Greece, Bolivia, and Peru. Below are details about several of the major incidents which the League of Nations was involved in. For further information, you will need to look at the map opposite.

- **Vilna:** Poland and Lithuania quarrelled over this city which had a mixed population but was predominantly Polish. Lithuania was created in the peace settlement and its capital was to be Vilna. The Poles objected and simply seized control. Despite Lithuania's protests to the League, nothing was done and Poland kept the city. The League had failed in its first major challenge.
- **Aaland Islands:** Sweden and Finland both claimed ownership of these islands, and it seemed as if war could break out between the two. The issue was eventually referred to the League and the islands were given to Finland.

- **Upper Silesia:** this area of land on the Polish and German borders had a mixed population. The League was able to solve the issue of ownership by means of a plebiscite. After the voting, the territory was divided between the two countries, who found the League's decision acceptable.

However, there was one incident which seemed to show the real weakness of the League. This happened over the island of Corfu in 1923.

The Corfu incident, 1923

This arose when an Italian general was killed when he was assisting in the redrawing of the borders between Albania and Greece. The leader of Italy, Mussolini, demanded reparations and an enquiry. The Greeks refused and Mussolini's response was to bombard and then invade the Greek island of Corfu. The League suggested that a committee of enquiry be set up and that 50m lire be paid into a Swiss account until the committee reported. However, Mussolini claimed that the League had no right to interfere and that Italy would leave the League if this interference continued. The League passed the issue over to the Conference of Ambassadors (this body had been set up at the end of the war as a temporary measure until the League established itself) and ordered the money to be paid directly to Italy. The authority of the League had been undermined. The message seemed to be that a powerful

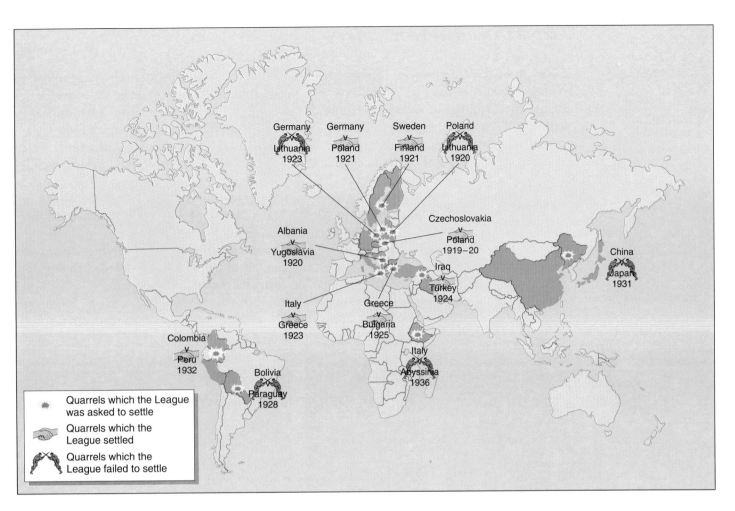

The successes and failures of the League of Nations by 1936

nation could resort to force and threats and its demands would be met. Source C shows what some people felt about the actions of Italy at the time.

THE NEW MEMBER

Mussolini   Poincaré   Cecil

C

This cartoon by David Low called 'The New Member' was published in September 1923

6   What were the successes of the League in the 1920s?

7   What evidence is there to show that the League was unable to prevent wars in the early 1920s?

8   Look at the map above. Some observers have said that the League was a complete failure from the very beginning. Does the map support or contradict this judgement? You must explain your answer carefully.

9   How did Mussolini undermine the authority of the League in the crisis over Corfu?

10 Look at Source C. What is the cartoonist trying to say about the Corfu incident?

The Manchurian crisis

It was in the 1930s when the League began to encounter problems that it could not solve. In 1931, Japan invaded the Chinese province of Manchuria and created a serious international incident. Both countries were members of the League and China appealed to the Council on the grounds that Japan had committed an act of aggression against a fellow member. By February 1932, the Japanese had occupied all of Manchuria and had renamed it Manchukuo.

Invading Japanese troops in China

The League's response to the invasion was to set up a Commission of Inquiry, which was led by Lord Lytton from the United Kingdom. It took the Commission seven months to publish its report which clearly condemned the actions of Japan. When the vote was taken to accept the report, only Japan voted against it. Directly afterwards, Japan withdrew from the Assembly and ended its membership of the League. Thus the League had failed its biggest test so far. Japan did not return Manchuria to China, and, just as over Corfu, it seemed as if a powerful nation could behave without fear of the consequences. The League had not even imposed economic sanctions, a weapon which some countries felt might have proved effective. However, many members felt that economic sanctions were not used because Britain and France were not prepared to go to war against Japan.

In many ways the failure over Manchuria sent out many signals to those who might wish to challenge the League. The next crisis to dent the authority of the League came when Italy invaded the weak African country of Abyssinia.

11 Explain why the League proved unsuccessful over the Manchurian crisis

The invasion of Abyssinia

Once again, the League had to face a serious problem caused by the aggressive actions of one of its member states. In 1935, Italy invaded Abyssinia following a border clash between the two countries at Wal Wal. (Part of Italy's African empire bordered on Abyssinia.)

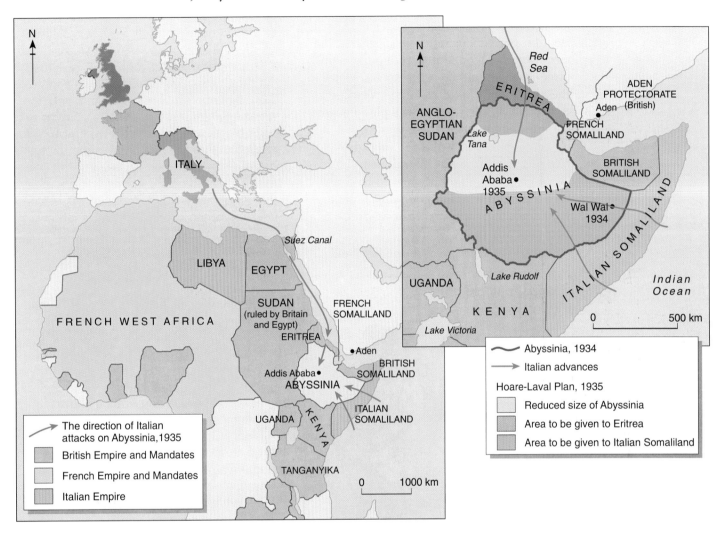

The British, French, and Italian Empires in North and Central Africa, and the Italian attack on Abyssinia. The detailed map shows the terms of the Hoare-Laval Plan.

The Italians had had designs on Abyssinia for many years and wished to enlarge their African empire. They were able to engineer a crisis and soon captured large areas of land. This was not surprising because they were using the latest in military technology (including poison gas).

Abyssinia appealed to the League and for once action was relatively speedy. Economic sanctions were applied and it was hoped that these would prevent nations from trading with Italy. Unfortunately, the sanctions did not include coal, iron, steel, and oil – the very materials a country needs if it wishes to fight a war! Some members even continued trading with Italy and of course those nations such as the USA and Germany who were not members of the League felt no pressure if they too continued to trade with Italy.

Britain and France repeatedly stated that they supported the actions of the League but they did little else to stop Mussolini. The crisis in Abyssinia was quite problematic for Britain. If Italy were condemned too sternly, then Mussolini might be tempted to ally with Hitler and the new found friendship between Britain, France, and Italy would be ruined. If

Britain had really wanted to stop Italy it could have prevented supplies reaching the Italian forces by closing the Suez Canal.

In late 1935, Britain and France did attempt to bring an end to the war. However, their solution turned out to be one which brought disgrace on both countries. Samuel Hoare and Pierre Laval, the two Foreign Secretaries, suggested that Abyssinia be divided into two parts – the larger area should be ceded to Italy and the remainder would become a smaller Abyssinia. When news of the plan became common knowledge, there was an international outcry and the infamous Hoare-Laval plan was abandoned. Nevertheless, this simply served to show the lengths to which Britain and France would go, in order to keep Italy as a potential ally (see Chapter 5 on appeasement).

The attitude of *Punch* to the Abyssinian crisis

THE AWFUL WARNING.

FRANCE AND ENGLAND (together). "WE DON'T WANT YOU TO FIGHT, BUT, BY JINGO, IF YOU DO, WE SHALL PROBABLY ISSUE A JOINT MEMORANDUM SUGGESTING A MILD DISAPPROVAL OF YOU."

Abyssinia was defeated and absorbed into the Italian Empire in 1936. The deposed Emperor of Abyssinia, Haile Selassie, made an impassioned speech to a special assembly of the League and accused the

Great Powers of breaking their promises to the small nations of the world. Abyssinia had not been saved by the promise of collective security. A further consequence of the Abyssinian crisis was the departure of Italy from the League.

▼

I was defending the cause of all small peoples who are threatened with aggression. Abyssinian warriors asked only for means to defend themselves. On many occasions I have asked for financial assistance for the purchase of arms. That assistance has been constantly refused me. The problem is a much wider one than that of Italy's aggression. It is the very existence of the League of Nations. Are states going to set up a terrible precedent of bowing before force?

Taken from the speech by Haile Selassie to the League of Nations Assembly, 30th June 1936.

12 Explain what economic sanctions are.
13 Why were economic sanctions so ineffective against Italy.
14 How had Britain and France shown themselves to be weak and selfish over Manchuria and Abyssinia?
15 The cartoonist in Source D is trying to make a serious point in a humorous way.
    i   What is the serious point?
    ii How is it made funny?
16 The cartoon is British and is critical of Britain and France. How reliable is this cartoon likely to be?

Two acts of aggression had weakened the effectiveness of the League, and by 1936 many felt that it was now a toothless organisation. The weaknesses of the League had become evident as the 1930s unfolded. By 1936, Germany had broken many of the clauses of the Treaty of Versailles and there were many in Europe who felt that another war would not be long in coming.

The League and Germany

War broke out in Europe in September 1939, only 20 years after the end of the First World War. Clearly, the high hopes and optimism of the League's founders were not met. Germany's aggressive acts after 1935 were never challenged by the League, and after 1938, the League was largely an irrelevant body ignored by the major powers of the world.

Germany was not allowed to join the League directly after the First World War and was informed that membership would depend on the acceptance of the peace settlement. There was widespread hatred of the Treaty of Versailles in Germany and it seemed that membership would take some time to achieve. Moreover, the feelings of France appeared to dominate European diplomacy, and this had resulted in the severe treatment of Germany. In 1923, the French occupied the Ruhr industrial area because Germany had been unable to pay the reparations. Troops were sent in and violence followed. Source E was published in a British newspaper.

Daily Mail cartoon about the occupation of the Ruhr by France in 1923

The League did not condemn the French action and the occupation lasted several months. The situation was solved when the USA, a non-member of the League, became involved and loaned Germany money to pay the reparations. After 1924, it did seem that relations between Germany and the League improved. Under the guidance of Gustav Stresemann, Germany accepted the Treaty of Versailles. By the Locarno Agreements (1925) it was accepted that Germany's frontiers with France and Belgium were not to be altered, the Rhineland would remain demilitarised and Germany's frontiers with Poland and Czechoslovakia would not be changed by force. These agreements paved the way for Germany joining the League in the following year.

There was continued optimism when Germany signed the Kellogg-Briand Pact in 1928, whereby countries promised never to go to war again. However, the hopes of the world were dashed the following year when the Great Depression began. In Germany the death of Stresemann added to their problems.

It was the Disarmament Conference of 1932-33, which saw a rift emerge between Germany and the League. Britain and France appeared to be rather slow in embracing the idea of disarming, and Hitler declared that Germany would completely disarm if France and Britain did. The Conference lasted several months and little progress was made. In October 1933, the Germans withdrew from the Conference and also announced that they were leaving the League. As far as they were concerned, it was Britain and France who had caused the failure of the Conference. The Disarmament Conference then broke up and with this the hopes of any lasting peace in the world seemed to evaporate.

Exclusive picture from the "Valley of the Tomb of the Kings."

David Low's comment in December 1928 on the slow pace of disarmament in the decade after the end of the First World War

PEACE (SADLY): "THIS LOOKS VERY LIKE THE POINT WE STARTED FROM."

Published five years later than Source F, in 1933, this cartoonist is commenting on the failure of the Disarmament Conference

PROFESSOR GENEVA WILL INTRODUCE KING KONG THE GREATEST MONSTER IN CAPTIVITY.

17 Look carefully at Sources F and G. If the main aim of the League was to secure peace and reduce arms, what do they tell you about the achievements of the League?

The League's failure to punish Japan and Italy over the invasions of Manchuria and Abyssinia sent the wrong kind of signals to Hitler. He saw that if he were to challenge the authority of the League there would be little to fear from the consequences of his actions. Although Germany was no longer a member of the League, Hitler's actions during the years 1935-38 broke the Treaty of Versailles and, therefore, he should have been resisted.

His first deliberate breaking of the treaty was to introduce conscription in 1935. He planned to build an army of some 550,000 troops, far in excess of the 100,000 permitted by Versailles. The League did nothing to stop this rearmament. During that same year Britain appeared to condone German rearmament when Germany was allowed to build 35% of Britain's naval tonnage. The Treaty of Versailles was broken again the following year when German troops were sent into the Rhineland – a flagrant violation of the de-militarisation clause. Once again the League did nothing in the face of military action.

The League's weakness was further shown when Austria was absorbed into Germany in 1938 and parts of Czechoslovakia ceded to her in the autumn of that year. To observers the League was no more than a paper tiger and the Treaty of Versailles had become impossible to uphold.

The events of 1939 showed the helplessness of the League (the seizure of Czechoslovakia, Memel, and the invasion of Poland); and when European war broke out in September 1939 it was impossible to defend the League.

Was the League at all successful? It was rather optimistic of the victorious nations in 1919 to think that they could maintain peace by excluding major powers. It was equally optimistic to believe that the absence of the USA was of no consequence. If the League were to succeed, then it had to include all nations, if not then the idea of collective security was illogical. There were enough indications in the 1920s that if the League were challenged then any response had to be speedy and above all firm.

You should now be in a position to write at length about the League of Nations. Answer the following question using the information from this chapter and the various sources it contains.

18 Some historians have said that the League of Nations failed because it gave in to force. Study all the sources in this chapter and use your own knowledge to explain whether you agree with this view.

Essay: 'The League of Nations was based on sound ideas but it had too many weaknesses and these proved to be its downfall.' Do you agree?
You may wish to refer to the following points:

membership

disarmament

economic sanctions

Great Depression

selfish members

militaristic states

5 The road to world war 1933–41

Twenty years after the Treaty of Versailles had been signed Europe was at war again. How did this happen? It is clear now that the Versailles Treaty left many problems for the future. By this time there were aggressive dictators in some countries, such as Hitler in Germany, and Mussolini in Italy. These leaders were determined to expand their countries by capturing territory. The way that the major powers attempted to solve these problems and deal with the dictators was not satisfactory. For example, in 1938 Britain and France refused to stand up to Germany over Czechoslovakia, they decided to 'appease' Hitler. This was one of the most controversial issues of this period. In order to understand why some countries wanted to expand, and why Britain and France behaved towards them the way they did, we have to go back to just after the First World War ended; to 1919.

1 Try to find out the names of the four leaders shown in Source A. Can you match each name to a person in the picture?
2 In what ways do the leaders of Britain and France appear to be different to the leaders of Germany and Italy?

A

A photograph taken in Munich, Germany in 1938. The picture shows the leaders of Britain, France, Germany and Italy. They have just signed an agreement which allowed Hitler to occupy a part of Czechoslovakia called the Sudetenland.

Germany after Versailles.

Chapter 3 tells you the terms of the Treaty of Versailles and how they affected Germany. Throughout the 1920s German governments were trying to overcome what they saw as the harsh treatment of Versailles. German foreign policy between 1919 and 1933, and then the policy of Hitler, can only be fully understood once the extent of German resentment of the Versailles Treaty is understood. No leading German politician publicly accepted the eastern borders (with Poland and Czechoslovakia) dictated at Versailles. All parties in Germany were agreed that the Versailles settlement had been unfair and that it should be overturned. But they differed in their methods.

In 1922 Germany signed the Treaty of Rapallo with the USSR. Germany and the USSR were both left out of the international community after the First World War, and it made sense to them both to make a treaty which was mostly about trade. Germany would exchange industrial goods for Russian food and raw materials. But the Rapallo Treaty also had some secret agreements which allowed the German army to train in the USSR, using tanks and other weapons which the Versailles Treaty had banned them from having.

The main problem for Germany was paying the reparations demanded by the Allies. In 1923 the Germans claimed that they did not have the money and stopped paying. The French Prime Minister, Poincare, did not believe this and sent French soldiers into the Ruhr area of Germany to take coal to France instead of the reparation payments.

B A photograph taken in the Ruhr in 1923. The picture shows some French soldiers posing outside a German bank in the city of Essen. Do the soldiers have any guns? What does this suggest?

But the situation was not as friendly as Source B seems to suggest. The German workers went on strike.

Wherever foreign soldiers appeared, German workers downed tools. The trains stopped running, the steelworks and factories emptied, the miners went home, farmers hid their food stocks, many shopkeepers locked up their premises...life came to a standstill.

The memories of a German living in the Ruhr in 1923.

This 'passive resistance' to the French occupation was unsuccessful. French engineers and miners were sent to the Ruhr. Some German civilians were killed and wounded in outbreaks of fighting. In September 1923, the Germans agreed to resume the reparations payments. This was a massive victory for Poincare and the French. They had forced the Germans to give way without the help of the other Allies.

The foreign policy of Stresemann, 1923–1929.

Between 1923 and 1929 German foreign policy was dominated by Gustav Stresemann. Gustav Stresemann was leader of the German Peoples Party (DVP). He was Chancellor of Germany for just four months in 1923. Then he became Foreign Minister until he died in 1929. Stresemann wanted to alter the Treaty of Versailles. He wanted to make Germany stronger. Here are some of the achievements of Stresemann.

a   In 1923 he appointed Dr. Schacht as special currency commissioner. Schacht introduced the Rentenmark. This helped to end the inflation crisis which had plagued Germany since the French occupation of the Ruhr.

b   In 1924 he negotiated the Dawes Plan with the USA. The reparations payments were reduced and Germany received loans of 800 million gold marks from the USA. This money helped to end the inflation crisis and was used to pay reparations.

c In 1925 he signed the Locarno Treaty (see Chapter 4.) This made the British and French feel much easier and so they moved some of their troops out of Germany, although the occupation did not fully end until 1930. This was an important change in the Versailles Treaty. Stresemann and the British Foreign Secretary, Austen Chamberlain, won the Nobel Peace Prize for their work in making the Locarno Treaty.

D

A British cartoon showing the signing of the Locarno Treaty in 1925. The characters are, from left to right, Briand representing France, Chamberlain of Britain and Stresemann of Germany. While they shake hands, Briand has a boxing glove behind his back and is ready to give Germany a 'knock out blow.' What does this cartoon tell you about how the British saw France and Germany at this time?

d In 1926 Germany was accepted as a member of the League of Nations.

e In 1929 Stresemann negotiated the Young Plan. This further reduced reparations payments. This was another important change in the Versailles Treaty.

f While he was negotiating with the Americans, the British, and the French, and accepting their loans, Stresemann was secretly building up Germany's armed forces; and because of this a German army 35 divisions strong existed even before the Nazis came to power.

Now it is for you to begin to decide how important Gustav Stresemann was.

3 In groups you are going to write newspaper obituaries of Stresemann following his death in October 1929. You should use the six points above to help

you. You should also find out all you can about the man and the period. Use as many different books as you can. Remember to use the contents and index and to 'scan read' where you can. Use the following headings to record information:
• Stresemann
• Treaty of Versailles
• Reparations
• Inflation crisis
• Treaty of Locarno

Each group will write for a different newspaper. These are: Berliner Tageblatt (world famous liberal newspaper), Le Monde (French national daily), New York Times (USA), Voelkischer Beobachter (Nazi Party newspaper). By the way, your editor will allow you just 200 words and one picture. You must think carefully about what you will say about Stresemann and how you will portray him.

Share these obituaries with the whole class, either report back or mount a wall display.

4 How similar were your obituaries? What does this show about different interpretations in history?

5 How important was Stresemann to Germany in the 1920s?

The problem of Italy, 1935–6

Before 1935 Italy was not seen as a threat to the balance of power or to peace. Most Italians thought that they had gained very little from the First World War; and after the War their economy was in a poor state. Benito Mussolini came to power there in 1922. He soon became a dictator. However, throughout the 1920s and early 1930s Mussolini did little that would upset the other powers. Instead he tried to prove Italy's power within the international community, for example in the League of Nations. Italy was seen as a country that could help to resist Germany. When the Austrian Nazi Party tried to take over in Austria in 1934 and Hitler was tempted to send German soldiers to help them, he was prevented by Mussolini. Mussolini rushed Italian troops to the Austrian border, threatening to use them against the Germans. It is worthwhile noting this incident, for it shows that Hitler retreated when he was faced by a country prepared to use force.

This view of Italy as a peaceful power changed in October 1935 when Italy invaded Abyssinia (see Chapter 4 for details). Once again the British and French were weak in their response. Through the League of Nations they imposed some sanctions on Italy, for example all imports from Italy were banned by the other League members; but these did not work. In December 1935 the British and French Foreign Ministers met and made a plan to solve the problem of Abyssinia. This was a private deal and involved acting without the League of Nations. When news of this Hoare-Laval Plan became known, it caused a storm of protest in Britain and Hoare was forced to resign. He was replaced by Anthony Eden who distrusted Mussolini and was in favour of stronger action against Italy. Eden was unsuccessful and

Italy could not be moved from Abyssinia. In May 1936 Abyssinia became part of the Italian Empire.

The results of the Abyssinian Crisis

The Abyssinian Crisis marked the end of the League of Nations Organisation as an effective peace keeping body. It also split Italy from Britain and France. Mussolini felt bitter at the way he had been treated by the western powers and he began to move closer to Germany. Some historians believe that failure to take strong action against Italy was a step along the road to war. They say that Italy could have been easily defeated in 1935 and that this would have been a lesson to both Italy and Germany. It would have shown that Britain and France were prepared to work together against aggression. Others have argued differently. They say that Italy might not have been so easy to defeat as it was quite well prepared for war in 1935. Anyway, it would have left a bitter and resentful Italy which may well have been a problem in the future.

The Civil War in Spain 1936–1939

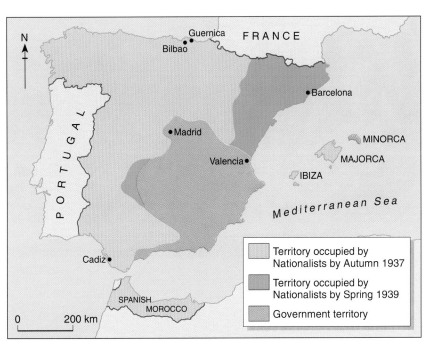

The Spanish Civil War, 1936-39

Since 1931 Spain had been a Republic with a Socialist government. This government followed policies of land redistribution and granted some independence to the areas of Catalonia in the north-east and the Basque province in the north. This government attacked the power of the Catholic Church and tried to reduce the power of the army. Divisions between the extremist political groups were turning to violence. In 1934 there was a Communist revolt in the northern province of Asturias. This was put down by the army. By 1936 street battles in the major towns and cities were common. These were between the right wing group called the Falange and the Communists. On 17th June 1936 three army Generals (Goded, Franco and Mola) led a mutiny of the Spanish army in Morocco. This spread to the mainland and a Civil War began. The Government or Republican forces were strongest around the capital city, Madrid, and the industrial area of Barcelona and Valencia. They were supported by all the left wing parties and the Basques and Catalonians, who wanted to keep their recently won independence. The rebels were led by General Franco. His force was made up of the army, the monarchists, the rich land owners and the devout Catholics. They called themselves the Nationalists. The fighting in this war was some of the most savage and destructive that Europe had ever seen. More than half a million Spaniards died in the war.

The Spanish Civil War was important for a number of reasons. Firstly, because it was a conflict between the two political extremes. As left and right fought each other in Spain, the Communist and Fascist countries of Europe became involved. Germany and Italy supported the Nationalists. Mussolini sent fifty-six thousand soldiers to Spain, disguised as volunteers. Hitler sent bomber aeroplanes and crews, tanks, and artillery. In 1937 Italian submarines sank merchant shipping in Spanish waters. The Republicans were helped by the Soviet Union, which sent munitions and military advisers. The Russian agency Comintern organised groups of volunteers from all over the world to go to Spain. These were called International Brigades.

Secondly, the Soviet leader, Stalin, became sure that Britain and France were not prepared to co-operate with the USSR to prevent the spread of Fascism. The governments in Britain and France wished to keep out of the fighting. Stalin was disillusioned with the western powers. He withdrew Soviet aid to the Republicans in 1938 and this allowed the Nationalists to capture more territory and win the war more swiftly than they might otherwise have done.

A third reason for the importance of the Spanish Civil War is that it was an unofficial rehearsal for any future conflict.

German and Italian troops and air crews were trained for war in Spain. There they could try out their weapons and tactics. The attack on the Spanish city of Guernica in April 1937 by German bombers showed the world the destructive power of modern military engineering. Newsreels of the destruction of Guernica, and other Spanish cities such as the capital Madrid, and the tragic loss of civilian life there, were shown in cinemas in Britain, France, and the USA. This confirmed British Prime Minister Stanley Baldwin's view that 'the bomber will always get through.' It strengthened the desire for peace in those countries.

E Some of the destruction done to part of Madrid after heavy German bombing raids during the Spanish Civil War, 1938

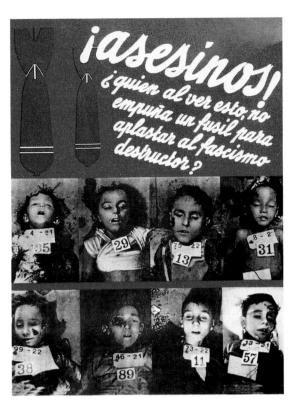

A poster issued by the Republicans to show the deaths caused by Nationalist air raids such as those on Guernica and Madrid. These eight children were killed in Madrid. The Spanish caption reads 'Murder! On seeing this, who won't seize a gun to crush the Fascist destructors?'

6 Explain why Germany, Italy, and the Soviet Union became involved in the Spanish Civil War.
7 Why did Britain and France stay out of the conflict?
8 What effect did the Spanish Civil War have on public opinion in other European countries? Why did it have such an effect?
9 Look at Sources E and F. How reliable are these sources for showing the effects of the bombing raids? What are the problems facing historians of the Civil War in Spain when they use sources such as these? Explain your answer fully.

Hitler's foreign policy, 1933–1939

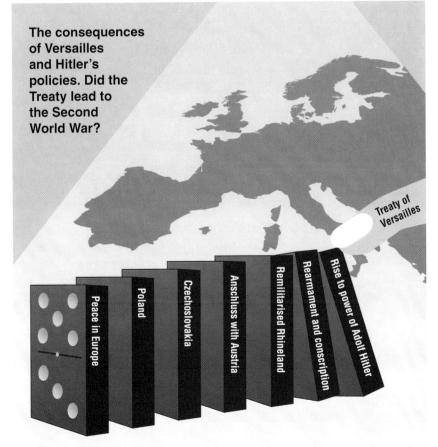

The consequences of Versailles and Hitler's policies. Did the Treaty lead to the Second World War?

Treaty of Versailles

Peace in Europe

Poland

Czechoslovakia

Anschluss with Austria

Remilitarised Rhineland

Rearmament and conscription

Rise to power of Adolf Hitler

The early years, 1933–1936

Adolf Hitler became Chancellor of Germany in 1933. His party (the Nazis) had gained many votes because they promised to reduce unemployment and make Germany strong again. Soon after his appointment as Chancellor, Hitler set about overturning much of the Treaty of Versailles. Hitler's first step was to appeal to the other powers to disarm. When they refused to do so, Hitler withdrew Germany from the Disarmament Conference (1932-34) and then in October 1933 he pulled out of the League of Nations (see Chapter 4). Hitler said this gave Germany the right to build up its armed forces because Germany could no longer rely on collective security through the League of Nations for defence. Germany carried on building up its armed forces. Although most of this was done in secret it soon became clear what Germany was doing. Yet few politicians in other countries objected. One who did was the British Member of Parliament, Winston Churchill.

G

Our neighbour Germany is arming fast and no one is going to stop her. That seems quite clear. No one proposes a war to stop Germany breaking the Treaty of Versailles. She is going to arm; she is doing it; she has been doing it. We want the measures to achieve parity. No nation in the world has a right to be in a position where it can be blackmailed.

From a speech by Winston Churchill to the British Parliament, March 1934.

10 Explain what Churchill is objecting to in Source G. What is he arguing in favour of?

Germany made a non-aggression pact with Poland in 1934. This was a promise made by both countries that any disagreements between them would be sorted out peacefully. They would not go to war. This was a clever agreement to make because it reduced the fears of the British and French. Then, in March 1935, Hitler announced that Germany had an airforce and that it was his intention to create an army of 550,000 men by introducing conscription. There was now no secret about German rearmament.

The reaction of Britain and France to German rearmament was weak. Representatives of these countries and Italy met in 1935 in a town called Stresa where they agreed to work together in order to preserve the peace in Europe. This became known as the Stresa Front against German aggression, but it did not last long. The British Government, still led by Baldwin, sympathised with Germany's right to rearm. It was reassured about Germany since the pact with Poland and was more worried about the power of France at this time. Since 1919 France had been more powerful than Germany and the British were concerned that France might become aggressive because of this power. In June 1935 Baldwin's Government made a naval agreement with Germany. This was called the Anglo-German Naval

Agreement. It allowed Germany to build as many submarines as Britain had and up to 35% of Britain's surface warships. Britain was afraid of a new arms race with Germany and so hoped to avoid one by giving concessions to Germany early on. This policy, of making concessions in order to avoid conflict, is called appeasement. Britain's action broke the Stresa Front. The French and Italians felt betrayed that they had not been consulted.

In March 1936 Hitler ordered a small number of soldiers to cross into the Rhineland, the area which was demilitarised.

This was a clear breach of both the Treaties of Versailles and Locarno. Hitler's excuse was that Germany was being threatened by the Franco-Soviet alliance of 1935. But he knew he was taking a great risk. The German troops had orders that they were to withdraw if they were opposed by the French. In fact the British and French did nothing. The French dared not act without Britain's support and the British Government took the view that the Rhineland was German anyway, so really they should be allowed to have soldiers

A photograph taken in 1936 showing German soldiers marching into the demilitarised Rhineland

there. As one senior politician in Britain put it, Germany moving troops into the Rhineland was really 'only going into her own back yard.' That was not how everyone in Britain saw the situation though, as shown by Source I from *Punch*, a popular magazine of the time.

THE GOOSE-STEP.
"GOOSEY GOOSEY GANDER,
WHITHER DOST THOU WANDER?"—
"ONLY THROUGH THE RHINELAND—
PRAY EXCUSE MY BLUNDER!"

 A cartoon from *Punch* magazine, 1936. It shows Germany as a big goose marching into the Rhineland. The German soldiers at that time often marched with a high kicking step. This was called the goose step. The original caption is a play on the popular children's rhyme 'Goosey, goosey gander.'

11 What is the goose wearing and what is it carrying? What are the flags on the buildings in the background?
12 What are the similarities between the goose in Source I and the German soldiers in Source H?
13 What is the piece of paper that the goose has walked over and torn? Why was this important?
14 Why did the cartoonist choose to show this Treaty rather than the Versailles Treaty?
15 What impression of Germany does the cartoonist give? Explain your answer.

1938, the year of appeasement

 A painting of Neville Chamberlain, British Prime Minister 1937–1940

16 Source J is a painting of Prime Minister Chamberlain which is now in the National Portrait Gallery in London. Before you read on find out more about Chamberlain. Think about the impression of Chamberlain you get from this portrait. What kind of character do you think is shown in the portrait?
17 What are the problems of portraits such as this for historians?

Appeasement is one of the great controversies of twentieth-century history. Historians still argue about whether it was the right policy to have followed, or whether it was a policy of great weakness. Appeasement has been seen by many historians as being the policy of Neville Chamberlain, Prime Minister of Britain from 1937 to 1940, but it did not begin with Chamberlain. By the time he became Prime Minister, the policy was well established. However, it was Chamberlain who had to deal with the most threatening of the dictators, Adolf Hitler. Chamberlain was the brother of Austen Chamberlain who had won the Nobel Peace Prize following the Locarno Treaty in 1925. He had been Lord Mayor of Birmingham where he had introduced many social reforms, including the building of council houses, schools, and public libraries. He had then become Chancellor of the Exchequer, the Minister responsible for taxation and spending. Chamberlain believed in social improvement and this is what he wanted to spend the nation's money on. He had a great desire to keep peace in Europe and was prepared to take an active personal role in foreign affairs.

The Austrian Anschluss, 1938

Hitler was able to use his influence over the weak Austrian Chancellor Schuschnigg. In 1938 Schuschnigg was forced by Hitler to appoint an Austrian Nazi, Seyss-Inquart, to an important post in his government. When Schuschnigg resigned over the Anschluss question, Seyss-Inquart took over as Chancellor, but the President refused to recognise his appointment. Austria was then troubled by civil disorder. Seyss-Inquart asked for Hitler's help in restoring order. Hitler ordered German troops to cross the border into Austria on 12th March 1938 and on the next day an Anschluss or union between Austria and Germany was announced. Once again this was something strictly prohibited by the Treaty of Versailles. How would the great powers react? Italy now had an African Empire. Mussolini was not closely tied to Britain or France. He was now more tolerant of Hitler's expansion. The British and French did nothing. Their governments seem to have been taken by surprise. Neither of them was prepared to risk a confrontation with Hitler over Austria now that the Anschluss had taken place. Hitler helped to divert opposition by claiming that without his actions Austria would have faced a civil war. In Britain, Winston Churchill once again spoke out.

Europe is faced with a programme of aggression, there is only one choice open, not only to us but to other countries, either to submit like Austria, or else take effective measures while time remains to ward off the danger...Where are we going to be in two years time, when the German army will certainly be much larger than the French army.

From a speech by Churchill in 1938 when he was an ordinary Member of Parliament.

The crisis over Czechoslovakia, 1938

By the time of the Czech crisis in the summer of 1938, Hitler was in a very strong position. Czechoslovakia had been created in 1919 from the old Austrian Empire. As well as Czechs and Slovaks, there were many German speaking people there. Three million Germans lived in an area called the Sudetenland where there was a strong Nazi Party. This Party pressurised the Czech Government to allow the Sudeten Germans self-rule or union with Germany. Hitler supported the Sudeten Czech Nazi Party in their aims, and, once the Anschluss with Austria had been achieved, the Sudetenland was almost surrounded by Germany. It soon became clear to everybody that Hitler would be prepared to go to war with Czechoslovakia over the Sudetenland. France had an alliance with the Czechs and might have to become involved. Britain might be forced to help France. In September 1938 it looked as though there would be a war. British school children were evacuated from the cities to safer rural areas. Trenches were dug in parks and gas masks were issued to the people to keep them alive should Britain be attacked by aeroplanes dropping gas bombs.

You must try to understand how the situation seemed to people at the time. It was only 20 years since the First World War had ended and every adult in Britain had vivid memories of the horror and misery of that war. The events of the Civil War in Spain, showing everybody the damage that could be done by aeroplanes, reinforced the Government's fear of the destruction and chaos that bombing raids would cause.

Neville Chamberlain took the decision to fly out to Germany to meet Hitler face to face. In September 1938 Chamberlain flew to Hitler's country home at Berchtesgaden. Chamberlain and Hitler agreed that all those parts of Czechoslovakia which contained more than 50% Germans should be handed over to Germany, and in return Hitler agreed not to attack Czechoslovakia before Chamberlain had time to convince the Czechs and the French of this plan. Chamberlain kept his part of the bargain and flew back to Germany later in September to inform Hitler of this. Chamberlain was surprised when Hitler then increased his demands by claiming the right to occupy the Sudetenland within eight days. Both the British Parliament and the French Prime Minister thought that they should now stand up to Hitler's

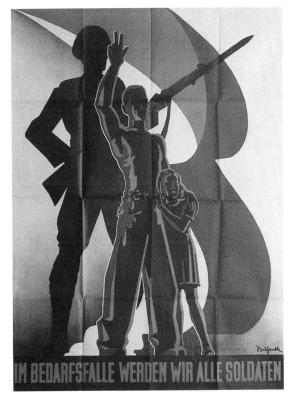

A poster distributed throughout Czechoslovakia in 1938. It reads 'We will all become soldiers if necessary'.

bullying. The Czechs were prepared to fight but they could not do so successfully alone. However, Chamberlain still wanted to avoid a war if possible. On 27th September he spoke to the British people on the radio (Source L).

> How horrible, fantastic, incredible, it is that we should be digging trenches and trying on gas masks here because of a quarrel in a far away country between people of whom we know nothing...I would not hesitate to pay even a third visit to Germany, if I thought it would do any good.

Part of Prime Minister Chamberlain's radio broadcast, 27th September 1938.

Chamberlain tried to avoid war again. He accepted Mussolini's idea of a four power conference at Munich to discuss the crisis. Britain, France, Germany, and Italy met in September 1938 to discuss Czechoslovakia. The Czech Government did not take part in the talks. Hitler was allowed to occupy the Sudetenland before the Sudeten Germans had voted on whether or not to join Germany. The Czech leader, Benes, was given no say. His Government could either accept the Munich decisions or fight alone. Chamberlain persuaded Hitler to sign a declaration that the Sudetenland was Germany's last territorial claim in Europe. He returned to Britain proudly waving this piece of paper.

> My good friends, this is the second time in our history that there has come back from Germany to Downing Street peace with honour...I believe it is peace for our time.

Part of a speech made by Neville Chamberlain on his return from the Munich Conference in October 1938.

Attitudes to appeasement

Anthony Eden resigned as Foreign Secretary over Chamberlain's dealings with Mussolini, but this was really because he believed Chamberlain was overruling him. Once out of the Cabinet, Eden spoke against appeasement. The other opponent of appeasement was Winston Churchill, who consistently warned of German rearmament and was in favour of tough action over Czechoslovakia.

> We have suffered a total defeat. All is over...I think you will find that in a period of time Czechoslovakia will be overrun by the Nazis. We have passed an awful milestone in our history, when the whole balance of power in Europe has been upset. And do not suppose that this is the end. This is only the beginning of the reckoning.

Winston Churchill's reaction to news of the Munich Conference, from a speech made to Parliament in 1938.

However, only Gallagher, the single Communist Member of Parliament, spoke against Chamberlain when he was about to fly to Munich to try to solve the Czech crisis. So we can see that there was considerable support for appeasement within Parliament. The public may have had different opinions of course, but Chamberlain received about 30,000 letters supporting his actions, and surveys at the time show there was considerable support for appeasement until March 1939.

An assessment of appeasement

Was appeasement a success or a failure? Was Chamberlain right to try to appease Hitler? There has been much disagreement about Chamberlain's appeasement of Hitler. Some politicians at the time (like Churchill) and many historians since, believed that Chamberlain had chosen the wrong policy. They believed that Hitler could never be appeased because he was determined to go to war.

> The blame [for the war] must rest with Hitler who had disregarded treaties and even his own undertakings and who committed aggression against his neighbours.

The historian M. Isaac criticising Hitler in 1965.

They thought that Britain should have taken much stronger action against Germany in 1938, when Germany was still weak. They also believed that Chamberlain was a poor leader because he would not listen to advice and preferred to act on his own. There is a lot of evidence to suggest that appeasement was a failure. Appeasing Hitler did not prevent war. War in Europe broke out in 1939. By allowing Hitler into the Sudetenland, Chamberlain strengthened the enemy. For the tanks and other arms Hitler's soldiers captured in Czechoslovakia were eventually used against Poland and France.

On the other hand, Chamberlain was not the first to use appeasement and we have seen that, by the time he came to power, appeasement was an established policy. By not opposing the dictators before 1937, Britain and France contributed to their aggressive demands and actions, and had made Chamberlain's task more difficult. For example, if Japan and Italy had been more vigorously opposed, then Hitler may have been more cautious. Germany itself could have been opposed early on. For instance, when the Rhineland was remilitarised in 1936, the German generals had warned Hitler against it. The German troops had orders to withdraw if they were opposed, but Britain and France did nothing. There is evidence that appeasement was a very popular policy in Britain. When Chamberlain returned from Munich in 1938, he was greeted with enthusiasm by politicians and the public, mainly because hardly anybody wanted war. Historians have pointed out that Chamberlain bought time to strengthen Britain's armed forces, especially the air force, so that it was better prepared for war in 1939 than in 1938. They say appeasement was the only policy in 1938 because Britain was weak and could not fight a war. British rearmament had begun in 1936 when Chamberlain, as Chancellor of the Exchequer, had introduced a four year plan. This meant Britain would not be ready for war until 1940. After Munich, Britain's spending on rearmament rose sharply. The production of aircraft rose from 240 per month in 1938 to 660 per month by September 1939. By the end of 1939, British aircraft production had overtaken that of Germany. In 1939 Britain also decided to raise a much bigger army, an army of 32 divisions which could play a part in a European war.

Britain was not ready for war in 1935, 1936, or 1938. The British economy had not been strong enough to support a large air force, army, or navy. Certainly the time gained by appeasement was put to good use in building the aircraft which would become vital in the defence of Britain. Another factor which helps explain why successive British Governments followed a policy of appeasement was Britain's Empire. This stretched as far away as India and Australia. Protecting the Empire was the main task of the British army and navy. The cost of protecting it was high. Governments were warned by the Foreign Office and military experts that Britain could not fight a war in Europe at the same time as protecting the Empire. Once the Japanese invasion of China had taken place (see Chapter 4) the defence of the Empire seemed to be the priority. To keep a free hand in the Far East it was vital not to be involved in a European war. This helps to explain why appeasement seemed to be the correct policy.

18 Study Source M What can you learn from this Source about Neville Chamberlain's view of the Munich agreement?

19 Study Sources M, N, and O.
   i In what ways do Sources N and O disagree with the evidence of Source M?
   ii Chamberlain and Churchill (Sources M and N) were from the same political party and both were Members of Parliament in 1939. Why did they have such different views about appeasement?
   Use the sources and your own knowledge to explain your answer.

20 Use the sources and your own knowledge to do the following task.

   Make two lists in your notes:

Arguments criticising Chamberlain	Arguments in favour of appeasement

The drift to war in 1939

In March 1939 Hitler took over more of Czechoslovakia and Hungary took the rest. Chamberlain told the British House of Commons that Britain would not go to war over Czechoslovakia. But now it was clear to everybody that Hitler was not to be trusted. Just seven months earlier he had signed a paper saying that the Sudetenland would be his last territorial demand.

The break up of Czechoslovakia in 1938 and 1939

▶

Czech citizens giving the Nazi salute as German troops invade Czechoslovakia in March 1939

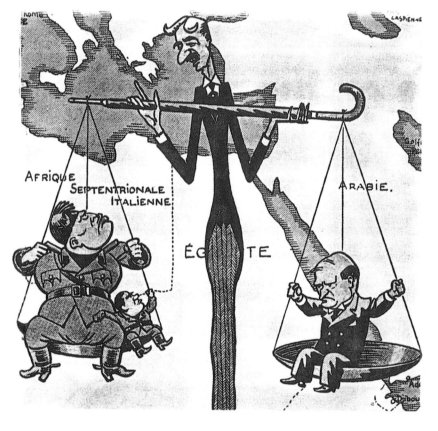

This French cartoon shows that some French people believed Chamberlain was prepared to bargain away anything to appease the dictators. 'Will Chamberlain now give French North Africa to Mussolini?', it asks.

21 Are the people in Source P happy at the arrival of the Germans?
22 Why do you think they are giving the Nazi salute?

Many British people began to lose confidence in the Government. They began to think that Chamberlain was weak. It seemed clear that Poland was where Hitler was likely to move next. Part of Germany had been given to Poland in 1919 and there were many German speaking people there. Chamberlain decided to offer a guarantee to Poland. The guarantee said that if Poland was attacked, Britain would come to her aid. The French Government said the same. This was a change of policy. Chamberlain would not use force to protect the Czechs, but was now ready to use it to help the Poles. Why did this change of policy take place in 1939? It is not as simple as Chamberlain not wanting to help the Czechs but being prepared to help Poland. Remember in 1938 the Government was receiving lots of advice to keep out of a European war, and Chamberlain was greeted as a hero when he came back from Munich. Perhaps Chamberlain had really believed that Hitler meant what he said about the Sudetenland being his last territorial demand.

In spite of the hardness and ruthlessness I thought I saw in his face, I got the impression that here was a man who could be relied upon when he had given his word.

Chamberlain's view of Hitler following the meetings of 1938.

Perhaps it was only when the rest of Czechoslovakia was taken over in 1939 that he realised negotiations would not work with Hitler. Many have criticised the guarantee to Poland. The Polish Government was a right wing dictatorship at the time and perhaps not worth fighting for. In any case there was no feasible way the British could do anything to help the Poles without the help of the Soviet Union.

23 Study Sources N and S and the map of Czechoslovakia on page 63. Explain the value of these sources in helping you to understand the importance of Czechoslovakia in 1938 and 1939.

24 Source S was published in 1938, but we are not told exactly when. Use your own knowledge to say at which point in the events this cartoon was published. Give your reasons.

Anglo-Soviet relations 1938-39

Since 1917 when the Communists took over Russia, relations between Britain and the Soviet Union had been cool. There were some trading alliances during the 1920s but little else. The leader of the Soviet Union after 1928 was Joseph Stalin. He was a dictator who concentrated on rebuilding the economy of his country and driving out any political opponents. He was not the kind of leader the British Government wished to deal with.

I must confess to the most profound distrust of Russia. I have no belief in her ability to maintain an effective offensive, even if she wanted to. And I distrust her motives, which seem to me to have little connection with our ideas of liberty.

Chamberlain on the USSR.

Stalin believed that Germany was likely to attack the Soviet Union at some time. There was a lot of evidence to support Stalin's belief. Hitler had written his ideas in a book called *Mein Kampf*. In this book he said that Germany must expand eastwards to find 'living space', and he also pointed out his hatred of Communists and his desire to defeat Communism for ever. What Stalin wanted most was an alliance with Britain and France against Germany. But to the Soviets it looked as though the western powers were not going to do anything to oppose Hitler. Britain and France's actions over Spain and Czechoslovakia convinced him of this.

A Soviet cartoon from 1938. The Englishman is telling the Czech not to let himself be shot by the German. Instead he should put his head into the noose. The noose is labelled 'give in'.

In 1939 Stalin invited the British Foreign Secretary, Lord Halifax, to come to the Soviet Union for talks. He refused. The year before the British Prime Minister had flown out to meet Hitler three times. Why was there such a difference in the way the British Government viewed Hitler and Stalin? Both were dictators. The British knew far less about the Soviet Union than they did about Germany, and they distrusted Communists. British intelligence told them that the Soviet army was so weak that Britain would be much better off making an alliance with Poland than with the USSR.

In August 1939 the British decided that they would send somebody to talk to the Soviet Government. They chose an Admiral called Reginald Ranfurly Plunckett-Ernle-Erle-Drax. They sent him by ship and train rather than by air. This way it took days to get to Moscow. Once there he met senior Soviet military officials and they asked him if the Soviet army could have permission to fight the Germans inside Poland? How would Britain feel about this? Drax had not been briefed and was not senior enough to make a decision. He did not know what to say and eventually had to return home to report to the Foreign Office. The talks broke down. Stalin was now sure the British wanted nothing to do with him. In September Germany and the Soviet Union signed the Nazi-Soviet Pact.

25 Read Source R. What reasons does Chamberlain give for not trusting the USSR?

26 How does this compare with the Soviet view of Britain in Source S?

27 Use these two sources and your own knowledge to explain why Anglo-Soviet relations were so strained during 1939.

The Nazi-Soviet Pact, 1939

Hitler did not take the guarantees made to Poland by Britain and France seriously. And really why should he? Britain and France had not taken strong action in the past and they were on the other side of Europe. There was little they could do. Although Britain and France had promised to protect Poland, Hitler knew it was only the Soviet Union which could do anything to stop him. Hitler ordered his generals to prepare to invade Poland. Before they could move, however, Hitler negotiated an agreement with the Soviet Union. Each country agreed not to fight each other. This agreement is known as the Nazi-Soviet Pact. The Nazi-Soviet Pact ensured that the Soviet Union would not stop Germany in Poland. The Pact also gave Stalin time to prepare for war.

> We secured peace for our country for one and a half years, as well as an opportunity of preparing our forces for defence if Fascist Germany risked attacking our country. This was a definite gain for Russia and a loss for Fascist Germany.

Stalin speaking in a radio broadcast in 1941.

In this way the Nazi-Soviet Pact achieved the same for the USSR as the Munich Agreement did for Britain and France. Soviet industry began producing armaments and by 1943 Soviet tank production had overtaken that of Germany.

A cartoon about the Nazi-Soviet Pact. This cartoon appeared in an English newspaper in September 1939.

Days after the Nazi-Soviet agreement was signed, Poland was invaded by both Germany and the USSR. The Polish guarantee had been a bluff which did not work. Because of it Britain declared war on Germany in September 1939. Many people thought this should have happened six months earlier

28 Read Source T. In what ways are Stalin's reasons for agreeing the Nazi-Soviet Pact similar to appeasement?

29 Look at Source U.
   i Who are the two men standing face to face?
   ii How are they behaving towards each other?
   iii How does their behaviour compare to the words they are speaking?

30 What is shown on the ground between them and what does it represent?

31 Study sources L, M, N, O, Q, R, and S. Many politicians at the time, and historians since, have criticised Neville Chamberlain for trying to appease Hitler and for then changing his policy towards Germany. He has been criticised for giving a guarantee to the Poles when the British were in no position to help Poland. He has also been criticised for failing to react positively to the USSR. Use the sources, and your own knowledge to write an *extended* answer (not an essay, a page or so) to explain whether you think Chamberlain has been unfairly criticised.

Japan's road to war, 1936–1941

Since 1931 the army had been very powerful in Japan. Japan's successes in Manchuria (see Chapter 4) strengthened their position and there were also some politicians in Japan who wanted to expand Japan's territory even further. The Emperor Hirohito supported expansion. In 1937 the Japanese army moved south from Manchuria into China and a full scale war began. The Japanese soon captured most of north-east China and they then went on to take Shanghai. By the end of 1938, Japan controlled most of eastern China.

Japan had clear aims in this expansion. It wanted the oil, tin, and rubber which the countries of south-east Asia possessed. In November 1938 Japan announced that China, Japan, and Manchuria would combine into one economic unit. This would be under Japanese leadership and would be known as the 'Greater East Asia Co-prosperity Sphere.' The outbreak of war in 1939 gave Japan the opportunity to extend this 'sphere'. In 1940 Japan signed the Tripartite Axis pact with Germany and Italy. Japanese soldiers invaded French Indo-China. The USA was very worried about Japanese expansion into the Pacific, an area the USA traded in and regarded as very close to home. Britain, the Netherlands, and the USA banned oil exports to Japan in response to its invasion of French Indo-China. Japan then took oil by force from Indonesia. This made a war with Britain and the USA very likely. Japan decided to strike first. On 7th December 1941 Japanese aeroplanes took off from aircraft carriers and attacked the US naval base at Pearl Harbor in Hawaii. Eight US battleships and three cruisers were sunk. 200 aircraft were destroyed and 2,000 people were killed at Pearl Harbor. The day afterwards, the USA declared war on Japan, and so did Britain. On December 11th Germany and Italy declared war on the USA. Germany had invaded the USSR in June 1941 and so, by December that year, a world war was being fought.

Japanese expansion, 1931–41 and the attack on the American base at Pearl Harbor, 7th December 1941

▼

Area under Japanese control by 7th December 1941

	Before 1918
	1931–1933
	By 1938
	1938–1941
——	International borders

0   1000 km

at the Equator

Interpretations of the causes of the Second World War

As with most events in history, the causes of the Second World War can be interpreted in different ways. Below are three interpretations.

a   The Second World War was the result of the First World War. The First World War had left bitterness in many countries and a strong desire for peace in others. The Treaty of Versailles was not satisfactory, especially because it took a lot of territory away from Germany. It was obvious that at some time the Germans would try to take this land back. When they did this, public opinion in Britain and France was in favour of peace because of the suffering during 1914-1918. This made strong action impossible.

b   The Second World War was caused by the actions of aggressive and expansionist countries who wanted to extend their power and territory. Germany, Italy, and Japan were each expanding between 1931 and 1941. There was little justification for this expansion, it was simply in the nature of the men and governments in power in these countries. Their expansion was bound to bring them into conflict with the other powers and cause a war.

c   The Second World War was caused by the weakness and misjudgement of Britain, France, and the USA. The USA tried to remain isolated from Europe and this weakened the League of Nations. Britain and France refused to act strongly against either Mussolini or Hitler. They were not firm in the League of Nations nor individually. This was partly because they were unprepared for war, but also because they were unwilling to fight. By appeasing the dictators, Britain and France simply made them stronger and so made a war more likely. Britain added to the likelihood of war by misjudging the USSR and failing to make an anti-Nazi alliance in 1939.

32   Which of these interpretations gives the best explanation for the causes of the War? Before you can answer this, you need to gather the evidence which supports each of the interpretations. It will be best if you work in groups, each group looking at one of the interpretations. There is a lot of evidence in this book, most of it in this chapter; but you will also need to look at other chapters and it will be helpful to investigate other books as well. Remember, you need to find evidence which supports the interpretation you are investigating. Each group could make a wall display about their interpretation, or give a presentation to the class. Could you organise a debate on the causes of the Second World War? As you carry out this investigation try to decide between the interpretations. Is any one of them better than the other two? Can you begin to offer an interpretation of your own, perhaps a combination of these? Remember that any interpretation may not be perfect and that historians still differ in their explanations of why the Second World War began.

6 The war years, 1939–1945

The war in Europe, 1939-1940

On 1st September 1939, German forces invaded Poland. Two days later Great Britain declared war on Germany. The war that many people had been expecting for several years had at last arrived. The German army used what became known as the blitzkrieg (lightning war), and within days had destroyed the Polish opposition. Blitzkrieg meant that motorised and armoured divisions (mainly tanks) attacked the enemy at weak, unexpected points which would have also suffered attacks from heavy bombers, artillery, and dive bombers. The intention was to surprise and demoralise the enemy very quickly and bring about a speedy surrender.

A Stuka dive bomber attacking an industrial target

A

The Poles had no armoured or motorised divisions. Poland's leadership still pinned their trust to the value of a large mass of horsed cavalry, and cherished a pathetic belief in the possibility of carrying out cavalry charges.

Liddell Hart *The Second World War*, 1970

When the Nazi-Soviet Pact of August 1939 was made, both countries had decided that they would divide Poland between themselves. Therefore, shortly after the German invasion, the Poles also had to face the Soviet forces on their borders. Defeat was inevitable for the Poles. On 28th September, Germany and the Soviet Union signed a formal agreement which split Poland between them. At this point German aggression in Europe ceased, although there were several incidents at sea. However, conflict in Europe did continue when the Soviet Union invaded Finland. The Soviet Union was expelled from the League of Nations as a result of this action. The conflict in Finland ended in early 1940 when the Finns and the Russians signed the Treaty of Moscow.

After the defeat of Poland, the British and the French anticipated a German attack in the west at any moment. None came. The period between the end of September 1939 and April 1940 has become known as 'the Phoney War', although at the time the British called it the 'Bore War' or the 'funny war'. The Germans called this phase of the war 'sitzkrieg'. Literally, this means stationary war.

The British hoped that the war could be restricted to as few countries as possible, and were confident that Germany could be defeated if there was an effective naval blockade. The British had seen the success of their blockade in the First World War and time was on their side. This policy proved to be totally wrong. The blockade was to be extended to prevent Swedish iron ore reaching Germany via Norway. Plans were drawn up but Hitler quickly outsmarted the British and he invaded Denmark on 9th April 1940, capturing the country in hours. The successful invasion of Norway soon followed and Germany had secured her iron ore route.

This *Daily Sketch* cartoon from April 1940 shows the Germans' desire for iron ore for use in their arms factories. To get it, they were prepared to invade neutral Denmark.

B

The British response to the German operation demonstrated confused strategic thinking, shifting objectives and poor command on the ground. The result was a decisive British defeat… growing pressure on Chamberlain, and demands for more effective control of the war.

From *1940 Myth and reality*, written in 1993 by Clive Ponting, a British historian discussing the German invasion of Norway.

The next phase of the war began on 10th May 1940 when German forces attacked the Netherlands, Belgium, Luxembourg, and France. (On this day Chamberlain resigned and was replaced by Churchill.) Britain had sent the British Expeditionary Force (BEF) over to France in September and these had joined with the French behind the Maginot Line. However, the British and French were taken unawares when the Germans made their thrust through the Low Countries. The French thought that they had constructed an impregnable wall in the Maginot Line and thought that the German panzers (tanks) would not be able to drive through the Ardennes Forest. The German blitzkrieg swept all before it once again and soon the Netherlands, Luxembourg and Belgium surrendered. The British forces found themselves surrounded near the port of Dunkirk and the road to Paris was clear for the Germans.

The German Blitzkrieg
September 1939 – June 1940

Map legend

→ German advances Sept. 1939
→ German advances April–June 1940
Germany and Italy (Axis Powers), 1 September 1939
Axis satellites and allies
Axis-occupied territories, 1939–41
USSR, September 1939
USSR-occupied territories, 1939–40
Neutral countries

0   500 km

Evacuation at Dunkirk

Before the start of the Dunkirk evacuation, the British had already brought 28,000 troops back to the mainland. The chart below shows the number of British and French soldiers evacuated during the last days of May and the first days of June. There was some ill-feeling between the two allies about who should have preference during the evacuation.

The British and French were most fortunate to be able to rescue so many of their soldiers. With hindsight, it can be seen that Hitler made a mistake at Dunkirk – he should have pressed on with his panzers rather than relying on the Luftwaffe to destroy the troops on the beaches. The British were fortunate that they could control the English Channel during the evacuation and were able to prevent the German navy and airforce from causing greater damage and chaos.

The British presented the retreat from Dunkirk (Operation Dynamo) as a magnificent victory when it was really a defeat. The evacuated soldiers had to abandon or destroy all of their heavy equipment – tanks, artillery, trucks and in many cases even their rifles.

The numbers of soldiers rescued from Dunkirk

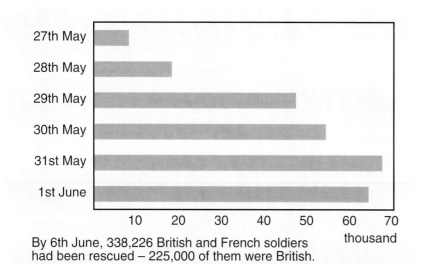

By 6th June, 338,226 British and French soldiers had been rescued – 225,000 of them were British.

The Dunkirk evacuation

After Dunkirk, Churchill made one of his most rousing speeches and you can understand why the British people rallied round him after such a demoralising defeat.

we shall fight on the seas and oceans; we shall fight with growing confidence and growing strength in the air; we shall defend our island whatever the cost may be. We shall fight on the beaches; we shall fight on the landing grounds; we shall fight in the fields and in the streets; we shall fight in the hills. We shall never surrender.

Winston Churchill, June 1940

Within three weeks of Dunkirk, the French surrendered. They were forced to sign the armistice in the same railway carriage where they had witnessed the Germans sign in 1918. Britain was now alone in its fight against Germany – only the Dominions and the Empire were there to give support.

▼ **E**

Personally, I feel happier now that we have no allies to be polite to and to pamper.

King George VI

However, when the war ended five years later, Britain was grateful to her eventual allies, some of whom endured far more than Britain did.

1　Explain what is meant by the term 'blitzkrieg'.
2　Why was Poland defeated so easily in September 1939?
3　Why do you think that the Germans called the 'phoney war' 'der sitzkrieg'?
4　In what ways do Sources A and B show that Germany was more prepared for war than her enemies?
5　Explain why the Maginot Line proved to be of no defensive use to France.
6　Explain whether you think that Dunkirk was a victory or a defeat for Britain.
7　Look at Sources C and D. In what ways does Source C support Source D?
8　In the light of Sources C and D, how can Operation Dynamo have been seen as a magnificent victory? Why do you think it was presented in this way?

Britain alone: Battle of Britain and the Blitz

Some historians have interpreted the Battle of Britain as the 'pivotal event of the war' (Calder). After the surrender of France, Hitler began to plan for the invasion of Britain – Operation Sealion. If he were to mount a successful invasion, then he needed to have control of the skies. Therefore, the RAF had to be destroyed. The table below indicates the respective strength of the two countries' airforces at the beginning of the battle.

Germany (Luftwaffe)	Britain (RAF)
1000 long range bombers	(fighters only)
261 heavy fighters	666 fighters
700 single seater fighters	750 in reserve
300 dive bombers	or grounded

Note: Only 33% of Fighter Command were Spitfires

Although the Germans had more aircraft, many were not suited for close aerial combat. The ME109 was the best German fighter and the Spitfire represented the best in British technology. The German pilots were quite experienced, having fought in the Spanish Civil War, Poland, and in the campaigns of April-June 1940.

During July, August, and September Britain had to face a massive onslaught from the Luftwaffe. The first weeks saw the Germans attack shipping, ports, radar installations, and Fighter Command bases. August 13th was given the name Adlertag (Eagle Day) by the Germans when more than 1,500 sorties were flown. This number was exceeded two days later when 1,800 were flown. The crucial two weeks for Britain were August 24-September 6th when losses outstripped aircraft production and 103 pilots were killed. Fortunately for Britain, the Germans changed their tactics on 7th September and began bombing London. The Battle of Britain was over and the Blitz had now begun.

Why did Britain survive the Battle of Britain ?

Clearly the German decision to switch their attack to London was important, but there are several other factors of equal importance. Britain possessed radar and was thus able to track approaching aeroplanes. Its own fighters could be deployed according to the radar findings and this often meant that British fighters could remain airborne longer than German aircraft which would have to return to base to refuel. Britain was also able to recover more pilots than the Germans and this proved to be especially significant at the height of the battle. Moreover, British aircraft production exceeded all expectations during the summer months of 1940.

Aircraft production in 1940

April	256
May	325
June	446
July	496
August	475
September	467

The Battle of Britain

(During the critical months 650 more fighters were produced than had been planned for. The Ministry of Aircraft Production, under the leadership of Beaverbrook, must take the credit for this.)

9 Look at the boxes below and explain how each contributed to the British victory in the Battle of Britain.

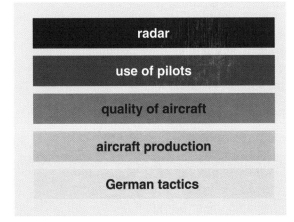

| radar |
| use of pilots |
| quality of aircraft |
| aircraft production |
| German tactics |

The Blitz

The first big air-raid took place on 7th September 1940 and the last one was on 10th May the following year. London and the major cities of the country were regular targets during this period and the raids caused huge devastation. The fear of the politicians in the 1930s had been that the 'bomber would always get through' and would cause massive casualties. Yet, by the time the first Blitz ended in May 1941, the casualties, though high, were only a fraction of those expected. Later in the War, almost 600,000 German civilians were killed in allied air raids. This figure is ten times greater than the number of British civilians killed during the Blitz and later attacks.

The bombing of Britain's cities did not break the morale of her citizens. There is evidence to show that it actually made the people even more determined to beat Hitler. That is not to say that the bombing was meekly accepted – in some cities there was 'trekking'. Towards the end of the day people would begin leaving the city in order to avoid the night-time bombing.

They would then return the next morning. (See Chapter 15 for further details.)

10 Look at the photograph of the bomb damage. How do the people seem to be reacting to the destruction? Why do you think this is?

11 How reliable do you think this photograph is?

12 Why do you think that the Blitz did not break the British will to continue the war against Germany?

13 Personal research: Try to find out as much as you can about the impact of the Blitz on a city near you. Consider its effect on – daily life, children, and the workers. You may have relatives who can be interviewed.

A cheerful South London family give the thumbs up sign to a newspaper photographer in 1940. They were sleeping in their Anderson shelter during an air raid when a bomb exploded right outside.

1941: The year of change

Enter the USSR

Britain endured the Blitz and by the spring of 1941, it was clear that the invasion threat was over. Nevertheless, Britain was still fighting Germany alone. The USA was giving help by means of the 'Lend-Lease' scheme (Britain leased bases in the Caribbean to the USA in return for more than fifty destroyers.) However, there was a distinct feeling that the war was a European one and that the USA should avoid direct involvement. Britain's isolation changed very suddenly on 22nd June 1941 when Germany made a surprise attack on the Soviet Union. Hitler's alliance with Stalin in 1939 had always been regarded as a marriage of convenience, and, by early summer 1941, Hitler at last felt confident that he would be able to rid the world of Communism. The destruction of the Soviet Union would also give Germany access to the wheatfields of the Ukraine and the oilfields of the Caucasus. There would also be living space (Lebensraum) for Germany. Hitler had had to delay his attack by five weeks because his troops were needed in Greece and Yugoslavia in order to help Mussolini's forces which had been unable to capture the two countries on their own. This delay proved to be quite crucial. Barbarossa was a three-pronged attack supported by 3 million men, who moved towards the cities of Leningrad, Moscow, and Stalingrad.

Initially the plan went very smoothly. The German armies employed the blitzkrieg tactic again, and Soviet forces were soon destroyed. German advances were quite astonishing and soon their targets were in sight. However, the Germans had not anticipated a winter campaign, and there was snow as early as September. By the end of November, large numbers of Germans were suffering from frostbite because they did not have the proper winter uniform. The cold weather was so intense that oil and diesel in the vehicles froze. The Germans found it increasingly difficult to keep their forces supplied and were unable to live off the land which they had captured because the Soviet people carried out a policy of 'scorched earth'. This meant that as they retreated they destroyed everything which could be of possible use to the Germans – food, animals, machinery, and weaponry. Before Christmas 1941, the Russians were able to make some counter-attacks, and did so in numbers far greater than Hitler had expected. Once again there had been miscalculations. By early 1942, although Germany had captured large areas of land, the USSR had not surrendered. The German invasion of the Soviet Union had widened the War.

Abandoned German vehicles on the Eastern Front

Winston Churchill had consistently opposed Communism since 1917, but on hearing of the invasion of the Soviet Union, he supported Russia.

> The Russian danger is our danger. Any person or state who fights against Nazism will have our aid. We shall give whatever help we can to Russia.

Winston Churchill

On 12th July Britain and the Soviet Union signed an agreement which pledged mutual assistance against Germany and no separate peace. Hitler had succeeded in bringing together two countries that had been antagonistic towards each other for several years. Now they were united against him.

Enter the USA

You have already read in Chapter 5 how Japan attacked the USA's Pacific fleet at Pearl Harbor on 7th December 1941. The following day the USA declared war on Japan. On 12th December, Hitler and Mussolini declared war on the USA. Roosevelt had had no intention of becoming involved in the conflict against Germany and was taken by surprise by Hitler's decision. So now the three major powers of the world (The Big Three) were ranged against Germany – the Grand Alliance had been created.

> [the involvement] of the USA makes amends for all, and with time and patience will give certain victory.

Winston Churchill

14 Look at the words in the boxes below and then answer the question: 'Why was 1941 a disastrous year for Hitler?'

Failure of the Blitz

Barbarossa

Scorched earth

Winter campaign

Counter-attacks

Pearl Harbor

Big Three

German Tactics

The Eastern Front, 1942-45

In the spring of 1942 the Soviet Union mounted a series of offensives in the hope of regaining territory. These failed and Germany went onto the offensive. Yet again Hitler made an error of judgement. He decided to seize not only Stalingrad but also the oil fields of the Caucasus. He had to divide his forces and the fighting around Stalingrad became extremely fierce. The Germans sustained heavy losses and more importantly had to divert more and more soldiers there. In November, a Soviet army led by Zhukov, counter-attacked and cut off the main part of the German forces. Von Paulus, the German Field Marshal in Stalingrad, wished to retreat, but Hitler refused to allow this. Von Paulus and his men had to fight on. By the end of January 1943, there was little else left for Von Paulus to do but surrender. 90,000 soldiers were left – Von Paulus' army had lost more than 200,000 men since being surrounded in November 1942.

The Russians tore the guts out of the German army.

Winston Churchill

Our children's children will look back through their history books with admiration and thanks for the heroism of the great Russian people.

Ernest Bevin, a member of the British wartime Cabinet

The German defeat at Stalingrad was a turning point in the war. Germany never seemed to recover and was always on the defensive thereafter.

The Eastern Front in the Second World War. The inset map shows the vast size of the Soviet Union compared to the battle zone.

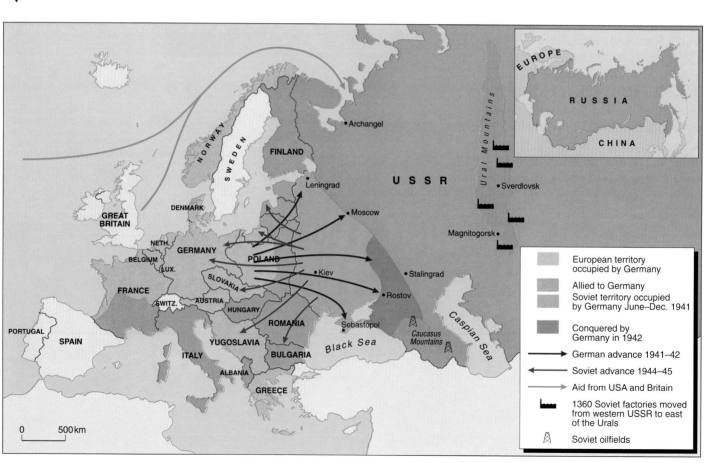

The Soviet Union began to grow steadily stronger. The USSR was able to produce military material even though it had lost large areas of land. The Soviets simply dismantled many factories and rebuilt them east of the Ural mountains. The military and industrial recovery of the Soviet Union can be seen by the amount of weaponry made available to its forces at the Battle of Kursk in mid-1943. Here they were able to field more than 3,500 tanks!

Churchill, Stalin, and the Second Front

▲ This German cartoon shows Churchill unwilling to cross the Channel and invade Europe despite Stalin's encouragement

Almost from the beginning, Stalin wanted Churchill to open a Second Front in Europe in order to divert German forces from Russia. Both Britain and the USA sent war material to the Soviet Union but this was not enough for Stalin. He suspected that Churchill and Roosevelt were both content to see Germany and the Soviet Union bleed each other dry. It must be remembered that the 'Big Three' were only united by their wish to defeat Germany. Before the War there was a record of poor relations between them and Britain and the USA were especially wary of the Soviet Union because they thought it would spread Communism across the world.

Churchill and Roosevelt met at Casablanca in January 1943 to discuss further strategy. Stalin was unable to attend as this was the crucial period in the German attack on Leningrad and Stalingrad. Each leader put forward his own demands: Stalin wanted a Second Front, the Americans wanted to defeat Japan, and Britain felt that Germany could be weakened if there were further campaigns in North Africa and then Italy. It was decided that the North African campaign should be completed and that Italy should then be invaded. There was some doubt about this plan because the Americans felt that the troops involved would be better employed in the build up for the eventual invasion of western Europe. Churchill's view was that if Italy was invaded then the Germans would have to divert even more forces from occupied France.

▲ The 'Big Three' at Teheran in 1943 – Stalin, Roosevelt, and Churchill

The first meeting of the 'Big Three' was at Teheran in November 1943. Here the eventual date for the Second Front was fixed at May or June 1944. It was also decided that the Soviet Union would declare war on Japan as soon as Germany was defeated. Preparations for the Second Front were meticulous. Churchill said that it was 'the most difficult and complicated operation that has ever taken place.'

Britain felt that the time was now ripe for the assault on Hitler's Europe. The Battle of the Atlantic had been won and the German U-boat menace was no longer threatening to strangle Britain. Britain had quickly adopted the convoy system but the German U-Boats responded by operating in 'wolf-packs' – groups of up to 40 submarines and were still able to sink many merchant ships. Almost 3000 British ships were sunk in the War, but advances in technology, such as asdic, radio location equipment and depth charges meant that the U-Boats were not able to starve Britain into surrender.

| US and British shipping losses | | U-Boat |
Year	thousands of tons	sinkings
1939	800	9
1940	4,400	22
1941	4,400	35
1942	8,200	85
1943	3,600	287
1944	1,400	241
1945	460	153

The Allies also had control of the skies and there were repeated raids on German cities and industrial centres. British air attacks on Germany increased in intensity after 1942, and, by the end of the War, most German cities had been devastated. British and American raids – sometimes with more than one thousand bombers – created havoc but, despite the damage and constant attacks, German industrial output did not diminish until the final months of the War. As in Britain, the bombing raids did not break the spirit of the people.

The campaigns in Africa were finally over and the Germans and Italians were under pressure in mainland Italy.

15 Why was the German spring offensive of 1942 flawed?

16 Read what Churchill and Bevin said about the Soviets in Sources F and I. Explain what they meant.

17 Explain what is meant by the term 'Big Three'?

18 Explain why there was suspicion between the 'Big Three'.

19 When the 'Big Three' met at Teheran, why did they feel that the time was right for opening the Second Front?

Operation Overlord

The opening of the second front was given a special codename – Operation Overlord, although the actual landings are now more usually called D-Day. The Supreme Commander of the allied forces was the American general, Eisenhower, and he had responsibility for the preparations for Overlord. In some ways this indicates the acceptance by Britain that it was no longer the greatest power in the world. Churchill was also beginning to realise this when he had his meetings with Roosevelt and Stalin. Britain was clearly the third of the 'Three'. For months before the invasion, American and British planes bombed German railway lines, factories, and cities with thousands of tons of bombs. On 6th June 1944, allied troops landed on the Normandy coast. They were carried by about 4,000 ships and by the end of the first day there were almost 130,000 soldiers ashore. The

The Allied invasion of Normandy in June 1944

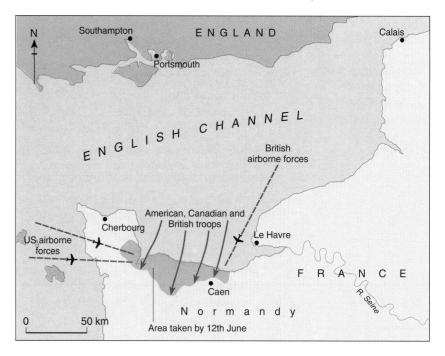

Germans had expected the invasion to come in the area around Calais and the allies had made as if to attack there. Fighting was extremely bitter but the allies were able to break through the German defences and were soon pushing inland.

The allied forces liberated Paris in August and by the end of the summer Belgium, Luxembourg and France were in allied hands. Hitler's last throw of the dice was made in December with a counter-attack through the Ardennes. The 250,000 German soldiers drove the allies back but the offensive, the Battle of the Bulge, petered out by the middle of January 1945. At the same time the forces of the Soviet Union were advancing rapidly across eastern Europe and it was on 25th April 1945 that soldiers from the US 69th Infantry Division met up with Russian soldiers from the 58th Guards Division. Germany surrendered on 7th May 1945. Hitler had killed himself a week before.

▲ Landing supplies on the invasion beaches in Normandy

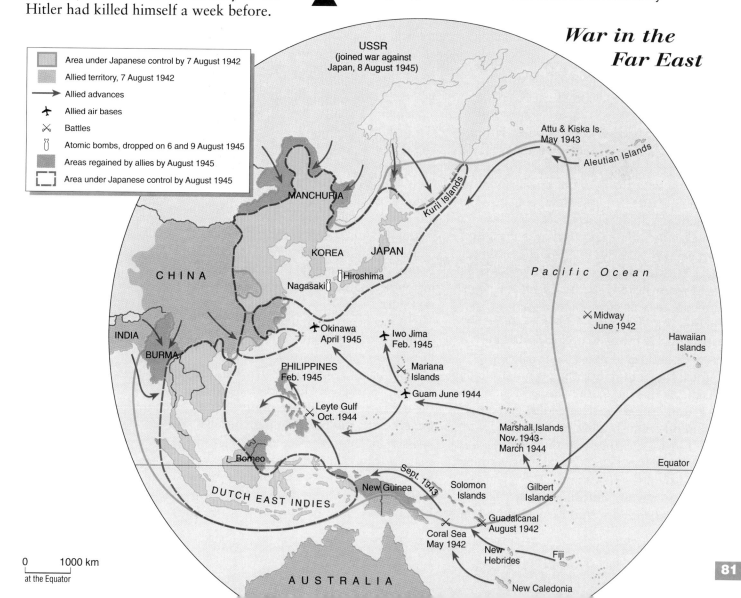

War in the Far East

▨	Area under Japanese control by 7 August 1942
▨	Allied territory, 7 August 1942
→	Allied advances
✈	Allied air bases
✕	Battles
☖	Atomic bombs, dropped on 6 and 9 August 1945
▨	Areas regained by allies by August 1945
⌐	Area under Japanese control by August 1945

USSR
(joined war against Japan, 8 August 1945)

MANCHURIA

KOREA   JAPAN

CHINA

Nagasaki ☖   ☖ Hiroshima

INDIA

BURMA

Okinawa
April 1945

Iwo Jima
Feb. 1945

PHILIPPINES
Feb. 1945

Mariana
Islands

Guam June 1944

Leyte Gulf
Oct. 1944

Borneo

DUTCH EAST INDIES

Sept. 1943

New Guinea

Solomon
Islands

Gilbert
Islands

Marshall Islands
Nov. 1943-
March 1944

Coral Sea
May 1942

Guadalcanal
August 1942

New
Hebrides

Fiji

New Caledonia

AUSTRALIA

Kuril Islands

Attu & Kiska Is.
May 1943

Aleutian Islands

Pacific Ocean

✕ Midway
June 1942

Hawaiian
Islands

Equator

0   1000 km
at the Equator

Japanese tanks enter Singapore in 1942

▶ The same scene in Hiroshima in 1945 after the first atomic bomb, and in 1995

Although the war against Germany was over, the conflict against Japan still continued. After the attack on Pearl Harbor (see page 68) Japan experienced many early successes. The map on page 81 shows the extent of their empire. Japanese military activity brought them into conflict not only with the USA but also Britain, its Empire, Australia, and New Zealand. The Americans did eventually recover from the shock attack on Pearl Harbor and there were naval victories in 1942 at Coral Sea and Midway. However, the Japanese still held many heavily fortified Pacific islands. To counter this advantage, American planners adopted the 'island hopping' strategy. US forces would capture key islands and build bases from which to attack the Philippines and eventually Japan itself. By this tactic, they hoped to surround Japanese strongholds and cut them off from supplies.

The first territory that the Japanese lost in the war was Guadalcanal. It was to be a foretaste of the fighting to come. The Japanese were fanatical in the defence of the island and lost 25,000 men. When the Americans recaptured the Philippines, the Japanese lost 170,000 soldiers. The strategy of island hopping seemed to be working but the Americans began to realise that it might take years before Japan could be defeated. There was also progress for the British and Imperial troops when Japanese forces were pushed out of India and into Burma after the Battle of Imphal.

To increase the pressure on Japan, the USA began to bomb the cities of the mainland. In one raid on Tokyo in March 1945, 83,000 people were killed, but the military leaders were unwilling to surrender. The tactics of the Japanese became desperate towards the end of the war when they began to use kamikaze attacks. In the battle for Okinawa, the kamikaze pilots sank 30 American ships. There seemed to be little hope of forcing a surrender and President Truman scheduled an invasion of the Japanese mainland for late 1945 or early 1946.

However, in July 1945, scientists successfully tested the first atomic bomb in the New Mexico desert. President Truman decided to use this weapon against the Japanese. On 6th August one atomic bomb (codename Little Boy) was dropped on the city of Hiroshima. Casualty figures vary and it is estimated that almost 100,000 people were killed instantly and at least 60,000 died later from burns, radiation or other wounds caused by the blast. Japan did not surrender. Three days later a second atomic bomb was dropped on Nagasaki killing a further 40,000 civilians. Four days later, the Japanese surrendered unconditionally. The Second World War was over.

There has been much debate about the dropping of the atomic bomb. Was President Truman justified in bombing Hiroshima and Nagasaki? The war did end after its second use. It has been said that the use of the bomb was immoral and unnecessary and that Truman and his advisers failed to think of the long term issues such as the potential arms race. Some observers have said that the bomb was dropped to intimidate the Soviet Union.

I told Secretary of State for War, Stimson, I was against it on two counts. First the Japanese were ready to surrender and it wasn't necessary to hit them with that awful thing. Second, I hated to see our country be the first to use such a weapon.

General Eisenhower's view, expressed in the summer of 1945

L

If the US were to be the first to release this new means of indiscriminate destruction upon mankind, she would sacrifice public support throughout the world, cause the race for armaments and prejudice the possibility of reaching an international agreement on the future control of such weapons.'

James Franck, University of Chicago, summer of 1945

20 Find out what is meant by the following:
  a island hopping
  b kamikaze
  c arms race
21 Compare the figures for civilian deaths after the raids on Tokyo, Hiroshima, and Nagasaki. Why do you think that there was little outrage after the raid on Tokyo?
22 Do you think that the atomic bombs should have been dropped? Use the sources at the end of this section and other information from this chapter to help you explain your answer.
23 Read Sources J, K, and L. In what ways are these sources similar and in what ways are they different?
24 Source J is the American President speaking to the people. Does this make it any more or less reliable than Sources K or L? Explain your answer.

J

We have used the bomb against those who attacked us without warning at Pearl Harbor, against those who have starved and beaten and executed American prisoners of war, against those who have abandoned all pretence of obeying international laws of warfare. We have used it in order to shorten the agony of war, in order to save the lives of thousands and thousands of young Americans.

President Truman addressing the American people on the radio on 9th August 1945.

7 World War to Cold War

The Second World War came to an end with the surrender of Japan in September 1945. Great Britain, the USA and the USSR had worked together to defeat the axis powers and many people were hoping that the world could look forward to a period of peace and prosperity. Yet, by 1950, the wartime alliance had fragmented and events in Berlin and Korea brought Britain and the USA to a position where war against the USSR was a distinct possibility.

▲ American and Soviet soldiers shake hands in 1945 at the River Elbe, where the two armies met

What had happened to create such a situation?

It should be remembered that the USSR had been treated with some distrust since the Communist Revolution. Many countries felt threatened by Communism and would have nothing to do with the Soviet Union. Membership of the League of Nations was not permitted until 1934, and this lasted only five years because of the Soviet invasion of Finland.

The creation of the wartime alliance against Germany came only when Germany invaded the Soviet Union in 1941. This invasion broke the Non-Aggression Pact which the two countries had signed in 1939. During the War, Stalin made many requests to the British and the Americans to open the 'second front' and he thought that the delay in invading mainland Europe was deliberate. Stalin felt that the USSR was being asked to take the brunt of the fighting so that it would be weakened after the War.

In February 1945, Roosevelt, Churchill and Stalin met at Yalta in the Soviet Union to discuss what should happen in Europe after the end of hostilities. The leaders were able to come to some agreements though discussions about Germany and Eastern Europe proved troublesome. The main points of Yalta were:

- Stalin would fight against Japan after the defeat of Germany, and there would be a reward of some islands in Asia.
- Stalin agreed to support the proposed United Nations which would be set up after the War.
- Germany was to be divided into four zones of occupation (French, Soviet, British, and American). Berlin (in the Soviet Zone) was also to be divided into four zones.
- Austria and Vienna (its capital) were to be divided in a similar way.
- It was decided that those Nazis responsible for the holocaust and other war crimes would be placed on trial.
- Those countries which had been occupied by Germany would be allowed to have free democratic elections as soon as possible.

However, there were disagreements over eastern Europe. Soviet forces occupied much of this area and Stalin had set up a Communist government in Poland. Stalin wanted recognition of his power in eastern Europe and claimed that he was protecting the Soviet Union's western border. Churchill and Roosevelt were forced to accept Stalin's demands and could only secure Stalin's promise to hold free elections.

There were criticisms of Churchill and Roosevelt for allowing Stalin to have so much influence in eastern Europe. Many Americans thought that Roosevelt had allowed Stalin his areas of influence in order to gain his help in the War against Japan.

▲ Churchill, Roosevelt, and Stalin at Yalta – the last meeting of the original Big Three

The new Big Three (Attlee, Truman, and Stalin) at Potsdam in July 1945

When the war against Germany was over, the leaders of Britain, the USA and the USSR met at Potsdam near Berlin to discuss the future of Germany and finalize the unresolved issues of Yalta. Since Yalta, there had been many changes. Roosevelt had died and had been replaced by Harry S. Truman. Unlike Roosevelt, Truman had a deep distrust of Stalin and was pessimistic about the success of any negotiations with the Soviet Union. Within days of the Conference opening, Churchill was replaced by Clement Attlee following Labour's landslide victory in the British General Election. By July 1945 the armies of the Soviet Union were occupying most of eastern Europe: Finland, Estonia, Latvia, Lithuania, Bulgaria, Romania, Hungary, Czechoslovakia, and Poland. Soviet troops had also occupied much of Germany including Berlin, and parts of Austria including Vienna. Stalin was unwilling to withdraw his forces from these territories.

At Potsdam, President Truman was informed that scientists in the USA had successfully exploded the atomic bomb. This news meant that the USA did not have to rely on Stalin's assistance to defeat Japan. It was evident that the distrust that had existed between Britain, the USA and the USSR before 1939 was returning now that the common enemy had been defeated.

However, there were some agreements at Potsdam:

- Germany and Austria were divided into zones of occupation, as agreed at Yalta.
- Leading Nazis were to be put on trial for war crimes and Germany was to be 'de-Nazified'.
- The USSR gained land from Finland.
- Estonia, Latvia and Lithuania became part of the USSR.
- Parts of East Prussia were absorbed into the USSR.
- Parts of Poland, Romania, and Czechoslovakia were given to the USSR.
- The Kurile islands and South Sakhalin in the Far East were returned to the USSR.

British Military Police put up new signs to mark the British Sector of Berlin

The Communist takeover of Eastern Europe

The Soviet acquisition of so much territory did worry Churchill and Truman but there was little that they could do to prevent it as Soviet troops occupied most of the land in question. Truman was against the idea of forcing Germany to pay huge reparations (as at Versailles) but was unable to prevent Stalin from taking his own payments from the Soviet occupation zone.

During the next few months, Stalin's intentions became clear. Soviet troops did not withdraw from eastern Europe and Communists took over the running of Bulgaria, Hungary, Poland, and Romania. There was a coalition government in Czechoslovakia where the Communist Party had won about 40% of the vote in the elections. Communist governments were also set up in Yugoslavia and Albania, although these two countries were not under the direct influence of Stalin.

The Iron Curtain

Tension between Britain and the USA and the USSR continued to grow, and, in 1946, the situation crystallized for the world to see. Stalin made a speech which claimed that Capitalism was a threat to the peace of the world and that he would defend the USSR by developing modern weaponry. The American response was to adopt a policy put forward by George Kenan, an adviser of the President. He suggested that the USA had to be firm and vigilant in *containing* Soviet expansion. Shortly after this, in March 1946, at Fulton, Missouri, Winston Churchill made his now famous speech.

From Stettin in the Baltic to Trieste in the Adriatic, an iron curtain has descended across the continent. Behind that line lie all the great capitals of the ancient states of central and eastern Europe. Warsaw, Berlin, Prague, Vienna, Budapest, Belgrade, Bucharest and Sofia all these famous cities and the populations around them lie in the Soviet sphere and are all subject... to a very high and increasing measure of control from Moscow. If the western democracies stand together in strict adherence to the principles of the United Nations Charter... no one is likely to molest them. If they become divided then catastrophe may overwhelm us all.

An extract from Winston Churchill's speech at Fulton in 1946.

A British cartoon, 1946

The Cold War had begun. It was a conflict between the USA and its allies against the USSR and its allies. It was a war in which the Capitalist west was ranged against the Communist east and a war where both sides were trying to extend their influence around the world. The two sides would avoid fighting each other directly in a 'hot war' but try any other means to prevent the other from gaining any advantage.

1 Explain the meaning of the following terms:

Communist Revolution

Nazi-Soviet Non-Aggression Pact

Second Front

Reparations

Coalition Government

Iron Curtain

Cold War

De-Nazification

What can be surprising about the fact that the Soviet Union, anxious for its future safety, is trying to see to it that governments loyal in their attitude to the Soviet Union should exist in these countries? How can anyone, who has not taken leave of their senses, describe these peaceful aspirations of the Soviet Union as expansionist tendencies on the part of our state?

Stalin's response to Churchill's speech, 1946.

Whoever occupies a territory also imposes on it his own social system. Everyone imposes his own system as far as his army has the power to do so.

Another comment by Stalin about the Soviet takeover of eastern Europe, 1946.

2 Why did the Allies wish to divide Germany into zones of occupation?
3 Why was Stalin unwilling to withdraw his troops from the countries of eastern Europe?
4 Look at Source A. What do you think Churchill meant when he said in his speech that 'catastrophe may overwhelm us all'?
5 Look at Source C. How was Stalin able to defend his actions by keeping his soldiers in eastern Europe?
6 Look at Source D. To what extent does Source D support the comments made in Sources A and C?

The Truman Doctrine

President Truman made clear the American position about the containment of Communism in March 1947 when he addressed the American Congress. He had been asked by Britain to help the government of Greece which was engaged in a fight against Communist rebels. The British could not afford the expense of a prolonged struggle and if they pulled out of Greece a vacuum would be left and the Soviet Union would be ready to fill it. Stalin was also threatening Turkey because he wanted to set up a Soviet naval base in the Dardanelles. Truman had to act. In his speech to Congress, he presented an image of a world threatened by the spread of Communism.

At the present moment nearly every nation must choose between alternative ways of life. The choice is too often not a free one. One way of life is based on the will of the majority and is distinguished by free institutions, representative government, free elections, guarantees of individual liberty, freedom of speech and religion and freedom from political oppression. The second way of life is based upon the will of a minority forcibly imposed upon the majority. It relies upon terror and oppression, a controlled press and radio, fixed elections and the suppressions of personal freedoms.

I believe it must be the policy of the USA to support free peoples who are resisting subjugation by armed minorities or by outside pressures.

An extract from Truman's speech to Congress in 1947.

This became known as the 'Truman Doctrine' and it was now clear how far the USA would go to resist the spread of Communism. Truman asked Congress for $400 million to be given to Greece and Turkey in the form of economic and military aid. The Doctrine became the basis of American foreign policy for about twenty years and convinced most Americans that they were locked in a mortal struggle with Communism.

An American military adviser examines a captured Communist machine gun during the Greek civil War

The Marshall Plan

The Truman Doctrine could use military aid to prevent the spread of Communism but Truman's advisers realised that if the rest of Europe was to be prevented from falling to Communism then massive economic help would also have to be given. In June 1947, George Marshall, US Secretary of State, announced what became known as Marshall Aid.

The United States should do whatever it is able to do to assist in the return of normal economic health in the world, without which there can be no political stability and no assured peace. Our policy is directed not against any country or doctrine but against hunger, poverty, desperation and chaos. Its purpose should be the revival of a working economy in the world so as to permit the emergence of political and social conditions in which free institutions can exist.

George Marshall's view of the purpose of Marshall Aid

Although the Marshall Plan was open to all countries, the Soviet Union refused American help and prevented its east European satellites from taking advantage of its benefits (except Yugoslavia, see Chapter 9). There was much enthusiasm in western Europe and in the summer of 1947, sixteen nations met in Paris to work out how best to use Marshall Aid. There were some members of Congress who objected to the prospect of billions of dollars being pumped into Europe. However, in February 1948, there was a Communist coup d'etat in Czechoslovakia and this ended any doubts that members of Congress had. Congress voted $17 billion over five years. The Plan was most successful and, by 1952, the economies of western Europe were prospering. The spread of Communism in Europe had been halted.

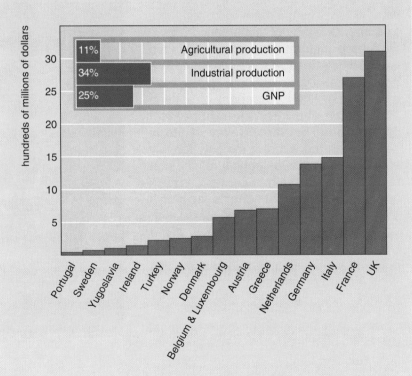

The large bar chart shows the amount of money given to each country under the Marshall Plan. The smaller chart shows the recovery of the western European economies, with growth shown as a percentage.

Berliners using money from the Marshall Plan to help rebuild buildings shattered by the War

The Soviet Union reacted to the Marshall Plan by creating its own economic organisation – The Council of Mutual Economic Assistance or Comecon. Eastern Europe was formed into a single economic group under the leadership of the Soviet Union.

The only Communist country to receive aid under the Marshall Plan was Yugoslavia, which maintained its independence from control by Moscow. Here flour is being sent to Belgrade

The Berlin Blockade

Germany had proved to be a stumbling block in relations between the Soviet Union and the USA at the end of the War. Stalin had wanted to impose massive reparations on the defeated country. He did not wish to see a rejuvenated Germany, because he feared that Germany might once again be a future military threat, whereas Truman saw Germany at the heart of any European recovery. It seemed as if the two superpowers were doomed to come into conflict over Germany. After the war, it had been anticipated that the four occupying nations would all share in the governing of Germany and Berlin. Britain and the USA merged their zones in 1948 to form Bizonia and there were also plans to incorporate the French zone. The three western powers then decided to reform the currency of their zones in order to help accelerate economic recovery. Stalin viewed these plans with fear and anger. The prospect of a strong Germany was alarming.

Stalin responded by blockading the three western zones of Berlin. Such a blockade was quite feasible because Berlin was more than 150km inside the Soviet zone. The blockade began on 23rd June 1948, when all road and canal traffic was forbidden access to Berlin. Two million Berliners were now cut off from the outside world and they needed more than 4,000 tons of food and fuel **each day**. Truman had a choice. He could just hand over West Berlin to the Soviet Union or use force to

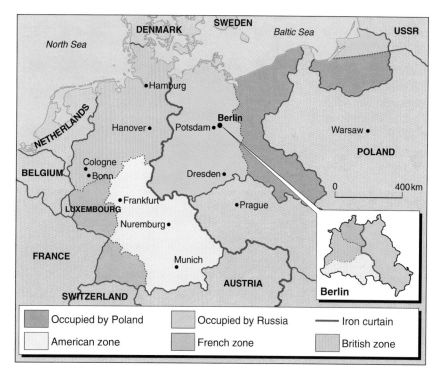

The division of Germany and Berlin after the War

supply the city. If he chose the latter there was a possibility that war could break out. A third choice emerged – the food and fuel needed by West Berlin could be flown in.

G

A British cartoon from 1948 about the Berlin airlift

THE BIRD WATCHER

Vital supplies are unloaded from an American aircraft during the Berlin airlift in 1949

During the next ten months, American and British pilots flew some 277,000 missions to West Berlin, landing about 8,000 tons of supplies per day. The airlift was a resounding success and Stalin lifted the blockade in May 1949.

The Soviet blockade had backfired on Stalin. The hostility which had existed between many Germans and Americans had now ended and the American action was a positive indication to the world of its willingness to fight Communism. The Berlin blockade also hastened the creation of a single state from the British, American and French zones.

The creation of two German states

The Berlin blockade had driven a wedge between the four occupying powers and the original intention of reconstructing Germany as one country was no longer on the agenda. The Federal Republic of Germany was formed from the British, American and French Zones in September 1949. The German Democratic Republic was created out of the Soviet Zone in the following month. The official division of Germany was final evidence that the wartime alliance was now at an end.

If proof were needed to signify that the world was divided into two distinct camps, then it could be found in the formation of the North Atlantic Treaty Organisation. The Berlin blockade convinced the USA and western Europe that a military alliance was needed to ensure their security. Those countries which joined – the USA, Britain, Canada, France, Belgium, the Netherlands, Luxembourg, Norway, Denmark, Iceland, Portugal, and Italy – agreed that 'an armed attack against one or more in Europe or North America shall be considered an attack against them all.' The alliance was seen as a guarantee against the expansion of the Soviet Union into western Europe and, most importantly, it was backed by the atomic might of the USA. President Truman persuaded Congress to grant $1.5 billion for military aid to NATO countries.

However, although Stalin had suffered several setbacks in 1949, there was one positive development for the USSR – the Soviet Union successfully tested its first atomic bomb. The arms race was about to begin.

In 1955, the Federal Republic of Germany was allowed to join NATO. This stirred up old fears in the Soviet Union and its satellites and it was decided that an equivalent to NATO should be formed – the Warsaw Pact. It was a defensive alliance but had its headquarters in Moscow.

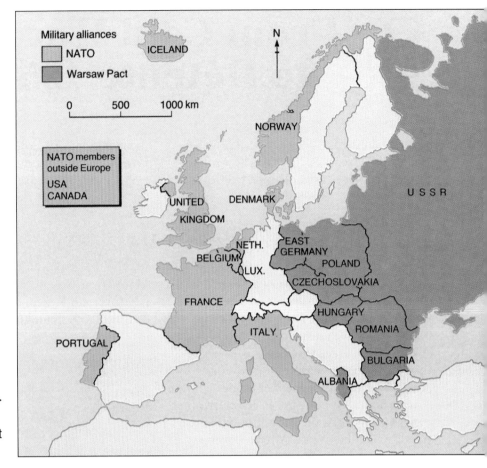

The opposing military alliances in 1955 brought about by West Germany joining NATO

7 Why did President Truman become involved in problems in Greece?

8 Look at the two ways of life described in the Truman Doctrine. Why do you think Truman painted such an image of the Communist way of life?

9 Look at the Marshall Plan. Explain in your own words why the USA decided to give such a huge amount of assistance to Europe.

10 Why was the Marshall Plan open to all countries of Europe?

11 Why was Stalin opposed to the reunification of Germany?

12 What were the consequences of the Berlin blockade?

13 Look at Sources F and G. How useful are these sources in helping you to build up a picture of the development of the Cold War?

14 Write a brief essay, about one and a half sides, using the following title: 'Why did the Cold War develop in the years 1945–1949?'

15 'The Berlin blockade was just an attempt by Stalin to secure control of West Berlin.' Study all the sources and use your own knowledge to explain whether you agree with this statement.

8 From Cold War to Détente 1950–1990

You have seen in Chapter Seven how a Cold War developed after the Second World War. This next chapter will look at the events of the Cold War and will show how tensions between the USA and the USSR eventually eased.

The War in Korea, 1950–1953

During the Second World War, Korea had been occupied by the Japanese. In 1945 the Japanese in the south of the country surrendered to the Americans, while those in the north surrendered to the Soviet Union. Elections were to be held for a united Korea, but in the meantime separate governments were set up. In the north there was a Communist dictatorship, which was aided by China and the Soviet Union. South Korea became a Capitalist dictatorship. However, in 1950 North Korean soldiers invaded South Korea. President Truman was very concerned about the spread of Communism in South East Asia. He was afraid that if one country became Communist then others would soon follow. This was called the 'Domino Theory'. Therefore, Truman decided to act quickly. He sent American soldiers to Japan and ordered American warships to stand by off the coast of Korea. In the United Nations the USA called for the condemnation of the North Korean invasion (see Chapter 13).

In 1950 the Soviet Union had withdrawn from the United Nations Security Council in protest at the UN's decision not to admit Communist China. This meant that they were unable to use their veto when the UN ordered troops into South Korea to fight the North Koreans and drive them back. The Korean War was a United Nations action but the USA provided most of the UN forces. Half of the soldiers were American and the USA provided 86% of the navy and 93% of the airforce. General MacArthur was in overall command of the UN forces in Korea, and he took his orders directly from Truman rather than from the UN officials.

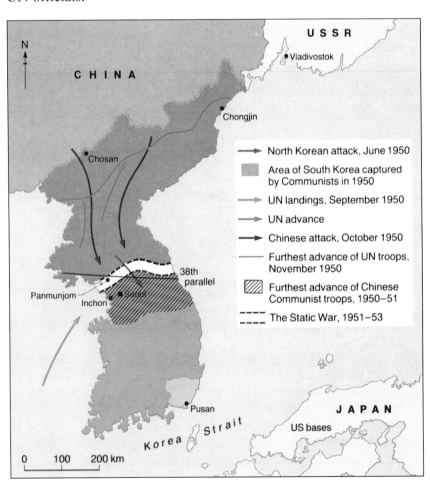

The map shows progress made during the War. At first the Communist forces were successful, and, by September 1950, only a small corner of Korea was not controlled by the Communists. MacArthur then

The progress of the Korean War, 1950-1953

landed troops at Inchon and the Communists were eventually pushed back into the North. Truman decided to pursue them into North Korea and so the UN troops invaded the North. This worried and angered the Chinese leader, Mao Zedong, and he sent a large Chinese army to attack MacArthur's soldiers. In 1951 the UN army was forced to retreat into South Korea. Now Truman and MacArthur differed. Truman did not want to become involved in a costly war in Asia, but MacArthur was all for carrying on into China and he even suggested using an atomic bomb against the Chinese. Meanwhile, the fighting was doing enormous damage to both North and South Korea. About a million Korean people lost their lives in the fighting and the USA suffered 142,000 casualties. By 1952 Truman had settled for containing Communism in North Korea. In 1953 a ceasefire was agreed upon and Korea was left as two separate countries.

The war had in fact been a war between Communism and Capitalism. Communist Chinese and Capitalist American soldiers had fought each other. After MacArthur's

American soldiers firing a heavy mortar at Communist positions in 1952

invasion of the North, the Soviet Union could say with some justification, that the USA was the expansionist country.

A Soviet cartoon, 1952, shows a bloodied US soldier in Korea and likens him to a Nazi German.

The fighting may have stopped in 1953, but the Cold War continued. The USA substituted economic aid for military aid, and between 1953 and 1955 the USA launched a programme of economic assistance for South Korea which amounted to $500,000,000 and this did a great deal to restore the economy of the South.

1 Describe how the USA became involved in the Korean War.
2 What did the War cost the USA? Try to think of more than just the cost in terms of lives and money.
3 Look at Sources A and B. What impression of the USA do they give? Why are the cartoonists trying to give such an impression?
4 How reliable are these sources as evidence of the USA's involvement in the Korean War? Explain your answer.

B

This Soviet cartoon is accusing the Americans of using nerve gas in the Korean War

Khrushchev and peaceful co-existence, 1955–1960

Stalin died in 1953 and from 1955 the Soviet Union was ruled by Nikita Khrushchev. He announced that the USSR intended to live in peaceful co-existence with the USA and the west. He said that he wanted to settle disputes by negotiation rather than through conflict.

In 1955 Soviet soldiers were removed from their zone in Austria, and the Warsaw Pact was formed. The Warsaw Pact was a defence treaty which was signed by the Soviet Union and the Communist countries of eastern Europe. Source C is an extract from the Treaty.

The members affirm their desire for a system of European collective security based upon the participation of all European states to safeguard the peace of Europe. The members shall consult with each other whenever a threat of armed attack on one or more of the members has arisen, in order to ensure joint defence and the maintenance of peace and security.

From the Warsaw Treaty, 1955

Despite Krushchev's words and the conciliatory language of the Warsaw Treaty, the Cold War continued. The USA and the west saw the Warsaw Pact as the Soviet Union's way of controlling Communist countries and, especially, of influencing their foreign policy. In 1956 there was a revolt in Hungary against Soviet control, which was put down by Soviet soldiers and tanks (see chapter 9). This increased tension between the super powers.

Then, in 1960, an American spy plane was shot down by the Soviet Union. The USA had developed special aeroplanes which could fly at high altitude and take secret photographs. They were called U-2 aircraft. The U-2 incident caused angry exchanges of words between Khrushchev and the American President, Eisenhower. Khrushchev announced that the U-2 had been shot down and that the pilot, Gary Powers, was being held captive and would be tried for spying. Khrushchev wanted Eisenhower to guarantee that the spy planes would not fly over Soviet territory again. Eisenhower refused to give this assurance. Khrushchev was now angry and demanded an American apology for the whole incident, and he also cancelled an invitation which he had made earlier to Eisenhower, inviting the President to the Soviet Union. This incident had caused great tension between the super powers.

This is a Soviet cartoon about the spy plane incident of 1960. It shows President Eisenhower painting a U-2 spy plane. What is Eisenhower trying to make the spy plane look like? What message is the cartoon giving?

An American U-2 spy plane

The Berlin Wall

The existence of West Berlin angered the Communists. West Berlin was a glittering example and outpost of Capitalism deep inside the Soviet zone. West Berlin was luxurious, prosperous, and bustling. The United States had poured $600 million into West Berlin to make it a shining example of their way of life. Khrushchev had been putting pressure on the western powers to move out of West Berlin. In 1961, the new American President, John Kennedy made a speech pledging American support for West Berlin.

> We cannot and will not allow the Communists to drive us out of Berlin, either gradually or by force. Our promise to Berlin is essential to the security of West Germany, to the unity of western Europe and to the faith of the entire free world.

From a speech made by President Kennedy of the USA in 1961.

In August 1961 hundreds of workmen suddenly appeared on the streets of Berlin and rapidly constructed a high wall which then separated the eastern and western parts of the city. In the following years many East Germans lost their lives trying to cross the Wall to get into the western part of the city.

(Chapter 9 covers this topic in much greater detail.)

This German cartoon from 1961 shows President Kennedy arguing with Khrushchev. It also shows the Chinese leader, Mao Zedong, urging Khrushchev to be more firm.

A shrine at a place on the Berlin Wall where a young East German was shot trying to climb over to the west

Cuba and the missile crisis of 1962

Cuba is an island in the Caribbean Sea, close to the coast of the USA. In 1959 Cuba became a Communist country when Fidel Castro overthrew Batista and became the new Cuban leader. Castro introduced a number of Communist reforms and he wanted to make Cuba much less dependent on American aid. In 1961 the USA backed an invasion of Cuba by the 2506 Brigade, a group of Cuban exiles and supporters of Batista. The attack at the Bay of Pigs in April 1961 was a disaster.

By nightfall on 18th April it was clear that the attack on the Bay of Pigs was doomed. Earlier attacks by US aircraft had not been successful in grounding the Cuban airforce. The exile forces were surrounded by 20,000 troops with artillery and tanks. The local population had not supported the invaders. The 2506 Brigade pleaded with the US for more aerial support, but President Kennedy, reluctant to admit his part in the affair, refused.

From a biography of Fidel Castro written by a British author in 1981.

One of the most disputed points about the invasion had been the promise made by Kennedy to give air support to the 2506. Some of the Cubans who accused Kennedy of betraying the Brigade based their arguments on this promise, but Kennedy denied that he ever suggested the US airforce be involved. The truth is that the Cubans received assurances from the US advisers that 'the sky will be yours.'

From a Spanish reporter working in Cuba in 1961.

Pepe San Roman: There is only one course of action open to me – to get the survivors back to the ships.
  US Adviser: Sorry Pepe, you've done everything you could... (pause)... You've fought well! Break off and scatter. Don't call me again.
  Pepe San Roman: We don't need any pats on the back, you bastard. What we need are your jets!

From a radio conversation between the leader of the 2506 Brigade, Pepe San Roman, and his US advisers. This conversation took place late on 18th April, when it was clear the attack was failing.

5 Study Source F. Why, according to this source, was the Bay of Pigs invasion 'doomed'?
6 Study Sources F and G. To what extent to these sources agree on the use of American air support in the invasion?
7 Study Sources F, G, and H. Source H is a conversation held at the end of the Bay of Pigs invasion. Do each of Sources F and G support the evidence of Source H? Explain your answer with reference to all three sources.
8 Using these sources explain why the Bay of Pigs invasion failed.

You have seen that the USA was the first country to develop and use a nuclear weapon. This monopoly could not last, however, and other countries began to develop their own nuclear devices. In 1949 the USSR produced its own atomic bomb. In 1952 Britain tested its first atom bomb and China exploded a test bomb in 1964.

In addition to this, in 1956, the USSR had launched the first satellite into space using a space rocket. If they could do this, perhaps they could place a nuclear weapon onto a rocket. Soon the USA and USSR were competing for dominance in the number and type of weapons they had. This was an arms race. A direct result of this arms race was one of the 'hottest' moments of the Cold War – the Cuban missile crisis.

would easily reach American cities. The Soviet Union had also been testing more powerful nuclear bombs. Soviet missiles in Cuba would tip the balance of power in favour of the Soviet Union. Kennedy insisted that the Soviets remove these missile bases from Cuba. Khrushchev replied in a series of letters to the American President.

Fidel Castro of Cuba and Nikita Khrushchev of the USSR embrace in friendship

After the Bay of Pigs invasion, Castro turned towards the USSR for aid. The Soviet Union was keen to aid Cuba because it gave them a friendly Communist outpost close to the USA. Then Khrushchev decided he would use Cuba as a base for Soviet nuclear missiles. In 1962 American spy planes photographed the missile bases in Cuba. Missiles launched from these bases

You have surrounded the USSR with military bases. You have rockets in Britain, Italy and Turkey which are aimed at us. You say you are worried by rockets in Cuba which is 90 miles away from the coast of your country, but Turkey is right next to us! Do you have the right to demand security by the removal of our rockets from Cuba and not give us the same right to security?

I make this proposal: we agree to the removal of our rockets from Cuba if you will make a declaration that you will remove yours from Turkey.

Part of a letter sent by Khrushchev to President Kennedy of the USA in October 1962. This was one of a series of letters between the two leaders.

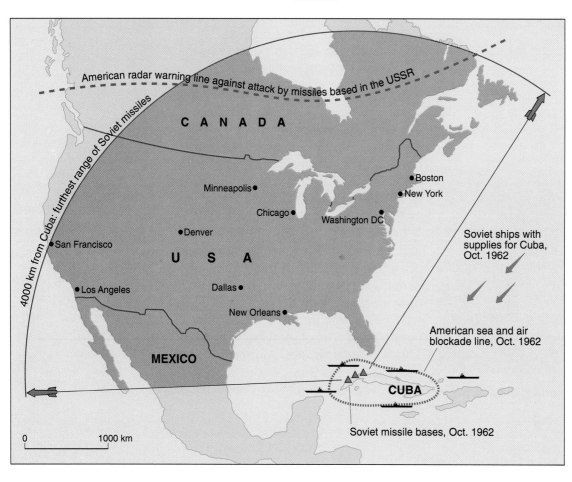

9 According to Source I, how did the USA threaten the Soviet Union?
10 How reliable an account of Soviet military policy in the early 1960s do you think Source I gives? Explain your answer by referring to both the content and origins of the source.

Kennedy would not make the promise. Instead he organised a quarantine area around Cuba into which no ships would be allowed if they were found to be carrying weapons. One Soviet ship, the *Kasimov*, was boarded and crates on its deck were opened. These crates contained parts of nuclear bombs.

The rest of the world waited anxiously while the two super powers decided what to do. For a while it did seem as though there might be a nuclear war. The Secretary General of the United Nations, Mr U Thant proposed that each leader do all they could to avoid the disaster that a nuclear war would bring.

J

The Soviet Union has always tried to strengthen the United Nations... We therefore accept your proposal, and have ordered the masters of Soviet ships bound for Cuba to stay out of the interception area, as you recommend.

From a letter sent by Khrushchev to U Thant, October 1962.

The crisis was over. The Soviet ships returned home. Kennedy had seemed strong. U Thant had provided Khrushchev with a way out of the crisis without losing face. However, out of the crisis came a closer relationship between the USA and the USSR. A Hot Line, a direct telephone link, between the White House in Washington and the Kremlin in Moscow was set up in 1963 to try to avoid future conflict. In the same year the USA and the USSR signed a Test Ban Treaty, which stopped further testing of nuclear weapons.

In Britain there was pressure against nuclear weapons from the Campaign for Nuclear Disarmament (CND). In the 1960s CND organised large protest meetings and marches directed against the British government's intention of spending hundreds of millions of pounds on nuclear weapons. After a decline in the 1970s, CND became more popular and more active again in the 1980s in response to the USA's intention of basing Cruise missiles on British soil. Some women who were particularly concerned about this set up a 'peace camp' at Greenham Common, one of the Cruise missile bases.

11 Describe the events of the Cuban missile crisis.
12 Why was neither leader at first willing to back down?
13 Which leader emerged stronger from the Cuban missile crisis, Kennedy or Khrushchev? Explain your answer with references to the sources and the text.
14 What good came out of the Cuban crisis?
15 Why do you think U Thant of the United Nations became involved?

A Soviet cargo ship bound for Cuba with missile crates on its deck

An analysis of the Cold War, 1950–1963

> The United Nations suffered 142,000 casualties during the Korean War to save South Korea from Communist domination. United States losses in three years were only narrowly outstripped by those suffered in Vietnam over more than ten years [see Chapter 12]. Since 1945, only the Cuban missile crisis had created a greater risk of nuclear war between east and west than in Korea. Korea remains the only conflict since 1945 in which the armies of two great powers, China and the USA, have met on the battlefield.

From a western historian, Max Hastings, writing in 1987.

16 Which posed the greater threat of a nuclear war, the Korean War or the Cuban missile crisis? Base your answer on Source K and use the knowledge you have so far gained from this chapter.

17 Make a time line from 1950 to 1963. Use one centimetre for each year and have the line in the middle of a page, with space above and below it. Now mark on to this time line the key events in the Cold War during this period. On the top half, mark all those events which worsened American/Soviet relations and increased tension. On the bottom half, mark those events which improved relations and eased tensions.

18 Détente means an easing of tension. Do you think there was any period of détente between 1950 and 1963? Explain your answer fully.

Détente during the 1970s and 1980s

During the period after the Cuban missile crisis there was an easing of tension between the super powers. This is known as détente. There were a number of reasons for detente:

a   The USA was involved in a long and costly war in Vietnam from the early 1960s until 1975. This was a war fought against Communism, but it did not involve the USSR (see Chapter 12). America's failure in this war taught them that even nuclear weapons and a massive economy cannot guarantee success in war.

b   The USA backed Israel whilst the USSR backed Egypt and Syria in the Middle East conflict (see Chapter 14). This enabled each power to defend its interests without direct confrontation.

c   The USSR, in particular, was finding difficulty in meeting the costs of competing with the USA in weapons building and in space exploration. The money spent on these expensive programmes was needed at home, to improve conditions for the workers. The success of the Polish workers union, Solidarity, in the 1980s showed the Soviet leadership that it could not afford to neglect the needs of the people for too long.

d   There was a split between the Soviet Union and the Chinese in 1960. This meant that the USA could now no longer see Communism as one enemy. For the Soviet Union, isolation from the Chinese made them look towards the USA, for they feared being the odd one out of the three super powers.

e   The most important reason of all was the possibility that a nuclear war might break out with the prospect of the almost total destruction of the human race.

In 1969 the USA and USSR made some progress towards limiting these weapons of mass destruction. They held the Strategic Arms Limitation Talks (SALT) and in 1972 the SALT 1 agreement was made between them. This limited the nuclear weapons of each country. The spirit of détente continued in 1975 at the Helsinki conference and SALT 2 was completed in 1979. However, SALT 2 was never ratified by the US Congress because of the Soviet invasion of Afghanistan.

▲ An American nuclear test

In 1979 Brezhnev took the decision to invade Afghanistan. Afghanistan was on the southern border of the USSR. It was a strongly Muslim country and the Soviet leaders were afraid that the militant Muslim nationalist groups there might have an influence upon the Muslims in the southern republics of the Soviet Union. Soldiers, tanks and helicopters were poured into Afghanistan in a war which lasted until 1985. The main effect of the Soviet invasion of Afghanistan is that it shattered détente and brought about renewed tension between east and west.

The 1980s were a time of more difficult relations, but nothing like the crises of 1950 and 1962 were ever reached again. The Soviet Union had invaded Afghanistan in 1979 and the USA intervened in civil wars in El Salvador, Guatemala and Nicaragua. New weapons, such as the American Pershing and Cruise missiles, were developed, and, in the mid 1980s, American President Reagan was hopeful of developing the Strategic Defence Initiative (SDI – later known as 'Star Wars') system for the USA to shoot down Soviet missiles in flight.

When Mikhail Gorbachev became the new leader of the USSR in 1985, there was a distinct change in Soviet foreign policy. Gorbachev needed to save some of the money that was being spent on defence. To do this he knew he must convince the USA of the Soviet Union's desire to reform. He removed Soviet troops from Afghanistan and from eastern Europe. Then, in 1989 and the early 1990s, the Communist regimes fell from power in eastern Europe and in the Soviet Union itself. With the almost total collapse of Communism the Cold War was finally over.

9 The USSR and Eastern Europe, 1945–1991

The Soviet view of the world

From 1917 until 1945 there was only one Communist country in the world; the Soviet Union. The leaders of the Soviet Union had a clear view of the history of their country. Even before the Communists took over, Russia had often been invaded by the west, including Sweden, Britain, France and, in the First World War, by the Germans. Germany had invaded again in 1941. In the wars which followed each of these invasions many Russians had died. In the First World War 1,700,000 Russian soldiers had died and 10 million Soviet citizens were killed in the Second World War. The diagram below shows more clearly the damage done to the USSR during the Second World War.

In 1918 and 1919, soldiers from Britain, France, and the USA were sent into Russia to fight against the Communists in the Russian Civil War. Then Russia was isolated by the western powers. The Communist leaders of Russia in 1919 were not invited to the Paris peace conferences and were not allowed to join the League of Nations. In 1923 Russia became known as the Union of Soviet Socialist Republics (USSR), or the Soviet Union. In 1938 and 1939, Stalin, the leader of the Soviet Union, tried to persuade Britain and France to agree to an alliance to stop the expansion of Nazi Germany. He was unsuccessful.

During the Second World War the Soviet Union formed a Grand Alliance with Britain and the USA. The leaders of these countries met three times during the War. At the Teheran Conference in 1943, Stalin asked the others to open a second front against the Germans as a matter of urgency. Soviet soldiers were bearing the brunt of the fighting and he felt that the western allies should do more. But a second front was not opened until June 1944, when the British and Americans invaded France. This made Stalin distrust the west even more. Then, during the Potsdam meeting in August 1945, President Truman announced to Stalin that the USA had just successfully exploded the first atom bomb. Truman had intended to frighten the USSR, but he only succeeded in making Stalin even more distrustful.

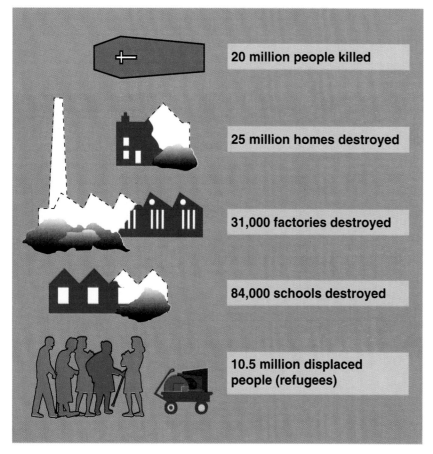

20 million people killed

25 million homes destroyed

31,000 factories destroyed

84,000 schools destroyed

10.5 million displaced people (refugees)

War damage done to the Soviet Union, 1941-1945

For the Soviets, the main aim at the end of the War was to make sure that their country would be safe in the future. They saw three ways of doing this, by

a   pushing the borders of the USSR and Poland further west

b   weakening Germany

c   making sure that the countries on their western border had governments which were friendly to the USSR. This meant setting up, or encouraging Communist Governments in these countries. These governments could then be influenced by Moscow.

The maps on pages 87 and 91 show how much of this was achieved. You can see that the western borders of the Soviet Union and Poland were moved further west. This was decided at the Yalta Conference in February 1945. Stalin met with Churchill of Britain and Roosevelt of the USA. They decided that Poland should gain land from Germany. Of course this also weakened Germany. At the Potsdam meeting it was decided that the two defeated powers, Austria and Germany, should be divided into four zones and occupied by soldiers from Britain, France, the USA, and the Soviet Union (see page 91). It was never decided how long this should be for. It was also decided that the USSR should receive reparations from Germany, as payment for the damage done during the War.

1   Explain why the Soviet Union felt threatened by the west after the Second World War.

2   Describe what the Soviet Union did to try to protect itself after the War.

It is important to realise that the Soviet Union's fears did not go away after 1945. The following sources are from much later, but they are giving a similar message about the Soviet view of the world.

A cartoon published in the USSR in the 1950s. It shows the NATO alliance marching towards the Soviet Union. They are led by US President Eisenhower. He is carrying a picture of Hitler, who had invaded the USSR in 1941.

We must understand that Russia is just as frightened of attack by the Western Alliance as we are of attack by the USSR. Part of her overall security is the belt of nations in eastern Europe. Any move by the western nations which suggested that they might help these countries to get their freedom would meet with instant action by Russia.

From the memoirs of Bernard Montgomery, written in 1958. Montgomery was a British Field Marshal. He is recalling his work in Germany just after the War and what this taught him about the Soviet view of the world.

Twice in this century the Russians have had to face an attack from the centre of Europe. Only they know the extent of their losses in the last war and the country is still governed by the men who fought it. The Russians have no intention of pulling down their defences in the west.

From a book about the Soviet Union written in 1972 by a Czech historian.

3 What can you learn from Source A about the Soviet view of NATO in the 1950s?

4 What 'defences' does Source C mean? Use Source B to help you to answer.

5 Source C was written in 1972 by a historian. When it says 'the Russians have no intention of pulling down their defences in the west', to what point in time do you think it is referring? Explain your answer.

6 Read Sources B and C and look carefully at Source A. Explain the similarities in the content of these three sources.

7 Sources B and C are written by people from very different backgrounds. How does this affect the reliability of the two sources when taken together?

How eastern Europe became Communist by 1948

In 1945 it was by no means certain that the countries of eastern Europe would all become Communist. In Czechoslovakia, Hungary, Romania, and Poland there were other parties in Parliament and Government alongside the Communists. Progress towards Communism was not the same in each country. We have to examine them in turn to understand what happened.

Poland

At Yalta the Great Powers decided what should be done about the government of Poland. Poland was an issue for each of them. In 1939 Britain had gone to war when Germany invaded Poland and throughout the War there were representatives of the Polish Government in exile in London. Churchill said that for Britain, Poland was a matter of honour. There were seven million Polish immigrants in the USA, which also made it important to Roosevelt. As you have seen, Poland was important to the USSR. Stalin said that for the Soviet Union Poland was 'a question of both honour and security.' In 1941 many Polish Communists fled to the USSR to escape the Germans. When the Soviet army entered Poland in 1945 they set up a government of Polish Communists in the city of Lublin. At Yalta it had been agreed that once Germany was defeated, this Lublin Government should be reorganised along more democratic lines. This did not happen. In 1945 Roosevelt wrote to Stalin and complained that the Yalta declaration was being ignored. The USA then sent an ambassador to Moscow to talk about Poland.

At Yalta we had agreed that the present Polish Government was to be reconstructed. Any one with common sense can see that this means the present Communist Government is to form the basis of the new one. No other understanding of the Yalta Agreement is possible. Despite the fact that we are simple people, the Soviets should not be regarded as fools, which is a mistake the west frequently make. We are not blind, we can see what is going on before our eyes.

Stalin speaking about Poland in 1945.

There were some non-Communists in the Polish Government until 1947, when there were elections. The Deputy Prime Minister was the leader of the Polish Peasants Party. But in the elections of 1947 the Peasants Party won just 28 out of the 444 seats in Parliament and the Communists were in control.

Bulgaria, Hungary, and Romania

In each of these countries Communist Governments, just like that in Poland, were set up. In Bulgaria the Communist Fatherland Front won 90% of the votes in an election in 1945. It then refused to allow any opposition members to join it in government and began to use harassment against its opponents. In Hungary the Smallholders Party (KGP) ruled until 1947 when the Communists took over. In Romania elections took place in 1946 and gave the Communists 372 seats out of 414. However, some results were forged! By 1947 the three main opposition parties had been destroyed.

Czechoslovakia

Of all the eastern European countries, only Czechoslovakia had a non-Communist government after 1947. There was a coalition government in Czechoslovakia. This meant that Communists and non-Communists shared power. In 1947 there was a severe drought in Czechoslovakia and the harvests failed. There was already an economic crisis. Living standards began to fall. There were demonstrations and a general strike. In 1948 many non-Communist ministers in the government resigned, hoping to bring down the Government. Instead of dissolving the Parliament the Communist Prime Minister, Gottwald, brought in more Communists to fill the posts of those non-Communists who had resigned. Now the Communists were in power. In the 1948 elections they gained 237 seats out of 300. Nobody can really say how fair the elections were, but soon afterwards the non-Communist parties were dissolved.

Why did so many east European countries become Communist?

There are two main reasons for this. Firstly, something that the Great Powers called 'spheres of influence.' At the end of any war it is usual for the victorious powers to divide up the spoils. When Churchill spoke of the Iron Curtain in 1946 (see Chapter 7) he was really talking of Europe divided into two spheres of influence. In the west was the sphere of British and American influence, two Capitalist and democratic powers. Eastern Europe was in the Soviet sphere of influence. Churchill had recognised this as early as 1944, when he met Stalin in Moscow and they made the 'percentages agreement'.

I said 'your armies are in Romania and Bulgaria. How would it be if you had most of the say in Romania and for us to have the say in Greece, and go fifty:fifty about Yugoslavia?' While this was being translated I wrote out on a half-sheet of paper:

	Great Britain and the others	Russia
Romania	10%	90%
Bulgaria	25%	75%
Greece	90%	10%
Hungary and Yugoslavia	50%	50%

I pushed this across to Stalin, who had by then heard the translation. There was a pause. Then he took his blue pencil and made a large tick upon it. It was all settled in no more time than it takes to set down.

Winston Churchill recalling a meeting with Stalin in 1944. The following day the Soviets changed the percentages on Bulgaria and Hungary in their own favour.

This recognition of each other's sphere of influence was very important. It meant that when Britain sent troops into Greece to fight against the Communist rebels, the Soviets could not stop them. It also meant that when Stalin encouraged Communist governments in Poland, Bulgaria, Hungary, and Romania, the west could not stop him.

Secondly, because these east European countries were geographically placed between the USSR and Germany/Austria they had been liberated by the Soviet army in 1945. Once the Soviets were in these countries it was far easier for them to influence the governments there.

Yugoslavia

The situation in Yugoslavia was different to the other east European countries. It was Communist from 1945 onwards, but was never dominated by the USSR. During the War, the Yugoslavs had a very strong resistance army of their own which fought against Germany. They were led by Joseph Broz known as Tito. Tito was helped and supplied by Britain and the USA, as well as by the Soviet Union. The Yugoslavs had freed their country themselves, and the Soviet army had not invaded Yugoslavia. After the War Yugoslavia became a Communist country under Tito. His Communist government was always more independent of Soviet control than the governments of the other eastern European countries. Tito would not be ruled from Moscow. In 1948 Stalin announced the removal from Yugoslavia of all Soviet economic and military advisers. This was an attempt to reduce Tito's power in the hope that he would be overthrown. Tito remained popular and stayed in power in Yugoslavia, receiving some aid from the USA. Nevertheless, Yugoslavia remained a Communist country.

What were the Communist countries like?

You have seen how quickly these Communist governments abolished opposition parties. These countries soon became one party states, and this means that the only political party allowed was the Communist Party. Any other party was unofficial and had to remain secret. Usually there were elections, but only to choose between different Communist candidates. The Churches and the trade unions were closely controlled, and there was little or no freedom of the radio, television, or newspapers. In particular, anybody who criticised the Government or was seen as an opponent of the Government was likely to find themselves in prison.

The Soviet Union dominated these countries. They became 'satellites' of the Soviet Union. In 1947 they were offered US economic aid from the Marshall Plan, but were forced by Stalin to turn this down. Once US aid had been refused, COMECON, a trading area of Communist countries, was set up to promote trade and economic recovery in the east. In 1955 the Warsaw Pact was signed by each European Communist country (except Yugoslavia) and the USSR. This was a defence treaty made in response to NATO (see page 93).

Interpretations of the Soviet Union's domination of eastern Europe

As with many events in history there is more than one interpretation of the domination of eastern Europe by the Soviet Union. Here are are two for you to consider.

a   The domination of eastern Europe by the Soviet Union was motivated by the Soviet Union's view of the world and its fear that the Soviet Union would be invaded again by the west. The Soviet Union had suffered more than any other country during the Second World War. Many events convinced the USSR that the west was being aggressive, for example, the Truman Doctrine, the Marshall Aid Plan and the formation of NATO. The only way that the Soviet Union could feel safe was by building a defensive 'buffer zone' of friendly countries along its western border.

b   The Soviet Union's domination of the eastern European countries was because the USSR wanted to extend Communism worldwide. The USSR had invaded Poland and the Baltic States in 1939. In 1945 the Soviet army was in most European countries and wished to spread Communism further.

It would have done had it not been for the Marshall Aid Plan and the formation of NATO which contained Communism in eastern Europe.

8   Describe each of these interpretations in your own words.

9   Which of these two interpretations gives the better explanation for the spread of Communism? You need to gather the evidence which supports both of the interpretations. There is a lot of evidence in this book, most of it in this chapter. However, it will be helpful to look at other chapters of this book and investigate other books as well. It will be best if you work in groups, each group looking at one of the interpretations. Remember, you need to find evidence which supports the interpretation that you are investigating. Each group could make a wall display about their interpretation, or give a presentation to the class. You could even stage a debate in class about this issue.

10 You should have noticed how each interpretation uses similar evidence to support its argument. Explain how the same evidence can be used to support different interpretations in history.

The problem of Germany, 1945–1961

Germany was divided into four zones in 1945. The Soviet Union occupied the eastern zone, which later became East Germany. This zone presented the Soviet Union with particular problems. Look back to the map on page 91.

11 The western allies looked upon this division as temporary. Do you think that the geographical position of the Soviet occupied zone would make the USSR see the reunification of Germany differently to the way the west saw it? Explain your answer.

An added problem was the position of Berlin, the German capital city. Although it was inside the Soviet zone, it was also divided into four zones. British, French, and American soldiers were in the western part of the city. West Berlin was supplied with food and fuel from the west by air, canal, road, and railway.

In 1947 President Truman of the USA provided American economic aid to western Europe. Then the British, French and American zones were combined into a single western zone. Some of the American aid went to the western zone of Germany.

From then on, the two zones, east and west, developed very differently. The Soviet Union had taken lots of industrial machinery and resources from the eastern zone as reparations for war damage. In this way the eastern zone was prevented from taking part in the economic recovery. In the west, American aid was allowing Germany to share in the economic rebirth of Europe.

The western powers decided to introduce a new currency into the western zone. This was done in 1948. This made the Soviet Union furious because they saw all these measures as strengthening Germany, which they wished to keep weak. In March 1948, the Soviets reacted. They prevented any movement of supplies into West Berlin. The blockade of West Berlin had begun. There were over two million people living in West Berlin. The western powers had to decide what to do with them. They could abandon them and allow a Communist take over, but this would seem like a defeat and might mean that other areas might fall to the Communists. Or they could try to keep the citizens of West Berlin supplied. If they chose to supply them, and broke down the Soviet road and rail blocks by force, then a war might result. They decided to keep West Berlin supplied by air. American planes were brought from Alaska, Hawaii and even Japan. They flew from bases in West Germany carrying the food and fuel that Berlin needed.

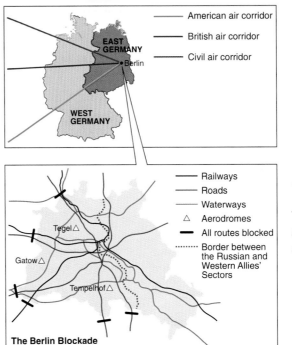

The Berlin blockade and the subsequent airlift

A photograph taken in 1948. It shows an American transport plane about to land in West Berlin.

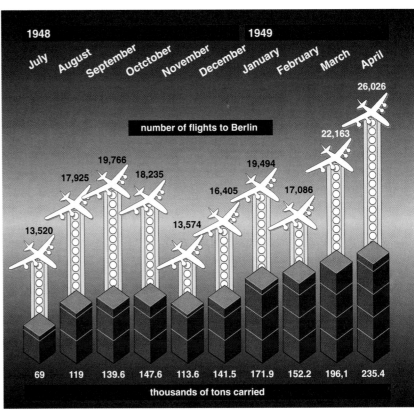

1948					1949				
July	August	September	Octctober	November	December	January	February	March	April

number of flights to Berlin

| 13,520 | 17,925 | 19,766 | 18,235 | 13,574 | 16,405 | 19,494 | 17,086 | 22,163 | 26,026 |
| 69 | 119 | 139.6 | 147.6 | 113.6 | 141.5 | 171.9 | 152.2 | 196,1 | 235.4 |

thousands of tons carried

Details of the Berlin airlift, 1948-1949

5,000 tons of coal were needed each day if West Berlin was to survive. At the height of this airlift, 1,400 aircraft per day landed in West Berlin, at the rate of one every three minutes. 79 men were killed in accidents, mostly American and British pilots and German ground crews, although some Soviet pilots also died. The airlift lasted until May 1949. West Berlin survived and the Soviets settled for control of the eastern zone of Germany and East Berlin.

Soon after the end of the Berlin crisis and the airlift, the Allies began to involve the Germans in the government of their own country once again. Power was given back to the German people in the western zone. The German leaders of the eleven western provinces were invited to set up an elected assembly. This became the German Federal Republic, also known as West Germany, and its first Chancellor was Konrad Adenauer. West Germany became fully independent in 1955.

In the east, the Soviet zone became independent in 1949. It was called the German Democratic Republic (GDR), also known as East Germany. It had a Communist government and was closely controlled by Moscow. West Berlin continued as a small enclave of the west inside East Germany.

West Berlin was a problem for the Soviet Union. There was no doubt that the West German economy was developing at a faster rate than that of the East. There were riots and fighting in East Berlin in 1953. Workers there had been forced to work longer hours for no extra pay. In June, thousands of workers roamed the streets burning Soviet flags and pictures of Stalin. Riots spread throughout East Germany and even the police joined the rioters in some cities. It took Soviet soldiers and tanks to stop the riots. Around 400 people died. The Communists blamed the revolt upon 'Fascists from West Berlin'. This was not the case, there was no plotting by the west to start protests in East Berlin. But the western part of the city did receive considerable American aid. The Americans were turning West Berlin into a showpiece of western Capitalism. West Berlin provided a window for the East Germans to see western prosperity and a door through which East Berliners could move into the west. The consequences of this were that each year about a quarter of a million East Germans emigrated to the west through East Berlin. Of course this made made the Soviet leaders distrust the USA even more.

East Germany had not been recognised by Britain or the USA. To do so would be to admit that Germany would always be divided. In 1958, Khrushchev, the Soviet leader, demanded that the western powers recognise the East German state (GDR) and move out of West Berlin. He gave them a six months deadline to do this. The western powers refused to act and Khrushchev could do nothing. In 1961 Khrushchev acted to stop the flow of East Germans to the west. First the East German Prime Minister made a speech to factory workers which hinted at what was to happen.

The frontiers of our country will be protected at any cost. We will do everything to stop the criminal activity of the headhunters, the slave traders of Western Germany and the American Spies!

From the speech by Walter Ulbricht, Prime Minister of the GDR, 10th August 1961.

Three days later hundreds of workmen appeared on the streets of Berlin and began building a wall along the boundary between the eastern and western halves of the city.

This is a picture of the Berlin Wall being constructed in 1961

A West German cartoon published shortly after the Wall had been built. The original caption said 'The final solution', says Ulbricht. 'The whole population has been evacuated to China. I announce the existence of total state security'.

12 Read Source F. What did Ulbricht mean by 'headhunters' and 'slave traders'?
13 Why do you think Ulbricht made this speech and who do you think it was really for?
14 Look at Source G. What impression of Ulbricht and the East German Government is it trying to give? Explain your answer.

Opposition to the Soviet domination of eastern Europe, 1953–1968

While Stalin was alive the Communist countries in eastern Europe were ruled in a very strict way. There were few freedoms and the secret police were powerful in each country. This style of rule is called Stalinism. The Soviet Union made sure that the Communist leaders of these countries were Stalinist in their methods. Each state had a secret police force and political

opponents were imprisoned. Stalin died in 1953. He was replaced by Khrushchev. Soon Khrushchev began to criticise Stalin. He abolished the NKVD, the Soviet secret police. This made Moscow's hold over their eastern satellites weaker. In 1955 Khrushchev met Tito, the Yugoslav leader, and tried to bring Yugoslavia closer to the USSR again.

Tito and Khrushchev meeting in Belgrade in 1955. Tito is the man in the uniform. Stalin had usually appeared in uniform at any public meeting. What impression do you think Khrushchev was trying to give?

Khrushchev said Stalin's criticisms of Tito had not been fair and he made it clear that 'there was more than one road to Socialism.' This made the eastern European countries feel that they had more control over their own future. Khrushchev made many more criticisms of Stalin in a speech at the Congress of the Communist Party of the Soviet Union in February 1956. All the faults of the Soviet Union were blamed on Stalin. Copies of this speech were supposed to be secret, but it was discovered by the USA who made the whole speech public in June 1956.

Many eastern European countries believed that this attack on Stalin gave them the right to develop Communism in their own way.

Poland, 1956

In June 1956 there was a revolt in Poland against Soviet domination. It was led by workers at the engineering factories in Poznan. Soldiers shot at the protesters and fifty people were killed. The Polish army was led by Soviet officers, but it could not keep order in Poland when it was opposed by large numbers of workers.

The Poles wanted Gomulka to lead them. Gomulka was a Communist who had been imprisoned by Stalin in 1948, but who returned to favour in 1956. He wanted an end to Soviet domination and wanted the Polish Communists to decide the future for the country. In October Gomulka was elected First Secretary of the Polish Communist Party.

Moscow was now very worried about what was happening in Poland. Khrushchev visited Warsaw and tried to win back support. At the same time, Soviet troops began advancing on the city. The workers and the police supported Gomulka and it looked as though there might be a civil war. But Khrushchev backed down. He was worried that fighting might spread to East Germany and that the west might intervene. Soviet troops withdrew and Gomulka became the Prime Minister of Poland.

Hungary, 1956

Just as Khrushchev feared, the Polish revolt spread. Hungary was the next Soviet satellite to rebel. In June 1953 Hungary had a new leader. He was Imre Nagy (in Hungarian Nagy means 'big', so Nagy was Mr. Big!). He took over from Rakosi, a Stalinist. Nagy introduced many reforms. There was an amnesty for political prisoners, the abolition of internment camps, and many social and economic reforms. This programme was called 'the

New Course'. However, the programme was not carried out in full. In 1955 Nagy was criticised by other Communists and called a 'right wing deviationist'. He was removed from office and expelled from the Communist Party.

So by October 1956 Hungary was split between the majority who supported Nagy and those who followed Rakosi and the Stalinists. Then the people heard news of the Polish uprising. This seemed to show the Hungarians the way forward. They tried to copy the Poles and get Nagy back in power. There were demonstrations in support of Nagy. 300,000 protesters were on the streets of Budapest shouting 'Imre Nagy to power' and 'Go home Russians'. Nagy's support came from the students, workers, and the army. But the police remained loyal to the Government. On 23rd October, the Hungarian Communist Government asked for Soviet help to put down this revolt. Soviet soldiers and tanks were in the cities. There was now fighting in Budapest and it began to spread across the country.

One group of youths tried to drive a car into the main gates of the radio station while others clambered onto the balconies. The defenders used tear gas and fire hoses. When this failed the AVO (the Hungarian secret police who remained loyal to the Government) began advancing onto the crowd with fixed bayonets. At about 9.00 pm the first shots were fired. Tanks and machine guns joined in, and soon the streets were littered with dead and wounded.

Some youths headed for the city park where they tied steel cables around the huge statue of Stalin and hooked them to a heavy lorry. With an enormous crash the statue broke off at the boots and was later dragged through the streets by a dustbin truck.

One badly wounded AVO policeman was taken from his hospital bed, kicked to death and hanged by his ankles from a nearby tree.

Advised by experienced Hungarian army officers, the young freedom fighters quickly learned the best way of dealing with Soviet tanks. As a column of tanks entered a narrow street, the Hungarians attacked the first and last tanks with petrol bombs. The others were then trapped between the two immobilised vehicles.

The Budapest revolt, October 1956. These extracts are taken from a British school history book written in 1968.

Stalin's statue after it had been removed from the Budapest city park. What else can you see in the picture? What are the people doing?

Near the cafe, lying in the middle of the road like a giant's football, was the head from Stalin's statue. It had been dragged there by a jubilant public as a mark of their triumph, displaying the traitor's head on a gargantuan scale. A gentleman was seeking to knock off a chunk with the aid of a pickaxe, and it occurred to Gyuri that he should take a souvenir as well. He queued up patiently behind the man, when the Soviet tank appeared. It roared into the middle of the square and opened fire on Gyuri.

From a novel written in 1992. The author is British with Hungarian parents. The story is set in Hungary in 1956 and the hero is a young Hungarian called Gyuri. Here Gyuri is in Budapest.

Nagy was brought back as Prime Minister and the fighting stopped. He formed a new government which included non-Communist politicians, and announced the end of the one party system in Hungary, and promised free elections. Political prisoners were released from prison. Free trade unions were to be allowed. By 1st November, newspapers not published by the Government were on open sale. Reforms were happening quickly. Nagy then announced that Hungary would withdraw from the Warsaw Pact and become a neutral country. He asked the USA to protect this neutrality.

Budapest in October 1956. You can see the corpse of a soldier in the foreground. What other evidence of fighting can you see?

On 30th October Nagy announced the end of the one party system in Hungary and declared his intention of forming a democratic coalition government along 1945 lines. He also promised free elections. An inner cabinet was set up including representatives of non-Communist parties. A national federation of free trade unions was formed, on a voluntary basis and with the right to strike. Cardinal Mindzenty was freed from prison the same day.

The next day a National Guard was formed in the Kilian barracks, Budapest. By 1st November un-censored newspapers were in the streets on sale openly, which had not been allowed before, and the Hungarian Christian Party was reformed.

The reforms of Imre Nagy, 1956.

This was too much for the USSR to accept. Soviet troops surrounded Hungarian towns and airports. On 4th November Soviet soldiers with six thousand tanks attacked Budapest. There was heavy fighting in Hungary for seven days. Nagy had to flee to the Yugoslav Embassy. He was later arrested and executed. The Soviets had maintained control of Hungary and sent a strong message to the rest of their satellites. Any attempt to move too far away from the Soviet idea of Communism would no longer be tolerated by Moscow.

Why did Khrushchev order Soviet soldiers into Hungary?

a The Hungarian rising was against the Soviet Union as well as against Hungarian Communists. By saying he would leave the Warsaw Pact, Nagy threatened the stability of the whole Soviet sphere of influence. If Hungary left the Warsaw Pact then so might Poland and then perhaps Czechoslovakia.

b Khrushchev was advised by the Chinese and other Communist leaders to take strong action.

c Khrushchev's own position in the Soviet Union was not totally safe and any sign of weakness over Hungary might have brought about his own downfall.

d Khrushchev was confident that the west would not intervene. Britain and France had problems in Egypt at this time. In November they had invaded Egypt (see Chapter 11) and so were not in a position to criticise the Soviets. The invasion of Egypt had split the western powers.

e Presidential elections in the USA made American intervention unlikely. All President Eisenhower did was protest.

I have noted with profound distress the reports which have come to me from Hungary. I urge in the name of humanity and in the cause of peace that the Soviet Union take action to withdraw Soviet forces from Hungary immediately, and permit the Hungarian people to enjoy the rights and freedoms granted to all people in the UN Charter.

From a letter sent by US President Eisenhower to the Soviet leaders on 5th November 1956.

A Socialist state could not remain a silent observer of the bloody reign of Fascist reaction in People's Democratic Hungary. When everything settles down in Hungary, and life becomes normal again, the Hungarian working class, peasantry and intelligentsia will undoubtedly understand our actions better and judge them right. We see our help to the Hungarian working class in its struggle against counter-revolution as our international duty.

From *Pravda*, the Soviet Government run newspaper, 23rd November 1956.

15 Describe the events in Hungary in October and November 1956.
16 Explain why the Soviet Union took stronger action in Hungary than it did in Poland in 1956.
17 Read Source I. What is the attitude of the writer towards the Hungarians? Explain your answer fully.
18 Read Source K. This source is a from a novel, a piece of fiction, which was written 36 years after the events in which it is set. How reliable do you think it is as a source of information about the Budapest rising of 1956? Use the other sources to help you explain your answer.
19 Source K might be useful to a historian for other purposes, not simply for information about the events. What uses do you think these might be?

20 Look at Sources J and L of Budapest in 1956. How would you describe the mood of each photograph?
21 Use Sources J, K, and L. Read through the text and sources again and try to work out exactly when the photographs were taken and exactly what point in the events Source K is based on.
22 Read Sources N and O. These two sources give very different interpretations of the same events. Describe these interpretations in your own words under two headings: 'The American view' and 'The Soviet view.' Use the sources and your own knowledge of the subject to explain why there are different interpretations of Hungary in 1956.

A photograph taken in the Czech capital, Prague, on 21st August 1968. It shows a young Czech protester raising the Czech flag above an invading Soviet tank.

▼

The Czechoslovak revolt, 1968

Since 1948, when the Communists took over, Czechoslovakia had been a 'model satellite'. The standard of living there had been higher than in most eastern European countries and the Czech Government had been obedient to the Soviets. In January 1968 changes began. Antonin Novotny was President of the country and First Secretary of the Communist Party. He was an old style Stalinist leader. In January 1968 Novotny was replaced as First Secretary of the Czech Communist Party by Alexander Dubcek. Between January and March, Dubcek and Novotny struggled for power. Dubcek wanted changes and many were made, including more freedom to individual firms and farmers' co-operatives. The changes were slow to take effect because of obstruction from the State bureaucracy. By March the newspapers were printing uncensored discussions of political and social problems. The coverage of the news by Czech radio and television became much fuller. Then Novotny resigned and General Svoboda became President of Czechoslovakia. Svoboda was a war hero. His name means 'freedom' in Czech. Now there were more reforms.

These included the creation of works councils in factories and increased rights for trade unions. Dubcek announced that there would be less censorship, less control by the secret police, and more open discussion. Dubcek called all this 'Socialism with a human face.' His ideas caused great excitement in Czechoslovakia during the spring of 1968. However, there was one area in which Dubcek said he would make no changes. This was in foreign policy. Dubcek declared that he had no intention of leaving the Warsaw Pact. In this way Dubcek was showing the Soviets that he was a Communist and he would not go as far as the Hungarians had tried to do in 1956.

But the Soviets were very worried by what they saw in Czechoslovakia. They were afraid that Czechoslovakia was becoming close to West Germany. It seemed to them that industrial relations between the Czechs and the West Germans were being strengthened from day to day. The new economic policy of Dubcek seemed to involve dependence on an increased contact with the west to a point which might allow Germany to begin to dominate Czechoslovakia and perhaps other countries in the Soviet sphere. Dubcek's assurances were of little comfort to the Soviets. In July 1968 Brezhnev, the Soviet leader, told Dubcek that American missiles had been discovered close to the West German border with Czechoslovakia and this meant that the West was going to invade. He asked Dubcek to allow Soviet troops into Czechoslovakia to protect the Czechs. Dubcek refused. In August Brezhnev ordered a mass invasion of Czechoslovakia by tanks and soldiers of the Warsaw Pact countries. The Czech Government decided not to offer any armed resistance to this invasion. They feared casualties amongst the civilian population. There was a great deal of passive resistance. The Czechs immobilised Soviet tanks, or painted them white. The Czechs tried to plead with the Soviet soldiers and there was a campaign of posters against the invasion.

A Czech street poster from 1968. Lenin, the leader of the Russian Revolution of 1917, is shown weeping as the Soviet tanks invade Czechoslovakia.

Young Czech protesters in 1969. They are congregating on the spot where a boy was killed. The posters in the background are supporting Dubcek and say 'Socialism yes. Occupation no!' The plaque by the flowers reads 'In the fight against the Soviet occupation here fell an unknown fourteen year old boy.'

Dubcek and Svoboda were taken to Moscow as prisoners. There they made a statement which said that after 'free comradely discussions' the Czechoslovak reforms begun in January would have to be given up. Demonstrations against the Soviet invasion and occupation went on until April 1969. Then the USSR forced Dubcek to resign and he was replaced by Gustav Husak. Once again the Soviets had exerted their control over eastern Europe.

23 List the reforms made in Czechoslovakia between January and August 1968.

24 Explain in your own words why the Soviet leaders were so worried about events in Czechoslovakia?

25 Look at Sources P and Q. What is meant by passive resistance? Why did the Czechs choose this method of protest against the Soviet occupation?

26 What were the similarities between Czechoslovakia in 1968 and Hungary in 1956? What were the differences?

27 Look at Source P.
i Why do you think Lenin is shown weeping?
ii Where has the poster been placed? What does this tell you about the poster?

Poland, 1980

You have read about the unrest in Poland in 1956. There were also strikes there in the 1970s, when 45 workers were killed and many more injured. A demand for a free trade union was started by workers in the Gdansk shipyard in 1980. This soon spread to workers all over Poland. The Polish Government eventually permitted this union, called Solidarnosk, which means Solidarity. Its leader was Lech Walesa. Walesa was a shipbuilder in Gdansk. He caused problems for the Communist leadership. Solidarity demanded better pay, shorter working hours, and lower food prices.

Shipyard workers! Hull fitters, welders, paint sprayers, plumbers, and you too, members of the intelligentsia, listen to me.

(Applause)

We demand that prices be brought down, back to their previous levels. And if they're not...then there'll be strikes tomorrow!

(More applause)

Lech Walesa speaking to a crowd of four thousand shipyard workers in 1980.

I went to the shipyard on behalf of the Government to define the conditions for negotiations. I remember that first meeting [with Walesa] very well. I entered the shipyard fearfully. The thousands of people at the gate and the difficulty of making my way through the crowd caused great tension. Frankly I imagined a different man: big, hard with a strong determined voice who would stand no opposition. Instead I found a man of medium height with a friendly smile. That friendliness touched me greatly at the time. His attitude to me was very important. It influenced the way I conducted our talk and reported back to my superiors.'

An eyewitness at the Gdansk shipyard in August 1980.

My husband comes home from work and says what they are saying in the District Committee (of the Communist Party) that the leader of the strike, Lech Walesa, has got a criminal record, is a drunkard and a scrounger.

An account written by a Polish woman in 1980.

Lech Walesa in 1981

In 1981 the Polish army took over the country. General Jaruzelski took over as leader. Solidarity was banned.

28 According to Source S what kind of man was Walesa? Is this supported by Source U?
29 What personal qualities did Walesa have which made him a suitable leader for the Polish workers at that time? Use the sources in your answer.
30 Do you think Sources R and S are likely to be reliable accounts of what happened at the Gdansk shipyard? Explain your answer.
31 Of what value is Source T to a historian studying these events?
32 Sources S and T give different impressions of Walesa. How would you account for these differences.
33 The Soviet Union did not become directly involved in the events of Poland in 1980-1981. Does this mean that events in Poland at that time were less serious than events in Poland and Hungary in 1956, or Czechoslovakia in 1968? Explain your answer.
34 How did the Soviet Union deal with revolts against Communist control in Eastern Europe between 1956 and 1980. Use material from all of this section in your answer.

Human rights in the USSR

The issue of human rights was one which had always figured in the USSR, and one which consistently aroused the objections of the west. Stalin had begun the Soviet Union's poor reputation on human rights during the late 1920s and 1930s with the persecution of the Kulaks, groups of richer peasants, and with the purges. The Soviet system was one which discouraged dissent and opposition. There were many prison camps and work camps (called Gulags) which were often full of political prisoners.

Between 1953 and 1964, when Khrushchev was in power, there was a little relaxation, but not much. Previously banned authors such as Bulgakov and Dostoyevsky could now be read and Alexander Solzhenitsyn was allowed to publish a novel called *One day in the life of Ivan Denisovich* which described the life of a prisoner in one of Stalin's Gulags. However, during this period the Churches in Russia were persecuted and some monks were beaten and sent into mental hospitals.

Women's rights increased significantly under the Soviet system. Women had full constitutional and voting rights from early on; in 1956 maternity leave from work was increased to 112 days and there were improvements to family allowances and more help for single parents.

Leonid Brezhnev (1964-1982) took a hard line against dissidents, such as scientists and writers like Andrei Sakharov and Solzhenitsyn, who criticised the USSR and its system for failing to respect human rights.

It was under Mikhail Gorbachev (1985-1991) that Soviet dissidents enjoyed their greatest freedoms. He gave people such as Sakharov their freedom, tolerated religion, and showed much greater respect for human rights.

The collapse of Communism in eastern Europe and the USSR, 1985-1991

After the death of Stalin in 1953, the leaders of the Soviet Union were less conservative. Both Khrushchev and Brezhnev were more liberal than Stalin in their dealings with eastern Europe and with the west. After the death of Brezhnev, two 'hard liners', Andropov and Chernenko, were in power in the Soviet Union for a short time. Then, in 1985, Mikhail Gorbachev became Chairman of the Communist Party. He was to be the most liberal leader of the Soviet Union. A new spirit of reform swept through the Soviet Government. Glasnost (which means openness) and perestroika (restructuring) became the new catch words of the Soviet Union. The country was opened up to more debate and criticism. Gorbachev was motivated by the need to reduce spending on the military. The USSR had economic problems and spending would have to be slashed if bankruptcy was to be avoided. The only way to do this was to convince the USA that the Soviet Union was reforming. Gorbachev announced the removal of Soviet troops from Afghanistan and eastern Europe.

There were changes in public opinion in the Soviet satellite countries at the same time. People became resentful of low living standards, poor wages, chronic shortages, and inefficient industry. It was the ordinary people who resented the privileges which the old style Stalinist system had brought to a few people. Traditionally, the Communist leaders in the east European countries reacted to this kind of opposition by clamping down on the protesters and tightening their control. But this was difficult to do after 1985. Gorbachev seemed to be encouraging the spread of the reform process. He believed glasnost and perestroika should also flourish in the countries of eastern Europe. One by one the Communist leaders fell from power. In East Germany Eric Honecker had held out against change for many years. Restrictions on movement between East and West Germany were relaxed and in 1989 the Berlin Wall came down. Eventually Honecker was removed and the two Germanys were reunited.

▶ Jubilant Berliners celebrate the reunification of Germany in October 1990. The flags say 'Germany United Fatherland'.

The most powerful symbol of postwar German divisions reopened yesterday after 28 years. Crowds from both sides of the city flocked in pouring rain to watch Helmut Kohl, the West German Chancellor, step into east Berlin for the first time and shake hands with Hans Modrow the East German Prime Minister. East German border guards wearing flowers joined the crowd in toasting the opening with champagne. In an atmosphere reminiscent of the opening of the border in November, strangers hugged and kissed.

From *The Times* newspaper, 23rd December 1989.

At the same time democratic changes were happening in Czechoslovakia and Hungary. In Romania Nikoli Ceausescu, who had been one of the most repressive Communist dictators, was overthrown after a bloody revolt in 1989. Ceausescu and his wife were executed by firing squad. In Poland change was more orderly. In 1989 power was handed over to moderate reformers and there were free elections the following year. In these elections Lech Walesa, the leader of the Solidarity Union formed by him in 1980, became the new President. The Warsaw Pact was no longer a possibility and it was abolished in 1991.

Eventually the desire for more freedom came back to the USSR where perestroika began. Parts of the Soviet Union wanted independence. First the Baltic states, Estonia, Latvia and Lithuania, then Georgia, Belarus and the Ukraine demanded self rule. Gorbachev spoke against this and tried to keep the Union

together. In 1991 there was a coup against Gorbachev. A group of army officers, KGB officers, and conservative politicians tried to take over. They failed, but Gorbachev was seriously weakened. Boris Yeltsin, the President of the Russian Federation, was now rivalling Gorbachev's power. By the end of 1991 the Soviet Union had broken up into 15 separate independent states.

Prague, 1991. The Soviet tank used as a memorial to the Soviet liberation of Czechoslovakia in 1945, has been painted pink on the collapse of Communist rule and is now being removed.

The new states formed from the former Soviet Union

Interpretations of the collapse of Communism

As with many events in history there is more than one interpretation of the collapse of Communism in Eastern Europe and the ending of the USSR's domination. Here are two for you to think about.

a   The collapse of Communism in eastern Europe was inevitable. There had always been opposition to both the Communist parties and to Soviet domination. For example, in Hungary in 1956, Czechoslovakia in 1968, and Poland in 1980. It was only a matter of time before one or more of the east European satellites freed themselves from Communism. Once this happened, the Soviet Union would not be able to keep control.

b   The collapse of Communism was the result of a deliberate policy by Gorbachev. He began with reform in the Soviet Union and encouraged the people of eastern Europe to reform.

When the first satellites began to change he did nothing to stop them and allowed others to follow. In 1956 and 1968 the Soviet Union was determined to keep control of its satellites, but by 1989 Gorbachev saw that they were no longer needed and allowed them to move away from the USSR.

35 Which of these interpretations gives the best explanation for the collapse of Communism? You need to gather the evidence which supports each of the interpretations. There is a lot of evidence in this book, most of it in this chapter. It will be helpful to investigate other books as well. It will be best if you work in groups, each group looking at one of the interpretations. Remember, you need to find evidence which supports the interpretation you are investigating. Each group could make a wall display about their interpretation, or give a presentation to the class.

10 *Towards a united Europe*

Reasons for European co-operation, 1945–1947

The Second World War ended in 1945 with the surrender of Germany and then Japan. Europe was devastated by a war that had lasted for six years. European countries had fought against each other. Many had been invaded, occupied and invaded again. Millions of people had died, been badly injured or made homeless.

European war dead, 1939–45.

Country	Number killed
Soviet Union	20,000,000
Poland	4,320,000
Germany	4,200,000
China	2,200,000
Yugoslavia	1,700,000
Japan	1,219,000
France	600,000
Romania	460,000
Hungary	420,000
Italy	410,000
United States	406,000
Great Britain	388,000
Czechoslovakia	365,000
Austria	334,000
Netherlands	210,000
Greece	160,000
Belgium	88,000
Finland	84,000
Bulgaria	20,000
Norway	10,000
Luxembourg	5,000
Denmark	1,000
Total 1939–1945	37,600,000
Total 1914–1918	17,000,000

There were hundreds of thousands of people who were now refugees. This means they had been moved away from their homeland. Also, almost every European country was heavily in debt. Germany and Italy were bankrupted by the war. Even the victorious powers, Britain and the USSR, were now in severe economic distress.

During the war the USA had supplied Britain and the USSR with huge amounts of aid through a system known as Lend-Lease. Supplies of weapons and other essentials flowed into Britain and the Soviet Union. It was to be paid for later. Lend-Lease to the Soviet Union ended in May 1945 and once the fighting stopped supplies to Britain also stopped.

Both Britain and the USSR asked the USA for loans to help them to revive their economies, but these requests were not fully met. The British and the Soviet Union reacted in different ways to the USA's decision. The Soviet Union had asked for one thousand million dollars of credit in August 1945. The Americans made it clear that any loan they might make would be on the understanding that the Soviet Government would make 'political concessions'. This meant that American films and books would be allowed into the USSR and other eastern European countries, and free elections would have to be held. This was known as 'dollar diplomacy.' It meant that the USA was trying to influence the USSR by using its economic power. But it did not work. The USSR quickly realised they would not get a loan from the USA. The Soviet Government decided to manage without. The Soviet hold over eastern Europe was stepped up and Soviet 'satellite' countries were exploited by the USSR. Chapter 7 explains in greater detail the divisions between the USA and USSR in 1945 and Chapter 9 shows how the Soviet Union dominated eastern Europe.

In Britain, the War made the Government reassess its position in the world. Britain and the USA had been close allies during the War. Even before the Americans became involved in the fighting, American Lend-Lease aid had been arriving in Britain. President Roosevelt had met Churchill, the British Prime Minister, in August 1941 and they had agreed the Atlantic Charter. This was a joint declaration about what the world should be like after the war. The British believed they had a 'special relationship' with the USA. When the economist John Keynes was sent to the USA in 1946 to negotiate a massive loan, it was honestly believed that he would come back having successfully secured the money which Britain needed. He did not. The USA would loan 3,750 million dollars on condition that Britain altered its policy in the Commonwealth (see Chapter 11). This loan was too small and was used up much more quickly than anybody had expected. Britain had to convince the USA that investment in Britain and Europe was essential. To do this the British Government decided to take advantage of American fears of Communism. Winston Churchill had been to the USA in 1946 and made his famous 'Iron Curtain' Speech (see page 87).

At this time, the USA was led by President Truman. Truman was new to foreign policy and he was surrounded by advisers who were anti-Communist. Many people in the American Government were worried about the spread of Communism. One of the few countries in eastern Europe that was not already Communist by 1947 was Greece. British soldiers were fighting in Greece. They were helping the Greek Government to fight against Communist rebels. In 1947 the British Foreign Secretary, Ernest Bevin, made it clear to the USA that Britain did not have the economic resources to carry on with this support. If Britain withdrew, said Bevin, Greece would become Communist. This seems to have affected Truman. In March he made a speech to Congress which made clear the extent of the Communist threat.

I believe that it must be the policy of the United States to support free peoples who are resisting attempted take over by armed minorities or by outside pressures. I believe that we must assist free peoples to work out their own destinies in their own way. The seeds of totalitarian regimes grow in the soil of poverty and strife, they are helped by misery and want. The free peoples of the world look to us for support in maintaining their freedoms.

From a speech made by President Truman of the USA in 1947.

This became known as the Truman Doctrine. Congress then voted in favour of aid to Britain. This aid programme was outlined by the US Secretary of State, George Marshall, and it was to become known as Marshall Aid. This aid was to be made available to Europe on condition that the European countries agreed upon a joint recovery plan (see also Chapter 7).

Before the United States Government can proceed much further in its efforts to help start the European world on its way to recovery, there must be some agreement among the countries of Europe. It would not be fitting for the USA to draw up a program designed to place Europe on its feet economically. This is the business of the Europeans. The initiative, I think, must come from Europe. The role of this country [the USA] should consist of friendly aid and support. The program should be a joint one, agreed to by a number of, if not all, European nations.

From the speech made by Secretary of State George Marshall, 1947.

This photograph shows the first Marshall Aid arriving in Europe in 1948. This is sugar from the Caribbean. Some of the Marshall Aid was in the form of goods and other aid was sent as money.

This cartoon appeared in a British magazine at the time the Marshall Plan was announced

D

The Marshall Plan

This was also known as the European Recovery Programme (ERP)

C

The day that the Marshall Plan was proclaimed, Britain moved into action. Key Foreign Office personnel drew up, within the next two weeks, a programme that involved Britain itself taking the lead to turn the Marshall Plan into a practical reality.

The British historian, Kenneth Morgan, writing in 1984.

The British Government responded quickly. Bevin organised a conference of Foreign Ministers in Paris in July 1947. The USSR rejected Marshall Aid. At first this Aid was open to all European nations, but the USSR would not allow the countries of eastern Europe to participate. They thought it was the USA's aim to dominate Europe.

THE TRUMAN LINE

5   What is President Truman doing in Source D?
6   What does Truman think the fence will do?
7   Compare the attitude of the cartoonist with Vyshinsky's attitude towards the Marshall Plan (Source E).

As is now clear, the Marshall Plan is clearly just another version of the Truman Doctrine adapted to the conditions of postwar Europe. In bringing forward this plan. the United States' Government counted on the co-operation of the governments of the United Kingdom and France to limit the freedom of choice in Europe.

Vyshinsky, the Soviet spokesman at the United Nations, commenting on the Marshall Plan in 1947.

8   What do Sources A and B say about the role of the USA?
9   Explain the link between Sources A, B, and C.
10 How useful are Sources A, B, C, and E for understanding the purposes of the Marshall Plan? Explain your answer by reference to the sources.
11 Sources C and E show two completely different reactions to the Marshall Plan. Describe these reactions. Use the sources and your own knowledge to explain why there were differences between them.
12 How important was the role of Britain in **a** influencing US attitudes to aid for Europe, and **b** organising the European response to the Marshall Plan?

The Paris conference led to the formation of the Organisation for European Economic Co-operation (OEEC) in 1948. This was made up of the sixteen countries receiving Marshall Aid (see page 90). The OEEC set itself three objectives.

a To distribute Marshall Aid.
b To encourage investment between European countries.
c To encourage trade between European countries.

This was the European Recovery Plan demanded by George Marshall. But some of the sixteen members of the OEEC wanted to go further towards European Co-operation. In 1947 three countries had already formed a customs union. These were Belgium, Luxembourg, and the Netherlands. This BENELUX customs union encouraged free trade between these three countries.

The Hague Congress, 1948

This was an un-official Congress which lasted for five days. It attracted over 800 delegates, all of which were greatly in favour of more European co-operation. These included Winston Churchill. Although not an official body, the Hague Congress made important progress towards European co-operation.
a It called for governments to work together for greater political and economic union in Europe.
b It called for a European Assembly where common interests could be discussed. This was achieved in 1949 when Belgium, Britain, France, Denmark, Ireland, Italy, Luxembourg, Norway, and Sweden signed a new Treaty and set up the Council of Europe. The Council of Europe met in Strasbourg. It was a meeting and talking place for the political leaders of the member countries. Some wanted it to have more power. The power to tell national governments what to do, for example. Others, including the British Government, had no wish for this.
c It called for a European Court of Human Rights which would help solve differences in people's rights from one country to another. This was established and it exists today, based at the Hague in the Netherlands.

The defence of Europe

The Brussels Treaty, 1948

Representatives from Belgium, Britain, France, Luxembourg, and the Netherlands met in Brussels. They made some agreements on cultural, economic and social matters. However, the real aim was military. The governments of these countries were concerned about possible Soviet aggression and they agreed that if one country were attacked the others would offer military assistance.

NATO

In 1949, during the crisis in Berlin, the USA was brought into the defence of Europe when it signed the North Atlantic Treaty Organisation (NATO). Many Americans and Europeans were still very worried about the spread of Communism from the Soviet Union into western Europe. NATO was a defence treaty designed to give western Europe the military support of the USA.

The Pleven Plan, 1950

In 1950 the USA had to move soldiers from West Germany to fight in the Korean War. President Truman called for a German army to take the place of the American troops. The French were worried by this. Germany had not been allowed to have an army after the war. The French President, Rene Pleven, produced a plan for a European army under joint control. This would be called the European Defence Community. However the British made it clear they would not join such a force. Britain preferred to rely on American support through NATO. Instead of a European army, Britain favoured Germany joining NATO and raising an army which would strengthen it. This was eventually achieved. Britain succeeded in keeping NATO alive and so avoided a European Defence Community.

The Schuman Plan and the ECSC, 1950

Up to 1949 Germany had not been included in any of these moves towards European co-operation, apart from receiving Marshall Aid. In 1945 Germany had been divided into zones administered by the Allies, Britain, France, the Soviet Union, and the United States (see Chapters 7 and 9.) This arrangement was meant to be temporary. In 1948 there was a major crisis in Berlin which led to the Soviets closing all land access to west Berlin. The Allies airlifted supplies to west Berlin and the crisis eventually ended. However, it convinced everybody that the partition of Germany would continue for some time. What was to be done with West Germany? There was now a West German Government and the economy was beginning to recover from the war damage. Many people were worried that a strong Germany might once again threaten the peace in Europe. Robert Schuman, the French Foreign Minister from 1948 to 1952, believed that French security could be achieved by creating common, shared goals between France and Germany. He came up with the idea of closely linking parts of the economies of Europe's two biggest powers, France and Germany. He wrote to Konrad Adenauer, the new Chancellor of West Germany, outlining his Plan. The Schuman Plan would create a European Coal and Steel Community to link the production of coal and steel in Europe, for the benefit of all and to ensure common targets which would bring the European nations closer together. The Schuman Plan was announced to the world in May 1950.

Schuman wrote that the purpose of his proposal was not economic, but political. In France there was fear that once Germany had recovered, she would attack France. He could imagine similar fears in Germany. Rearmament always showed first in the increased production of coal, iron and steel. If an organisation such as he was proposing were to be set up, it would enable each country to detect the first signs of rearmament.

Schuman's plan was along the lines I had been suggesting for a long time concerning the integration of the key industries of Europe. I informed Schuman at once that I accepted his proposals whole-heartedly.

Konrad Adenauer's reaction to the letter sent by Robert Schuman outlining the need for co-operation in coal and steel production.

The French Government proposes that the whole of Franco-German coal and steel production be placed under a common 'high authority' within a framework of an organisation open to participation by other countries of Europe.

The pooling of coal and steel production will provide for the setting up of common bases for economic development as a first step in the federation of Europe.

Robert Schuman describes his plan in a speech in Paris, 1950.

13 What has the cartoonist in Source H drawn to represent the Coal and Steel Plan and what will it make?
14 What will the Coal and Steel Plan do for France and Germany?
15 What is the attitude of the cartoonist towards the Schuman Plan? Explain your answer.

PONT DE LA CONCORDE

There was an immediate response to the Schuman Plan. The leaders of the BENELUX countries and Italy agreed with Adenauer and Schuman that there were great benefits to be had. Not only would there be economic advantages but integration would bring a greater chance of peace to Europe. In 1951 Belgium, France, Italy, Luxembourg, the Netherlands, and West Germany signed the Treaty of Paris which established a European Coal and Steel Community (ECSC). Britain was invited to join but decided not to do so. By 1952 there was a 'common market' in coal, iron ore, scrap metals, and most steels between the six ECSC countries.

This is a cartoon from a British magazine published in 1951 and is about the Schuman Plan

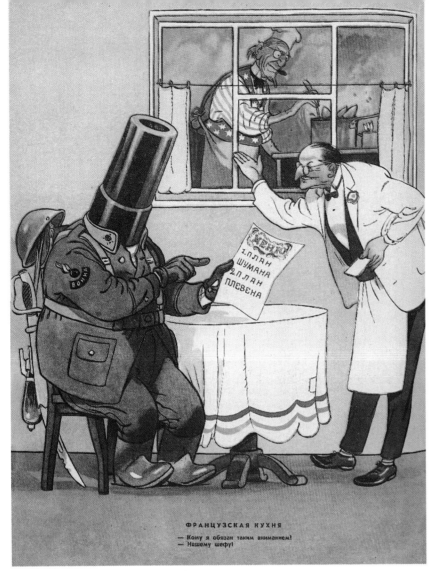

ФРАНЦУЗСКАЯ КУХНЯ
— Кому я обязан таким вниманием!
— Нашему шефу!

This is a Soviet cartoon from 1951. The scene is a French restaurant. The customer is 'war'. War tells the French waiter how pleased he is to see the Schuman Plan and the Pleven Plan on the menu. The waiter tells him that he should thank the chef. The chef is the USA.

16 Look at Source I. How can you tell that the chef is the USA?
17 How can you tell that the customer is 'war'?
18 Why has the cartoonist made a link between the Schuman and Pleven Plans and war? Explain your answer.
19 What is the cartoonist's attitude to the USA? Explain your answer.

The Treaty of Rome 1957 and the EEC

During the 1950s, the ECSC countries enjoyed thriving economic success. Many of their leaders wanted to extend economic integration to other products besides coal and steel. They wanted to set up common markets in lots of goods. The biggest obstacle to common markets was the existence of customs barriers, and these would have to be abolished. In 1957 the leaders of the ECSC six met in Rome and signed two treaties. The first set up the European Atomic Energy Community (EURATOM). This organised joint research centres to pool knowledge and work together on atomic research. The second treaty set up the European Economic Community (EEC or Common Market). The aims of this organisation were to set up a customs union for the six and to make trade easier among the members. It was also hoped that one day it would lead to full political unity in a kind of United States of Europe.

The aim of the Community is to set up a Common Market. This will promote the development of economic activities, a continuous and balanced expansion, an increased stability, a raising standard of living and closer relations between member states.

From the Treaty of Rome, 1957.

Did the economies of 'the six' benefit from integration?

A graph comparing economic growth (measured as GDP) in the six ECSC/EEC countries and Britain. (GDP = Gross Domestic Product, or how much is produced in a country in one year.)

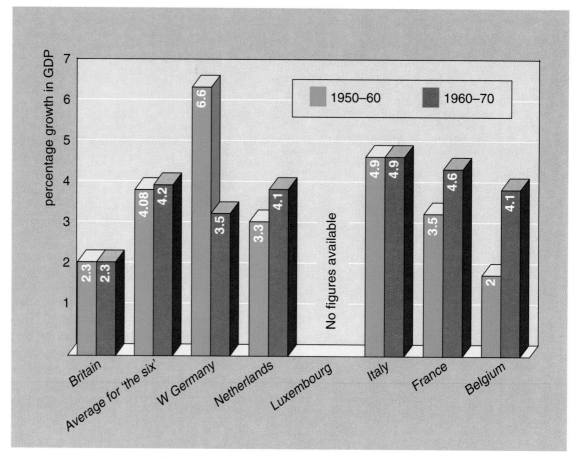

20 Look carefully at the graph. Which economy grew most in the 1950-60 period? By how much did it grow?

21 Which economy grew most in the 1960-70 period? By how much did it grow?

22 How did the British economy compare to the six in both periods?

23 Does the graph show that the economies of the six benefited from integration? Explain your answer.

The graph shows a number of things. The economies of the six were certainly growing in the period 1950 to 1970. They were growing faster than the British economy. Britain was not a member of the ECSC or the EEC. Does this mean that integration brought about the increased growth? No, it does not. It is not such a simple conclusion as that. The graph is measuring how much these economies were growing, it does not tell you why they grew. As a source, the graph is

reliable but it is not very useful for answering the question. Integration had contributed to the growth of these economies. The ECSC had been such a success that the Common Market was almost inevitable. The EEC would provide a Common Market of over 150 million prosperous people. Britain was left out of this market, but tried to join in 1961–2, 1967–8 and 1972–3.

24 Describe the steps made towards European Integration between 1947 and 1957.

Why did Britain decide not to join the Common Market in 1957?

Bevin was a key person in the first moves towards European integration. Once he had seen the establishment of the OEEC he became suspicious of integration. Britain took a distant view of the ECSC in 1951 and did not join the EEC in 1957. Why

Britain and Europe, 1948-73

were successive British governments reluctant to join in the integration movement until 1961? There were a number of reasons. It was not simply party political. The attitude of Britain's two main political parties towards Europe have been very close, as the diagram shows.

It was Attlee's Labour Government which said no to coal and steel co-operation in 1951 and a Conservative Government which decided against the Treaty of Rome in 1957. The Conservatives tried to gain entry to the EEC in 1961 and Labour tried again in 1967. Here are a number of reasons why Britain said no to Europe in the period 1950-1957.

a   Britain was still closely linked to the Commonwealth. There were strong ties with each of the former Empire countries and with the Commonwealth as a whole. This Commonwealth was a large free trade area in which Britain had a favoured position. Britain imported a great deal of its food from the Commonwealth. This food was relatively cheap. Entering a European Common Market would mean that Britain would have to place import duties on products from the Commonwealth.

b   Britain had stronger links with the USA than any European country. Britain and the USA shared a common language and culture. They had been close allies during the War. The British always felt that a 'special relationship' existed between them and the Americans. Since 1949 the NATO alliance had tied the USA yet closer to Britain as well as to Europe.

c   Europe, the Commonwealth and the USA provided three areas for British foreign policy to consider. They have been described as three circles of foreign policy. British Governments had great difficulties in deciding which of these three circles they should make the priority. Look at the diagram on the next page.

1948
Marshall Aid OEEC

1951
ECSC Formed

1957
EEC Formed

1961–1967
Britain twice tries to join EEC

French say no

1973
Britain joins EEC

Year	Government	Prime Minister	Decision
● 1948	Labour	Attlee	Leading role in OEEC
● 1951	Labour	Attlee	Not to join the ECSC
● 1957	Conservative	Macmillan	Not to join the EEC
● 1961	Conservative	Macmillan	Tried join the EEC
● 1967	Labour	Wilson	Tried join the EEC
● 1973	Conservative	Heath	Eventually joined EEC

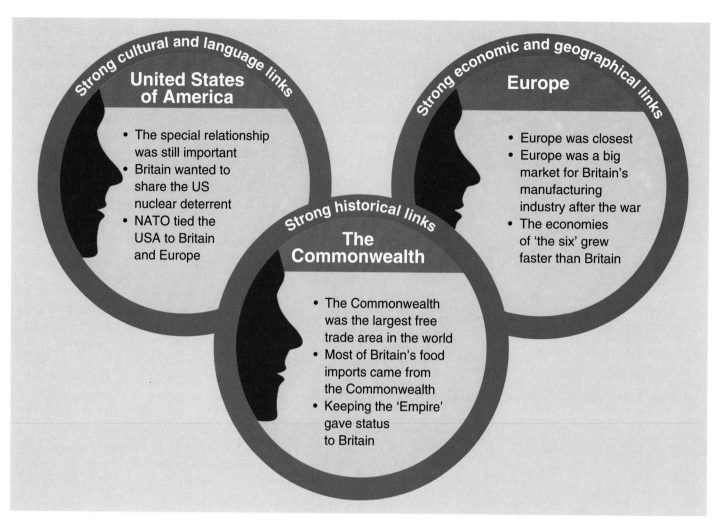

The three circles of British foreign policy. Choosing between these three circles was the main problem for British governments from 1945 onwards.

d Britain was a island and not genuinely part of continental Europe. The British were not so familiar with the concepts of crossing borders and co-operating. It is significant that four of the leaders of the six ECSC countries came from border areas of Europe. Schuman was from Alsace in eastern France and had been educated in a German school when Alsace had been under German control. Adenauer was a Rhinelander. The Italian leader Gasperi was born and educated in Trentino when it was under Austrian rule. The Belgian, Spaak, had seen his country invaded and occupied in two world wars. These men were convinced by their lives experiences that European peace would be secured by co-operation and integration. Such experience was absent in the British leadership.

e The Labour Government decided not to join the ECSC in 1950 because it believed it should protect the jobs of British workers. It felt that placing the production of British coal and steel under a 'higher authority' as Schuman proposed might mean the closure of British coal mines and a loss of jobs.

f Successive British Governments were afraid of submitting Britain to any foreign authority. The British were in favour of economic co-operation and free trade but drew the line at that. Their commitment to Europe went no further. They were against giving power to the Council of Europe as this could over rule national parliaments. They were worried when Schuman, Adenauer and others spoke of political union or of a Federal Europe. It was this issue, of national sovereignty, that prevented Britain from joining the Common Market in both 1951 and 1957.

I am speaking about the suggestions that the United Kingdom should join a federation on the continent of Europe. This is something which we know in our bones we cannot do. Britain's interests lie far beyond the continent of Europe. Our people play their part in every corner of the world. These are our family ties. But does this mean we are turning our backs on Europe? Certainly not.

Anthony Eden, the new British Foreign Secretary, speaking in the USA in 1951 about Britain's role in the world.

25 Look at Source K. Where does Eden say Britain's interest are?
26 Which of the 'three circles' do you think he feels is most important to Britain at this time?
27 Does Source K give the impression that British foreign policy was at all undecided? Explain your answer.

Britain's changing policy towards Europe, 1957–1973

The British Government quickly changed its policy towards Europe. In 1961 and 1967 Britain tried to gain entry to the EEC but was not successful. Britain eventually joined the EEC in 1973. Why did this change happen?

a   Britain was attracted to the idea of a European Free Trade area. Once the EEC had been formed in 1957 Britain worked to form a rival group. In 1959 Britain, Austria, Denmark, Norway, Portugal, Sweden, and Switzerland formed the European Free Trade Association (EFTA). EFTA did not have any of the political aims that the EEC had, but it provided a market of 38 million people. EFTA was a good idea. It made trade between Britain and the other members easy. But these were not the countries which British industry was trading with. Between 1958 and 1964 Britain's trade with EFTA increased by 72%, but British trade with the EEC increased by 92%, even though it was not a member. Also, EFTA was a small trading area compared with the 170 million people in the EEC. Britain had joined the wrong community!

b   The USA was very much in favour of the EEC and was encouraging Britain to join. In 1962 Dean Acheson suggested that Britain had lost its Empire but not yet found a role. It was yet more pressure on Britain to join the Common Market.

Britain has attempted to play a separate power role. That is a role apart from Europe. A role based on a 'special relationship' with the United States. A role based on being the head of a 'Commonwealth' which has no political structure, or unity, or strength. This role is about to end!

Dean Acheson speaking about Britain's position in the world in 1962. Acheson had been the United States Under Secretary of State in 1947, and he had played a big part in persuading President Truman to give aid to Britain and Europe.

c   The British Commonwealth was beginning to be seen as a problem. In 1947 India had become independent and had divided into two countries; India and Pakistan. In 1965 there was a war between India and Pakistan,

Britain was unable to do anything to stop this war. In 1965 Rhodesia had declared itself independent and the Commonwealth was unable to do anything about it.

d It was becoming clear that Britain was no longer a world power. The Suez crisis of 1956 (see Chapter 11) proved that Britain could not act independently if the USA disagreed. The two superpowers, the United States and the Soviet Union, did not need to consult with Britain on any major issue. Perhaps Acheson was right. Despite its nuclear weapons, on its own Britain was not a world power.

It was not easy for Britain to gain entry into the EEC. The first attempt was made in 1961-1962, when Harold Macmillan was Prime Minister. It was stopped by President de Gaulle of France. De Gaulle vetoed Britain's entry. He said no to the British entry because he thought Britain was not European enough to join the EEC. In Britain de Gaulle was criticised for this, but examination of the evidence shows him in a different light.

De Gaulle became President of France in 1958. He was as committed to the principle of national sovereignty as the British leaders of the early 1950s. De Gaulle tried to stop the political integration of the EEC. He tried to change it into an association of independent countries working together for economic benefit. This squared with Britain's view. De Gaulle welcomed Britain's application to join. He thought Britain's entry into the EEC would alter the balance in favour of the kind of EEC he wanted. He also hoped to build a European Security Community, independent of the USA, based on British and French power.

David Sanders' view of de Gaulle. Sanders is a British expert on international politics. He wrote this in 1990.

Britain had decided to purchase an American nuclear missile system called Skybolt. In 1962 the Skybolt system was cancelled. De Gaulle saw this as an opportunity for Britain to move closer to France and develop an Anglo-French nuclear weapon. Macmillan thought differently. He flew to the Bahamas to meet US President Kennedy. He agreed to buy the Polaris missile system from the USA as a replacement for Skybolt.

It is possible that the Polaris Agreement may have been the excuse that de Gaulle was looking for in order to prevent Britain's entry into Europe. Or the agreement may have been seen as a symbolic decision by Britain that caused the French President to change his view of the desirability of Britain's membership of the EEC.

From David Sanders, 1990.

A Polaris submarine is launched. These submarines were equipped with Polaris nuclear missiles. They were difficult for an enemy to find and the missiles could be fired from underwater. Britain had bought Polaris from the USA in 1962, in the middle of talks to enter the EEC. Polaris became Britain's main nuclear deterrent.

Britain tried again to enter the EEC in 1967. This attempt was made by Harold Wilson's Labour Government. Once again Britain was unsuccessful. This time it was because a British diplomat, Sir Christopher Soames, leaked details of a confidential talk he had had with de Gaulle. The talk was about the terms of Britain's entry. De Gaulle hoped that Britain and France together could alter the direction of the European Community. De Gaulle became furious when Soames leaked this to the German Government. Because of the row that followed, Britain did not bother to press its entry request. Once again the British newspapers blamed President de Gaulle.

"I suspect you of driving under the influence of America."

28 How is de Gaulle shown in Sources O and P? What do you think the cartoonists think of de Gaulle? Explain your answer.

29 What impression of de Gaulle does Source M give you?

30 How would you explain the differences between Source M and Sources O and P?

31 What reason do Sources N and P suggest for de Gaulle's veto of the British entry in 1962?

32 President de Gaulle was criticised in the British press for vetoing Britain's entry into the EEC. Use all the sources and your own knowledge to explain whether these criticisms were justified.

Two cartoons which appeared in the British press in 1967

In 1973 Britain joined the European Community. De Gaulle was no longer President by then. Britain's entry was not welcomed by everybody in Britain as Source Q shows.

'My dear! One doesn't marry for LOVE! One makes a GOOD marriage arranged by one's parents who know best!'

Cummings 'Daily Express'

In 1975 there was a referendum in Britain to decide whether to remain inside the EC. The people were asked to vote yes or no. The majority of those voting in this referendum voted to remain in.

 A cartoon from the *Daily Express* newspaper, 1973. The Prime minister, Edward Heath, and the Foreign Secretary are shown dragging a very reluctant Britain to a wedding with Europe.

European integration since 1973

The original six ECSC countries formed a European Economic Community. This organisation grew in size and scope after 1957. By 1973 the EEC had grown. It had combined with Euratom, the organisation for European co-operation on atomic energy and other associated organisations to become the European Community. Later it became known as the European Union. Denmark and Ireland joined the European Community in 1973, along with Britain. This created a larger and stronger Community which could be seen as a fourth Superpower in the world, competing with the USA, the Soviet Union, and China.

Later entries were made by Spain, Portugal and Greece. In 1995 Austria, Finland and Sweden joined. By 1996 there were fifteen members of the European Union.

A French cartoon called the fourth mountain. Can you see how the European countries combined become bigger than any of the other three?

-. *Le quatrième Sommet.*

There has also been greater social and political integration within the European Union since 1973. In 1989 the Maastricht Treaty was signed by the members. This introduced a single market and the Exchange Rate Mechanism (ERM) as a step towards a single European Currency (the ECU or Euro).

Maastricht made the teaching of the history of the European Union compulsory in all schools and it also included a Social Chapter of workers rights. Britain would not sign the Social Chapter and quickly dropped out of the ERM. To many Europeans it looked as if Britain was still not fully committed to Europe. Had de Gaulle been right?

How the European Union works

The European Union has two decision making bodies, the Council of Ministers and the Parliament, and a civil service of its own called the Commission.

The Council of Ministers is where real power lies within the EU. Here the ministers of each country's national Parliament meet to decide future policy. Voting in the Council is according to the size of the country, so that big countries like the UK get more votes than the smaller countries. The Council's resolutions are passed on to the European Parliament.

The European Parliament is made up of members (called MEPs) from every member country. In each country there are direct elections to the European Parliament. The Parliament meets in two cities, Strasbourg in France and Brussels in Belgium. Many issues are debated, but the Parliament can only suggest amendments to resolutions from the Council of Ministers. It cannot make laws of its own.

Each year there is an Inter-Governmental Conference or IGC. Each year it is in a different member country, and that country sets the agenda.

The European Commission is based in Brussels. Its job is to put the laws decided by the Council and Parliament into practice.

The European headquarters at the Point Schuman in Brussels.

In Britain the European Commission is often criticised by the media because of the laws it puts into practice. This has led to negative attitudes about the European Union. Many of the other European countries think that the British do not really want to be members of the EU.

Problems facing the European Union

Because it started life in 1951 as a free trade union, the European Union has not yet moved very far towards political integration. The issue of national sovereignty is just as important now as it once was to Attlee and to de Gaulle. The Union has to decide how it can become more integrated without risking the loss of those cultural differences which make Europe the place it is.

Qualified Majority Voting in the Council of Ministers means that it is possible for a few countries to block legislation. This hinders progress. The right of veto is also a problem for the Union. Veto means that just one member can say no and stop an entire policy from going ahead. This was all very well in the early days when there were six members, but is rather more problematic now that there are fifteen. In 1996 there was still no common currency and no common foreign policy. Moves towards a European Defence Plan came to nothing. When the Berlin Wall came down in 1990 (see Chapter 9) and Germany was re-united, East Germany automatically became a member of the EU. It is difficult to gauge what the reaction of the fifteen members will be when Poland or the Czech Republic asks to join. The question is being asked, 'how large can the EU become?'

ON THE NEED FOR A STRONG, UNITED EUROPE.

The policy of European Integration is really a question of war and peace in the twenty-first century. I know that some do not wish to hear this. My warnings may contain an unpleasant truth. But it is no use burying your head in the sand. We have no wish to return to the nation state of old. Nationalism has brought great suffering to our continent; just think of the first fifty years of this century. We need Europe to give weight to our collective influence in the world. We can only achieve our common interest if we speak with one voice and combine our strength.

ON THE ENLARGEMENT OF THE EU.

We don't want a 'superstate' with central control. It does not exist and it never will. The enlargement of the Union is about 'European identity.' Czechoslovakia and Poland are central European countries. I find it unthinkable that the western border of Poland must always be the eastern border of the European Union.

ON BRITAIN'S ATTITUDE TO FURTHER INTEGRATION.

The slowest ship must not be allowed to determine the speed of the convoy. If some members are not prepared or unable to take part in steps towards integration, the others must be allowed to move forward and develop increased integration.

From a speech by Helmut Kohl, the German Chancellor, made in 1996.

33 Read Source S. Describe Kohl's attitude to the enlargement of the EU.

34 What did Kohl compare Britain to? What does this tell you about Britain's attitude towards European integration in 1996? What did he think the other European countries should do?

35 What did Kohl mean by 'a "superstate" with central control'? Why do you think Germany did not want this?

36 Why did Kohl speak about war and peace in Europe?

37 Some observers became very worried about the German threat in this speech by Chancellor Kohl. Why do you think this was so?

38 **Essays:**

i Why did European co-operation begin in the period 1947 to 1957? What have been the benefits for the European Union since 1957?

ii Describe Britain's policy towards Europe between 1947 and 1996. What are the reasons for the changes in Britain's European policy?

39 Research:

The European Union is constantly developing.

i Find out who your MEP is. Contact him or her to find out more about European issues.

ii Where was the last IGC held and what did it discuss?

11 *Britain's changing role in the world, 1945–1983*

Anthony Eden and Clement Attlee read of Hitler's death in April 1945

Source A was taken during the San Francisco Conference. Attlee and Eden were influential in British Foreign policy from 1945 to 1957. Attlee was Prime Minister from 1945 until 1951. Eden was Foreign Secretary from 1951 to 1955 and he then became Prime Minister until 1957. This was a time of great change in Britain's role in the world; a time when British statesmen, like Eden and Attlee, were trying to find a suitable role for Britain in a world which had been changed dramatically by the Second World War.

The Labour Government, 1945–1951

The situation facing Britain in 1945

In 1945 Britain emerged victorious after the Second World War. British soldiers had played a major part in the defeat of both Germany and Japan, and now 5,000,000 of these soldiers were stationed all over the world. Britain had not been invaded and its towns and cities had escaped the kind of devastation found in France, Germany, and the USSR. About 400,000 British people had been killed, which was half the number lost in the First World War. The Commonwealth remained intact, with those parts of it which had been occupied by Japan being recaptured in 1945. Britain was regarded as a world power and British politicians took their place with the leaders of the USA and USSR in the peace making process which soon followed the end of the fighting in Europe.

On the other hand, the British economy had been severely damaged by the War. The physical destruction to houses, factories and shipping had cost 25% of Britain's national wealth. Many foreign assets had been sold to pay for wartime imports. British factories had not been able to modernise and re-equip during the war years. Most importantly, Britain's balance of trade had altered massively during the War. The balance of trade is the balance between what a country sells abroad (exports) and what it buys from abroad (imports). Before the War Britain had sold lots of manufactured goods to other countries, but during the War British industry had to make weapons for the armed forces. So British exports fell. By 1945 British exports were £350 million, less than half the 1939 level. At the same time, its imports had reached £2,000 million. This meant a trade deficit of £1,650 million. Britain had borrowed money to fight the War, and in 1945 owed over £3,500 million to the USA.

The General election of July 1945 returned a Labour Government with a big majority. Clement Attlee became the new Prime Minister. His Foreign Secretary was the rough, tough, former leader of the Transport Workers Union, Ernest Bevin. This Government had some definite priorities. At home it wanted to improve the Welfare State. This included the introduction of the National Health Service

which would cost a lot of money. In foreign affairs, Labour was less committed to the USA than the Conservatives had been and wanted to see as much independence as was possible in parts of the Commonwealth. At the same time, Attlee realised that the resources of the Commonwealth would be vital to the restructuring of the British economy. There was one other large problem facing the government. Although they were Socialists, Attlee and Bevin both disliked and distrusted Communists, especially the Soviet Union. They believed that Britain had to keep a large armed presence in Europe to prevent the spread of Communism. This gives you some idea of the situation facing Britain in 1945 and is summarised in the diagram.

Britain's position in the world in 1945

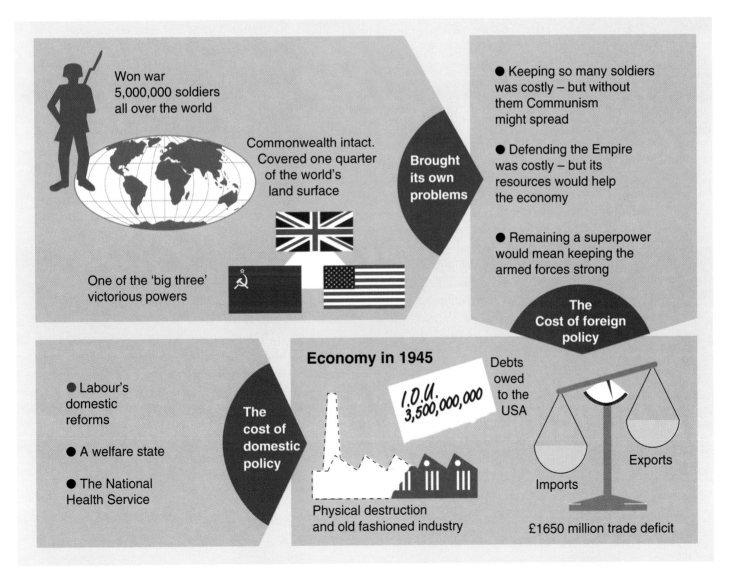

Labour's European policy

"THEN WAS THE TUG OF WAR."

A British cartoon about the Greek Civil War

In 1946 British soldiers were in Greece and in Turkey helping the governments there to fight against Communist rebels. This was part of the Cold War between the Soviet Union and the western allies. Source B shows the Greek Civil War as a struggle between Communism and Democracy. Britain could not afford to carry on supporting these governments, but was afraid of the spread of Communism if British troops were withdrawn. Bevin managed to convince President Truman of the need for American aid for Britain and Europe. An aid package was developed and became known as the Marshall Plan. You can read more about these events in chapters 7 and 10.

One of the conditions imposed by the USA was that the European countries receiving Marshall Aid had to co-operate with each other over how the aid was to be used. This meant that some kind of economic co-operation was needed. Bevin was a key figure in bringing together the European Foreign Ministers to start this process of European economic co-operation in 1947.

In 1950 the French and German governments announced that they were going to join together to form a common market in coal, iron, and steel. They invited other countries to join as well. This became the European Coal and Steel Community in 1951. Britain refused to join and, therefore, began to distance itself from the movement towards European co-operation. Dennis Healey, who was a Labour Party Foreign Affairs adviser in 1951 and later became Foreign Secretary, has described this decision as a great mistake.

Labour's policy towards the Commonwealth

The British Empire was still the largest in the world, yet it was clear by the end of the Second World War that the situation was rapidly changing. Many countries, for example Australia, Canada, New Zealand, and South Africa, had become dominions. This gave them much more say in their own government. The English monarch was still their monarch and there was a Governor-General who represented him or her, but these countries each had their own Parliament. They had been members of the British Empire until 1931, when the Empire became known as the British Commonwealth.

The Statute of Westminster of 1931 gave the dominions the right to alter their own constitutions and even to leave the Commonwealth if they wished. Most of them decided to stay in the Commonwealth and were still members in 1945, except Ireland, which became a Free State with dominion status in 1922 and decided to leave the Commonwealth.

Independence in India 1947

In 1945 there were still many countries in Asia, Africa, and the Middle East which were ruled over directly by Britain. India was governed by the British Secretary of State and a Viceroy. The Viceroy ruled in India on behalf of the monarch and in consultation with the British Government in London. Since 1918 there had been a growing number of Indians wanting independence from Britain. The man most associated with the movement for Indian independence is Mahatma Gandhi. He was an educated Indian who was able to argue forcefully with the British whilst at the same time remaining an inspiring and popular leader of millions of Indians. Gandhi believed in non-violent protest which included days of strikes and fasting (hartals), refusal to pay taxes, boycotting of British goods, and deliberate law breaking in order to be sent to prison. Such campaigns lasted until 1947. In 1919 Gandhi had joined the Indian Congress Party, which campaigned for independence. The Congress was made up mainly from well educated Hindus. There was also a Muslim League which represented the Indian Muslims and which began to press for an independent Muslim country.

Between 1919 and 1939 there was some movement towards independence, but it was not enough for most Indians. In 1917 the Secretary of State for India, Montagu, said that Britain supported the inclusion of Indians in all branches of the administration of India, and this would gradually move India towards self-government. The 1919 *Government of India Act* set up elections for Indians and they were allowed some say in government at local level. In 1929 the Labour Government set up a round-table conference on the future of India to which Indians as well as British politicians were to be invited. The 1935 *Government of India Act* gave wider powers to elected Indians, but the British Viceroy continued to be Head of State and had power over defence and foreign affairs and could still act alone in cases of emergency. This did not go far enough for most Indian nationalists.

In 1939 the Viceroy declared war on Germany without consulting a single Indian politician. Indians reacted differently to this. Gandhi was a pacifist and opposed any involvement in the War. Other members of Congress sympathised with the British but insisted that support for Britain could only be given in return for real progress towards independence. When it became clear that the British would give no promise, all the Congress leaders, including Nehru, who was to become India's first Prime Minister, resigned from office and refused to co-operate. The Muslim League, led by Jinnah, pledged their support for Britain and many Muslims joined the British army. Jinnah hoped to win British support for the idea of a separate and independent Muslim state of Pakistan. Chandra Bose, who was the leader of the Indian Nationalist Party, took advantage of Britain's difficult position and joined with the Japanese against the British.

 This is an anti-British poster issued by the Japanese. The words, which are written in two Indian languages, say: 'Set the devils right with a stick'.

1   Look at Source D. What is the British army officer doing?
2   The man in the bowler hat is meant to be Winston Churchill. What position did Churchill hold in 1942? What is he shown doing in the cartoon?
3   What is the attitude of the cartoonist to the British?
4   Who is the poster aimed at and what feelings is it trying to stir up?

The Japanese threatened to invade India in 1942 and the British Government offered full independence to India once the War was over. This was done to try to gain the support of Congress, but it failed. Congress demanded full independence at once and launched the 'Quit India' campaign. This was an enormous non-cooperation movement which led to the deaths of over 1,000 Indians and nearly 100,000 were arrested. The British regained control of India and, by 1945, the Congress Party was quite weak. The Muslim League, which had helped the British in the War, had more influence with the British once the War was over.

Prime Minister Attlee was very much in favour of granting full independence to India. He recognised how expensive it would be to remain in India. He hoped that an independent India would stay inside the Commonwealth. The problem now was differences between the (Hindu) Congress Party which wanted one large Indian state, and the Muslim League which favoured an independent Pakistan for the Muslims. A plan was put forward in 1946 but the Muslims rejected it and began 'direct action' for a separate Pakistan. This led to serious rioting in Calcutta, in which thousands of people were killed. In December 1946 the British cabinet were

A Quit India demonstration in 1943

informed that a civil war between India's 92 million Muslims and 255 million Hindus might break out at any time and that Britain could not hope to retain control of the country after March 1948 at the latest. Attlee now had to decide when Britain should pull out of India and how this could be achieved in as orderly and dignified a way as possible. Attlee made a public announcement that Britain would not stay in India after the middle of 1948 and he appointed Lord Mountbatten, cousin of the Queen, as the new Viceroy.

Mountbatten was given power to make all of his own decisions on the spot.

To avoid a civil war, Mountbatten decided that India would have to be partitioned. Mountbatten's main achievement was in persuading Nehru, the leader of the Congress Party, that partition was necessary. In August 1947 the *Indian Independence Act* was passed. It set up two new dominions, India and Pakistan The period of British rule in India was over. Burma and Ceylon soon followed India in becoming independent.

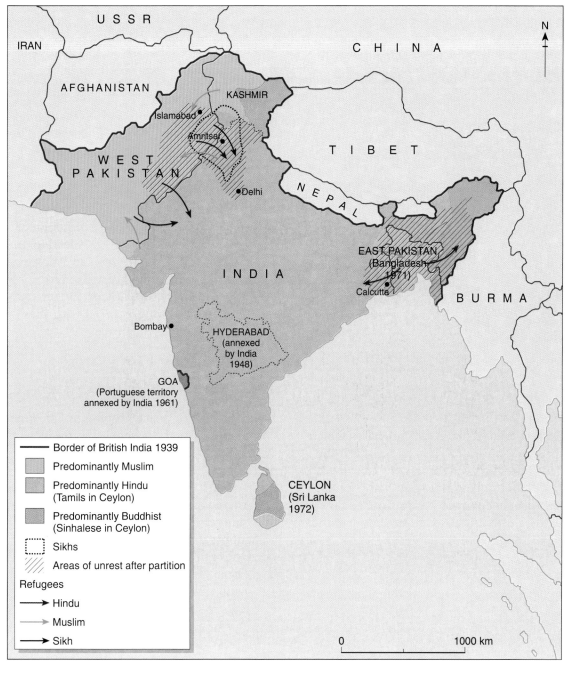

The religious and political division of British India at the time of independence from British rule. The control of Kashmir continues to be disputed by India and Pakistan. They fought wars over the territory in 1948–9, 1965, and 1971. Kashmir is now divided between the two countries and contains a UN peacekeeping force.

Labour's policy in the Middle East

Palestine, 1945-1948

The background to the problem

Palestine had been looked after by Britain since 1919. It was one of the League of Nations Mandated Territories created at the Treaty of Versailles after the First World War. Before this it had been part of the Turkish Empire and many Palestinian Arabs lived there. The British had made certain promises to these Arabs to gain their help against the Turks. These included a promise by Sir Henry McMahon, the British High Commissioner in Egypt, that Britain would 'recognise and support the independence of the Arabs.'

At the same time, however, Britain was also making promises to the Jewish community. Many Jews were settling in Palestine and wanted a Jewish homeland there. In 1917 the Foreign Secretary, Lord Balfour, made a promise to the Jews.

His Majesty's Government view with favour the establishment in Palestine of a national home for the Jewish people, and will use their best endeavours to facilitate this.

Letter from Lord Balfour to Lord Rothschild, a leading member of the Jewish community in Britain.

So Britain had made two promises which affected Palestine. They had assured the Jews that they were in favour of a Jewish homeland in Palestine, and had promised independence to the Arabs. In 1922 the League of Nations made further demands of Britain.

Great Britain shall be responsible for placing (Palestine) under such conditions as will secure the establishment of a Jewish national homeland and the development of self-governing institutions, and also for safeguarding the civil and religious rights of all the inhabitants of Palestine.

Details of the British Mandate, 1922.

5   Study the promises made by Balfour and McMahon. How might these create problems for Britain in the future?
6   Did the League of Nations Mandate (Source F) make either of these promises impossible? Explain your answer.
7   What extra demands did the Mandate place on Britain?

Between 1922 and 1945 there was a great deal of Jewish immigration to Palestine. In 1928 there were 150,000 Jews in Palestine, by 1937 the number had increased to 400,000. Outbreaks of violence were common and Britain was faced with the problem of keeping the peace.

The situation after 1945

The problems of peace keeping in Palestine became much worse after the Second World War. The Nazi Holocaust, in which millions of Jews were slaughtered, had three effects.

a   There was a great increase in the number of Jews coming into the country; many of these were refugees from Europe.
b   There was also a great increase in sympathy for the Jews amongst non-Jews in Europe and the USA.

c The 650,000 Jews now in Palestine became much more militant in their quest for an independent homeland. In 1946 the Jewish terrorists of Irgun bombed the British Military Headquarters in Jerusalem, killing 88 people. Public opinion in Britain was not in favour of remaining in Palestine if it meant British soldiers being killed. There were also other pressures on Attlee to withdraw. American President Truman wanted Attlee to allow 100,000 Jews to enter Palestine, but Attlee thought this might lead to a civil war. Attlee knew how much it would cost to remain in Palestine and he also knew that Britain could not afford that cost. In 1947 Britain announced that Palestine was to be handed over to the United Nations Organisation, this effectively ended the British Mandate. Palestine was no longer Britain's problem.

▲ The King David Hotel in Jerusalem blown up by Jewish terrorists. this was the British headquarters building.

Labour and the USA

Many British governments had taken for granted the support of the USA, believing that there was a 'special relationship' between the two countries, based on their common language, religion, and culture. Many historians feel this 'special relationship' has been exaggerated. The problems which Attlee's Government encountered in its dealings with the USA shed light on the relationship between these two countries.

As soon as the war ended, the USA stopped Lend-Lease to Britain. Attlee sent the economist Keynes to the USA to negotiate a loan. Keynes was successful, but the loan too little and was soon used up. Perhaps the American Government was reluctant to loan money to a Labour Government which it believed might spend it on Socialist policies. By 1947, however,

Marshall Aid was coming from the USA into Europe, and Britain received the largest portion of this aid (see Chapter 10).

The USA put great pressure on Britain to reduce its Empire and open up the Commonwealth to free trade and competition. Obviously, the USA was looking to extend its markets and trading area. Britain had to give in to this pressure to some extent, in order to gain the economic aid it needed from the USA. You have read how the USA pressurised Attlee over Palestine.

Defence was a great issue at this time. The USA was the only country in the world which possessed an atom bomb in 1945 and Britain saw co-operation with the USA in atomic technology as being vital to the defence of Britain. In 1946 the US Government passed the *McMahon Act* which made sharing atomic secrets with any non US citizen an act of treason. This was a bitter blow to Britain. Bevin said, 'we must have one [an atom bomb] and it's got to have the bloody Union Jack on it!' The USA did not want to be directly involved in Europe, yet by 1949 the USA was formally tied to the defence of Europe when the North Atlantic Treaty Organisation (NATO) was formed. In part this was because Bevin had managed to convince Truman that Europe would become a Communist stronghold without American involvement; and in part it was a reaction to the Berlin blockade organised by Stalin in 1948-9, (see Chapter 7). The formation of NATO eased Britain's defence problems enormously.

In 1950 Britain showed itself to be a loyal ally of the USA. North Korea, backed by the Soviet Union, had attacked South Korea. The USA called for action to be taken against North Korea by the United Nations. Britain supported this. The British Government sent soldiers to Korea to aid the American troops sent there as part of a United Nations force. Although the British contribution was tiny compared to the USA's, Britain did provide valuable air and naval support for the UN force (see Chapter 8).

Did Labour follow a successful foreign policy?

In this period, Britain lost India, Burma and Ceylon, had to hand over Palestine to the UNO, and was continually seeking economic aid from the USA. In some ways Labour's policy seems to have been a disaster. But you must remember the damage done to the British economy during the War. Britain was almost bankrupt in 1945. To have remained in India and have kept troops in Greece and Palestine was simply not an option for Attlee and Bevin. In any case, Labour favoured giving independence where possible and were carrying out promises made earlier. Labour did have a number of successes. They retreated from India and Palestine with a degree of dignity. They managed, crucially, to bring the USA closer to Europe through the Marshall Plan and NATO. Perhaps the one mistake made by Bevin was not to join the ECSC in 1951. By deciding not to join this European movement, Labour began a trend which was to delay British participation in the European Community for more than twenty years.

8   Describe the foreign policy problems faced by the Labour Government in 1945.

9   Use the words in the boxes to explain how successfully Labour had overcome these problems by 1951.

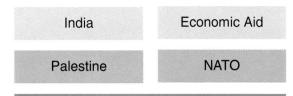

10 Make up a 'balance sheet' of Labour's successes and failures in your note book. On balance, do you think Labour had a successful foreign policy between 1945 and 1951? Explain your answer.

1951–1964, a testing time for Britain

Labour lost the 1951 General Election, and for the next thirteen years Britain was ruled over by Conservative governments. In 1951 Winston Churchill became Prime Minister again and his Foreign Secretary was Anthony Eden. Some people thought this would mean a stronger foreign policy as these two had been Britain's leaders during the Second World War. However, the Conservatives had much the same problems as Labour. The British economy was not strong enough to support a strong foreign policy.

Suez, 1956

The main incident during this period of Conservative government, and an occasion when Britain tried to follow a strong policy, was the Suez crisis of 1956. Suez is the area of Egypt which contains the Suez Canal, linking the Mediterranean and Red seas. The Canal was built in the nineteenth century by British and French firms and, until 1956, it was owned and operated by an Anglo-French company. The Suez Canal was vital to British trade in the 1950s as it avoided the need to sail right round Africa to get to the Far East. In 1955 the leader of Egypt, President Nasser, began to buy weapons from the USSR. In retaliation, Britain and the USA withdrew the financial aid they had been providing to Egypt. In 1956 Nasser announced that the Egyptians would nationalise the Suez Canal. This meant that the Egyptian Government would own the Canal and could use the profits from it to replace the aid Britain and the USA had been giving. This was not illegal, but it obviously threatened Britain's status as a world power. If Britain were still a strong world power it would not be treated like this by a small country such as Egypt. This was the view taken by Eden, who was Prime Minister in 1956. Eden had been Foreign Secretary in Neville Chamberlain's Government and had resigned in 1938 because he disapproved of the way Chamberlain treated Mussolini. Eden had believed in a tough approach to dictators in the late 1930s (see Chapter 5). In 1956 Eden looked upon Nasser as a dictator who should not be appeased. He said that Nasser 'has his hand on our windpipe'. 'I don't care whether it's legal or not,' he said, 'he's not going to get away with it'. In private he went even further. He once shouted at one of his advisers 'I want him destroyed, don't you understand?'

In October, the British, French, and Israeli Foreign Ministers met in France and made a plan to invade Egypt. The Israelis would invade first, then the British and French would send ships and soldiers to Egypt in the pretence of protecting the Canal and keeping it open to shipping. In late October the British bombed Egyptian airfields and on 5th November paratroops landed along the Canal zone. They could not keep the Canal open, however, because the Egyptians sank ships there which blocked the canal completely. The Americans were furious at Britain and France. They condemned Britain in the United Nations where a resolution was passed calling for a cease fire and for Britain's withdrawal. Many investors in currency began to sell British money and this put even more pressure on Eden to withdraw. The US President, Eisenhower, told Eden that he must withdraw and that the USA would do nothing to stop the run on the British pound until he did so. Britain and France were forced to withdraw from Egypt. The incident had been badly conducted and left Britain embarrassed.

Headlines which appeared in British newspapers about the Suez crisis, 1956

Evening Standard

41,183   MONDAY, NOVEMBER 5, 1956   ●● Twopence

Paratroops take Port Said airfield, then fan out

FIRMLY IN AFTER TOUGH FIGHTING

Red Devils fight Nasser's tanks

BIG NEW FRENCH FORCE MAKES AIR DROP THIS AFTERNOON

Wave after wave of British and French paratroops today landed in Egypt. The main force, dropping from 600ft., seized the airport of Gamal, five miles west of Port Said. They have had some very tough fighting, said the Allied C.-in-C., General Sir Charles Keightley, this afternoon. But, he added, the paratroopers are now firmly established, and are setting out from the airfield.

There is an unknown number of British casualties said the general. "I shouldn't think they are very high," he added. French known casualties are six wounded.

FORCES WILL LINK UP

And General Keightley revealed that another French drop had been made this afternoon. "It is a big drop, landing close to the other one," he said. "If all goes well it will form a combined front south of ...

... landed at 3 p.m. local time.

... mentioned the Third Battalion Parachute Brigade as having ... tough battle with Egyptian ... with mortars and tanks. The ... still had an "adhesive fight-

THE HOUSE OF COMMONS BEGINS WITH A STORM

Tempers were quickly roused in the House of Commons this afternoon, even before the normal business had got under way. Before question hour started, Mr. Anthony Wedgwood Benn (Soc, Bristol S.E.) presented a petition "signed by some hundreds of citizens."

He called on the Commons to take immediate steps to urge the Government to comply with the terms of "all resolutions of the United Nations Security Council, the General Assembly and the Charter of the United Nations in its entirety."

The Queen will miss Royal Show

The Queen, the Queen Mother and the Princess Margaret will not attend tonight's Royal Variety performance because of the international situation.

WEATHER—Mostly dry

ATTACK BEGINS

RAF bomb 4 Egypt air bases: NAVY sink Nasser frigate

BRITISH and French forces began an air and naval bombardment of military targets in Egypt at 4.30 p.m. yesterday, it was officially announced last night.

Early this morning the Admiralty announced that H.M.S. Newfoundland, 8,800-ton cruiser, engaged on shipping protection duties, had sunk an Egyptian frigate in the Gulf of Suez, southern end of the Suez Canal.

The frigate, it was stated, failed to answer a challenge to stop. "She was therefore sunk and survivors were taken aboard the Newfoundland," said the Admiralty.

This was the Egyptian President Nasser's second loss in a day.

War flashes

4.30 is zero hour

WE'RE GOING IN

By GUY EDEN and SKETCH WAR BUREAU

BRITISH troops are poised this morning to reoccupy the Suez Canal bases, they left in 1954.

An Anglo-French force of Marines, Commandos and assault troops was lying off Port Said early to-day in a huge fleet of landing craft supported by warships and aircraft carriers.

President Nasser has rejected outright the Anglo-French 12-hour ultimatum given at 4.30 p.m. yesterday.

He refused "under any circumstances" to allow our troops into Egypt to act as a buffer police force ... invading Israeli ... Marshal Bulganin, the

Air, sea armada poised

70/6

EDEN'S VICTORY!

MIDNIGHT CEASE-FIRE: WE NOW CONTROL THE CANAL

BRITAIN and France control the Suez Canal this morning. By midnight last night, when the cease-fire ordered by Sir Anthony Eden took effect, the Allied forces had:

Destroyed or scattered Egypt's army units defending the Canal, wrecked 95 per cent. of her air force and sunk or seriously damaged her navy.

The midnight cease-fire was announced to the Commons at 6.7 last night by Sir Anthony Eden amid a tumult of cheering at his great and resounding victory.

An unconditional cease-fire was accepted by both Egypt and Israel, said the Prime Minister. So he ordered the cease-fire from midnight. "UNLESS OUR TROOPS ARE ATTACKED."

And if United Nations talks are favourable, Britain and France will let an international police force take over in Egypt in the next few days.

Throughout the world the cease-fire was hailed as a personal triumph for Sir Anthony—except in Moscow, where the news was ignored in radio bulletins.

A French communiqué issued in Paris at midnight said the Anglo-

1 UN police force to take over soon?

2 3 a.m. talks on a new demand by Nasser

◀ Egyptian ships sunk in the Suez Canal in order to block it to shipping

The effects of Suez

Nasser emerged as the strongest and most popular leader in the Arab world. He had taken on Britain and France and won. He now had complete control of the Suez Canal. Many Arab states began to turn away from the western powers and looked to the USSR for help. Britain had suffered a blow to its status. It was now clear to the whole world that Britain was not the force it had been before the Second World War. Britain could not have its own way. Most importantly, the Suez crisis showed that the British Government could not act without the support of the USA. Eden was a broken man, his health had suffered during the crisis and he resigned as Prime Minister in 1957.

A Soviet cartoon about the Suez crisis. The British lion and French cockerel have had their tails pulled off by an angry Egyptian Sphinx

Many of the lessons of Suez should have been obvious before the events of 1956. Britain did not cease being a world power because of Suez. Britain's decline had been happening since the First World War. The two World Wars had seriously weakened Britain's economy. On the other hand, the USA and the USSR had emerged as superpowers after 1945. The Labour Government of Attlee and Bevin had recognised this and they had tried to follow an appropriate foreign policy. Perhaps it needed Suez, or something like it, to convince the British people that Britain's world role was changing.

11 Describe the events of the 1956 Suez crisis.
12 Why did Eden feel so strongly about Nasser?
13 Look at Source G. What kind of headlines do you think might have appeared in newspapers in Egypt and in the USA at this time? Suggest at least two headlines that might have appeared in each of these countries.
14 Describe the main effects of the Suez crisis on Britain.
15 Do you think Eden's policy on Suez was a complete failure? Explain your answer.
16 What other tactics might Eden have used?

Europe, 1951–1964

In 1956 the six members of the ECSC began talks which led to a bigger common market. Britain was invited to join these talks and to join the Common Market, or European Economic Community, which was set up in 1957. The British Government decided not to join. Britain still regarded the Commonwealth and the special relationship with the USA as more important. The Government was also worried about handing over decision making power to a European body. Britain did join the European Free Trade Association, EFTA, in order to increase trade with some other European nations.

However it soon became clear that a mistake had been made. Britain was trading less with the USA and the Commonwealth, and British trade with the EFTA countries was not as great as was trade with the Common Market countries. Britain was outside the EEC but British firms were selling into the Common Market and British shoppers were buying

EEC produce. (Chapter 10 contains more detail of these changing trade patterns.) In 1961 Britain began the negotiations with the EEC that would enable Britain to join. However, the Prime Minister, Harold Macmillan, was also still committed to the USA when it came to the defence of Britain and in 1962, at the same time as negotiating Britain's entry to the EEC, he was buying nuclear weapons from the USA. This was too much for the French President, de Gaulle, who thought it proved Britain was not a true European nation. In 1963 Britain's entry was prevented when the French vetoed the application.

17 Until 1961 the Conservative Government's policy towards Europe was very much like Labour's had been between 1947 and 1951. Why were these British governments, with such different political views, so similar in their policy towards Europe? Explain your answer.
18 Why did Macmillan try to join the EEC in 1962 and why was he unsuccessful?

The Commonwealth, 1951–1964

During the 1950s there were growing demands for independence from many of Britain's colonies, especially in Africa. The Gold Coast was the first British colony in Africa to become independent. In 1950 the British offered places in a Gold Coast Parliament to the Africans living there. The Gold Coast Africans were led by Kwame Nkrumah who began an "Independence Now" movement. His party won a majority in the 1951 elections and afterwards he worked with the British. In 1957 the Gold Coast became independent and was called Ghana. Malaya, in the Far East, also became independent in 1957. Prime Minister Macmillan recognised that more African countries were likely to become independent. He made a speech in 1960 which spoke of a 'wind of change' sweeping across Africa.

Fifteen years ago nationalism spread through Asia. Many countries there pressed their claims to an independent national life. Today the same thing is happening in Africa. The wind of change is blowing across this continent. Whether we like it or not, this growth of national consciousness is a political fact...our national policies must take account of it.

Harold Macmillan speaking to the South African Parliament, 1960.

Post-war European colonies in Africa, together with their dates of independence

In 1960 Nigeria became independent, and then, in 1963 and 1964, Kenya, Malawi and Zambia became independent countries.

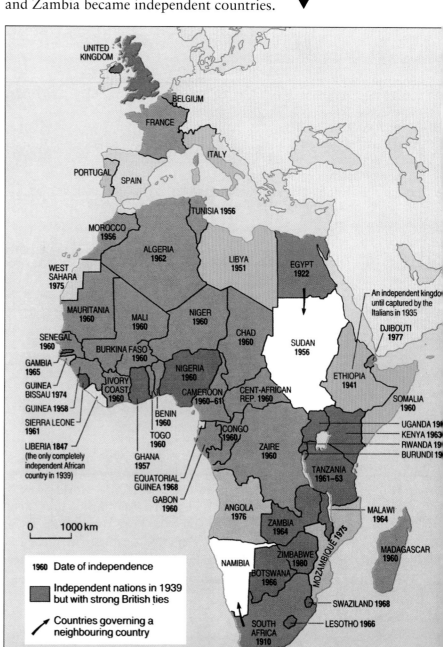

Interpretations of British policy

Was the loss of African colonies a sign of Britain's weakness?

Most historians think this was not the case. Britain's position can best be understood when it can be compared with the experience of other European countries. Independence movements were strong all over Africa during the 1950s and 1960s, not just in the British colonies. The French had problems in Algeria from 1954 to 1962. The war there was extremely costly for France who had to send thousands of soldiers to Algeria, and the killings and brutal tortures which were carried out made the French Government very unpopular. In the Belgian Congo, the independence movement turned to violence in 1959 and Belgium granted independence the next year. Zaire, as the Belgian Congo was known after 1960, had not been prepared for independence. Within five days of independence being granted, white settlers were attacked and the native army mutinied. The Belgian army returned and there was a civil war with fighting between rival African groups. A separate state of Katanga was set up and white mercenaries were brought in to defend it from the rest of Zaire. There was chaos. United Nations soldiers were sent to Zaire in 1961 and remained there until 1964. When they left, more fighting broke out.

Compared to the French experience in Algeria and the Belgian handling of Zaire, Britain staged an orderly and dignified withdrawal from its African colonies. On the whole they were not forced out,

though there had been a great deal of violence in Kenya where a terrorist group called the Mau Mau were active. More importantly, they left behind the basis of governments which had a good chance of continuing once the British rulers had left. All of these newly independent countries stayed as part of the British Commonwealth and, therefore, Britain could still trade with them on favourable terms.

In 1959 Cyprus became independent after the British decided that they could not afford to stay on in the country to keep the peace between warring Greek and Turkish Cypriots.

Suspected terrorists detained for trial in Cyprus in 1956

19 List the British colonies which became independent between 1951 and 1964
20 Describe Britain's policy towards Africa in this period.
21 What arguments can you use to justify Britain's policy towards its colonies between 1951 and 1964?

Lost an empire and not found a role, 1964–1995

By 1964 Britain had had time to consider its position in the world. The relationship with the USA was still strong, but it was an unequal relationship. Britain needed the USA more than the USA needed Britain. The Empire no longer existed. You have seen how many colonies had become independent since Indian independence in 1947. This did not stop. More were

becoming independent, for example Singapore in 1965 and Aden in 1967. In 1965 the white government in Southern Rhodesia asked the British to grant them independence. Labour Prime Minister Harold Wilson refused to do so, as Ian Smith, the leader of the white Rhodesians, would not allow black Africans to take part in government. Smith made a declaration of Rhodesian independence in 1965, called a Unilateral Declaration of Independence, or UDI. Britain tried to bring down the Smith government by imposing economic sanctions on Rhodesia. At the same time black guerrilla fighters from neighbouring countries went into Rhodesia to help the black independence movement there, whilst the South African Government supported Smith. The situation drifted into a war which lasted until 1980. Then, after talks in London, Rhodesia became officially independent. It was called Zimbabwe and had a black Prime Minister, Robert Mugabe. Although eventually solved with British help, in the 1960s the Rhodesian problem had seemed insoluble. Also, in 1965 India and Pakistan had gone to war and neither Britain nor any other Commonwealth country had been able to prevent the war, or bring it to an end. These events showed that the Commonwealth could bring more problems than benefits.

It was becoming clearer that Britain's role was in Europe. In 1967 there was a second application to join the EEC, but it failed. Then in 1973 Britain was allowed to join the EEC. (Chapter 10 has more details of this.)

Since 1973 Britain has directed most of its energies towards Europe and has conducted foreign policy as part of a group of nations (for example through the EEC or NATO) rather than alone.

The Falklands War, 1982

The exception to the trend of Britain acting as part of Europe, NATO, or the United Nations occurred in 1982 in the South Atlantic Ocean. The Falkland Islands had been seized by Britain in 1765 and had been a Crown Colony since the 1830s. In 1982 a population of about 1,800 English speakers lived there. However, the Falklands were also claimed by Argentina, who called them the Malvinas. For a number of years there had been a diplomatic dispute between Argentina and Britain over ownership of the Falklands. Then, in April 1982, the

It is not very easy to take a decision which commits your country to fight a war eight thousand miles from home. But Argentina invaded the Falkland Islands. I knew exactly what we must do – we must get them back. Their people were our people. Their loyalty and devotion to Queen and Country had never faltered. As so often...it was not, what should we do? But, how could it be done.

From Margaret Thatcher, British Prime Minister at the time of the Falklands War. This was written ten years later as the foreword to a book about the military operation to re-take the Falklands.

Argentinian Government ordered its soldiers to invade the Falkland Islands.

The United Nations Organisation recognised that this invasion was a breach of international law and ordered Argentina to withdraw. Economic sanctions were applied against Argentina.

This was not enough for the British Prime Minister, Margaret Thatcher. She ordered a task force of ships with aircraft and soldiers to set sail for the Falklands, which were 8,000 miles away from Britain. The British were so

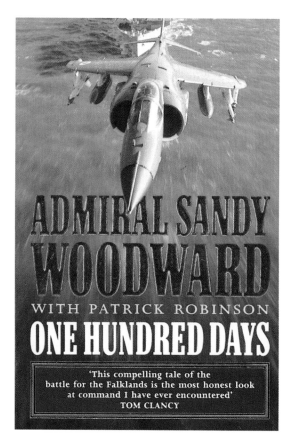

The front cover of a book about the Falklands written by Admiral Sandy Woodward, who was the task force commander during the War. This is the book which contains Margaret Thatcher's foreword.

unprepared that battle plans for the invasion were being prepared on board the ships as they sailed towards the South Atlantic. After six weeks of fighting the islands were recaptured. There were losses of men, ships and planes on both sides. Some British ships were sunk by the Argentine airforce, which use aeroplanes bought from the USA and French made missiles.

22 Read Source I. What reasons does Margaret Thatcher give for ordering the task force to recapture the Falklands?

23 What is the attitude of Thatcher in Source I?

24 Source I was written ten years after the events it is referring to. How might this affect the reliability of the evidence it contains. Explain your answer fully.

25 Study Source J. Source J was written ten years after the events too. How reliable do you think it might be as an account of the Falklands War? Explain your answer fully.

▲ Protests against Britain sending the task force to the South Atlantic

Results of the Falklands War

Mrs Thatcher's Government came under heavy criticism at the time. Many thought that the United Nations should have been allowed to resolve the problem. This would have taken longer but probably would not have resulted in bloodshed. Importantly, by ignoring the UN, Britain was showing a lack of faith in the ability of this organisation to solve conflict. There was an outcry when an Argentinian warship, the *General Belgrano*, was sunk by a British submarine. The *General Belgrano* had been sailing away from the Falklands when it was attacked. 368 sailors lost their lives in this incident. However, the eventual success of the operation did much to improve Thatcher's popularity and she was re-elected as Prime Minister. In the long term, Thatcher left British governments with the cost of remaining in the Falklands. Soldiers had to remain there to protect the inhabitants from any further Argentinian attack. The costs of this have been very high and show the problems of trying to follow a world role without a rich economy.

Assessment of British foreign policy, 1951–1995

During this period Britain lost its Empire but kept links with the newly reconstructed Commonwealth. Britain succeeded in joining the highly successful common trading market provided by the European Union. Most important of all, Britain, on the whole, managed to avoid becoming involved in any large scale foreign conflict. This avoidance of war was vital, for on the two occasions in which Britain did find itself involved in conflicts, in Suez 1956 and the Falklands 1982, the results were unfavourable. For neither the loss of status nor the great expense inflicted by these two conflicts was desirable to British governments.

12 Vietnam, 1945–1975

Vietnam's fight for independence was long and arduous, costing the lives of hundreds of thousands of her people. Firstly, there was a struggle against France, who had controlled Vietnam as a colony since the latter part of the nineteenth century. Secondly, after the withdrawal of the French, Vietnam was divided into two. North Vietnam became Communist and South Vietnam remained Capitalist. There now followed a conflict with the USA, who wanted to prevent South Vietnam from being taken over by the North. The USA pumped in millions of dollars to prevent Communism from spreading into South Vietnam, and also sent in its armed forces to support the South. The final phase in the struggle came after the USA had been defeated and had been forced to withdraw, when the North and South reunited under a Communist Government.

The struggle against France

During the Second World War, the French colony of Vietnam was taken over by the Japanese. The reaction of some Vietnamese nationalists was to form a League for Vietnamese Independence, also known as the Vietminh. Ho Chi Minh, a Communist, led the Vietminh in their fight against the Japanese occupying forces. On 2nd September 1945, Ho Chi Minh declared Vietnam's independence from French colonial rule. This was resisted by France who had no desire to give up any of their colonies in Indo-China because they were rich in minerals and were thus a source of income. Vietnam was also a market for French goods. The French began to re-establish their control over Vietnam but soon found that the Vietminh were prepared to fight them. The French were able to capture the towns and cities but were unable to defeat the Vietminh in a full pitched battle, because the Vietminh adopted guerrilla tactics. They were never drawn into head on battles, used hit and run methods, and, whenever possible, gained the confidence of the local peasantry. In this respect, Ho Chi Minh and his followers were imitating the tactics of Mao Zedong of China.

Ho Chi Minh preparing for a guerrilla attack against the French

The French found that the war against the Vietminh was expensive in lives and money. Between 1946 and 1952, they had suffered some 90,000 casualties and had spent several hundred million francs. By 1950, the French had decided that they would have to rely on financial support from the USA if they were to keep control of Vietnam. President Truman agreed to grant $20 million in 1950 and over the next four years, the French received more than $2.6 billion in their fight against the Vietminh. The Americans had become involved because they were concerned that

Chinese Communist influence might spread into Vietnam and other parts of Indo-China. They wished to halt the spread of Communism and were beginning to follow a policy which was known as containment.

Despite all the funds that they were receiving from the USA, the French were still unable defeat the Vietminh. In 1954, a new strategy was adopted and a plan was drawn up to tease the Vietminh into a full scale battle. The French forces concentrated themselves around Dien Bien Phu, hoping the Vietminh would then enter open conflict. However, instead of open battle, the French found themselves besieged and, after several weeks, were forced to surrender. The French then realised that they could not regain their former colony and at the Geneva peace talks in May 1954, they gave up their claim to Vietnam.

Geneva Conference

However, the surrender of the French at Dien Bien Phu did not mean that Vietnam was now an independent country. The countries involved in the peace talks were the USA, the USSR, Great Britain, France, and China and the key decision was that Vietnam should be temporarily divided at the 17th parallel until 1956, when elections would be held to determine its future. (It was decided to divide Vietnam into two because the French had been in control of most of the south and the Vietminh the north.) Ho Chi Minh agreed to the Geneva decisions because he felt that the Vietminh would win any general elections.

The involvement of the USA

President Eisenhower of the USA refused to sign the Geneva agreements. He and his advisers believed that Communism was spreading like 'ink on blotting paper' and Vietnam would be the next place on the paper. For the Americans, the 'Domino theory' was gaining currency and they had no wish to see Vietnam 'knocked over'. Vietnam had to be defended and thus prevent other countries in Asia from being 'knocked over' in turn.

The 'Domino theory'

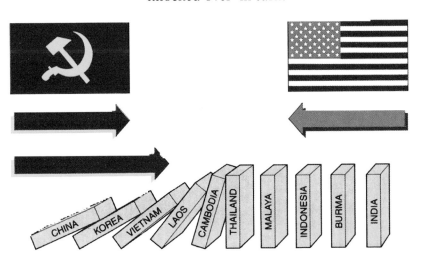

A group of American advisers were sent to South Vietnam in 1954 and their main aim was to ensure that its people did not support the Communist North in the approaching elections. In 1955, a new President of South Vietnam, Ngo Dinh Diem, was chosen. Diem was staunchly anti-Communist and the USA were happy to support him throughout the 1950s.

However, Diem was unwilling to run South Vietnam democratically. He employed many of his relatives in key positions and there was little freedom of speech. Diem did not attempt to improve the lot of the peasants and the fact that he was a Roman Catholic and the majority of the population was Buddhist did not endear him to them. However, the USA continued to back Diem because of his anti-Communist stance. In 1956, Diem cancelled the promised elections about reunification and held a referendum to indicate that he had the support of his people. Diem rigged the votes and the results showed that 98% of the people voted for him. (In Saigon, Diem claimed that 605,000 had voted for him, yet there were only 405,000 registered voters!)

During the next four years, Diem ruled South Vietnam like a dictator and antagonised people of all classes. There were various groups who opposed Diem and they came together to form the National Liberation Front in 1960. The NLF, also known as the Vietcong, contained many Communists and a specific set of goals was drawn up. Economic reform, reunification with the North and genuine independence were promised, and there would be a Government which would represent all classes and religions. The NLF began a terror campaign against Diem's Government in 1960 and assassinated more than 2,000 officials in that year. The NLF was given aid by Ho Chi Minh's North Vietnamese Government so that it could continue its guerrilla activities.

The Kennedy years

Let every nation know, whether it wishes us well or ill, that we shall pay any price, bear any burden, meet any hardship, support any friend, oppose any foe to assure the survival and success of liberty.

An extract from President Kennedy's inaugural speech.

President Kennedy saw the spread of Communism as a threat to the 'free world' and he was, therefore, determined to halt the spread of Communism into South Vietnam. Kennedy was a believer in the 'domino theory' and he made the decision to increase help to South Vietnam. The help was to be in the form of money and 'military advisers'. He also wanted Diem to introduce reforms so that the people of South Vietnam would not find Communism an attractive proposition.

By 1963, there were 16,000 American 'advisers' in South Vietnam and financial aid had been tripled in three years. Kennedy had introduced the 'strategic hamlets' programme in order to win over the South Vietnamese peasants (this was rather crude – peasants were moved away from the Vietcong and their new village was surrounded by barbed wire and guarded by the South Vietnamese army.) The programme failed and served only to increase the hatred towards Diem.

That same year, there were several occasions when Buddhist monks protested against the lack of religious tolerance in South Vietnam. Diem was a Roman

A Buddhist monk burns himself to death in protest against Government discrimination of Buddhists

Catholic who tended to appoint only Catholic people to Government posts. This was in a country where the majority of the population was Buddhist. The Buddhist monks committed suicide by pouring petrol on themselves and igniting it.

The opposition to Diem's regime continued to grow. In November 1963, with the help of the Americans, several South Vietnamese generals seized power from Diem, whom they murdered. (Eventually a new leader of the South emerged – Thieu – who became President in 1967.) This for America ended one phase of the war because by the end of the same month, President Kennedy had also been assassinated.

1 Explain the following terms: Vietminh, containment, Domino Theory, referendum, Vietcong, and guerrilla tactics.

2 Why were the French unable to keep control of Vietnam?
3 Why was there unrest in South Vietnam in the 1950s and early 1960s?
4 Why did the USA become involved in the Vietnam conflict?
5 In what ways did President Kennedy try to halt the spread of Communism in South Vietnam?

Johnson and the escalation of the War

Kennedy's successor, Johnson, felt unable to withdraw American military advisers from South Vietnam. He was a firm believer in the 'domino theory' and hated Communism. Johnson wished to secure South Vietnam and could only do so by increasing American aid but he needed Congress' support. Johnson won the support of Congress, but in a fortunate manner. Some North Vietnamese gunboats attacked two US destroyers in the Gulf of Tonkin. Johnson claimed that America had been the victim of unprovoked attacks and he wished to prevent any further

aggression. Congress passed the Gulf of Tonkin Resolution and Johnson likened it to 'grandma's nightshirt – it covered everything'.

The first American bombing of North Vietnam began in February 1965. 'Operation Rolling Thunder' was the codename for the bombing and for almost three years the Americans pounded North Vietnam. American bombers also attacked the Ho Chi Minh trail – the supply route of the Viet Cong from the North to the South. Shortly after Rolling Thunder began, the first American combat troops were sent to South Vietnam. By the end of 1965, there were more than 180,000 American troops fighting in the South. By the end of 1967, there were more than 500,000 troops in the South and it was estimated that the war was costing the USA $28 billion per year.

The division of Vietnam and the main Vietcong supply routes from the North

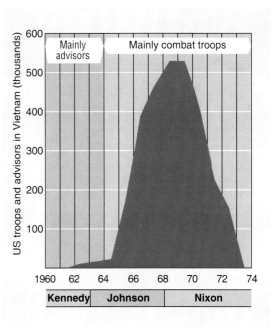

You can kill ten of my men for every one I kill of yours, but even at those odds, you will lose and I will win.

Ho Chi Minh when he was fighting the French.

 A Vietcong patrol in South Vietnam in 1966. The Vietcong used both men and women as fighters.

The bombing campaign quickly escalated and by 1967, the USA had dropped more bombs on Vietnam than the Allies dropped in the whole of the Second World War. The Ho Chi Minh trail was attacked but the Vietcong were still supplied by the North. There was a network of some 30,000 miles of tunnels which allowed the supplies to pass through to the South.

The American troops found the ground war impossible to win. The Vietcong employed guerrilla tactics and were able gain the support of the South Vietnamese people. The USA tried to gain the support of the peasants by offering medical help, farming advice, and technological assistance – a policy which became known as 'winning the hearts and minds', but it was a policy which could not compete with the simple approach of the Vietcong. The Vietcong adopted the ideas of Mao Zedong, the Chinese Communist leader.

 A Vietcong supply convoy of reinforced bicycles - each one could carry 500 lbs

C

The enemy advances, we retreat; the enemy camps, we harass; the enemy tires we attack; the enemy retreats, we pursue.

Mao Zedong.

Opposition to the war

In the USA opposition to the war grew slowly.

> We are there to strengthen the world order... Let no one think that retreat from Vietnam would bring an end to conflict. The battle would be renewed in one country then another. The central lesson of our time is that the appetite of aggression is never satisfied.

President Johnson defending the decision to fight in Vietnam.

> The picture of the world's greatest superpower killing or seriously injuring 1,000 non-combatants a week...is not a pretty one. It could produce a distortion in the world image of the United States.

Senator Fulbright, a leading opponent of the War speaking in October 1966.

By April 1967, there were huge anti-war parades in many American cities and in October 200,000 people marched to the Pentagon demonstrating against the War.

The turning point in the War was the Vietcong's Tet Offensive of 1968. On 30th January 1968, 67,000 Vietcong troops stormed 100 South Vietnamese cities and towns and took over twelve American military bases. The US Embassy in Saigon even came under severe attack. The American forces quickly recaptured most of these places but the problem for the American commanders was that the Vietcong attacks had been witnessed on television by the American public. The American people could see for themselves that the War was not being won.

A young American soldier shot by a sniper is helped to safety by his comrades in the city of Hué during the Tet Offensive of 1968

The American news reports showed the fighting in the grounds of the Embassy, the destruction of cities like Hué and the worst report showed a South Vietnamese policeman shoot a Vietcong prisoner in the head. Within weeks of the Tet Offensive, opinion polls showed that only 26% of Americans approved of Johnson's handling of the war – a fall of 14%.

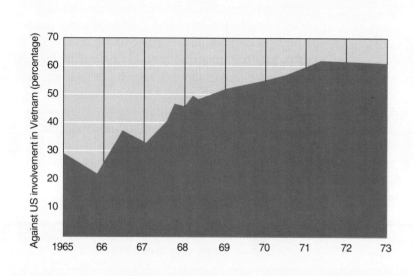

The growing unpopularity of the Vietnam War in the USA

On the streets of America the chant of the demonstrators was 'Hey, hey, LBJ, how many kids did you kill today?' (LBJ was President Lyndon B. Johnson.) After the Tet Offensive the number of demonstrations against the war increased rapidly. The students of America were especially vocal – more than 40,000 of them at 100 colleges protested against the war. Sometimes the demonstrations became violent.

Many young men protested by burning their draft (call up) cards. Many refused to register for the draft and even left the country to avoid joining the army. At the height of the war, several thousand men were prosecuted for refusing to be drafted into the army. The most famous of these was the boxer, Muhammad Ali. Soldiers protested against the war by deserting – many thousands did so during the course

of the conflict. Soldiers were even known to kill their officers if it was felt that lives were put at risk on what they thought were meaningless missions. Some soldiers turned to drugs to overcome fear and anxieties. It is interesting to note that working class males were twice as likely to be drafted as were middle class males, and that African Americans made up about 20% of the soldiers even though they were only 10% of the population.

The media helped to mould public opinion against the War after the Tet Offensive. Every day dreadful scenes of fighting and carnage were brought by television into the living rooms of the American public. When the people could see American GIs being killed, their enthusiasm for the War began to diminish. One of the most disturbing incidents of the War which turned the public against continued involvement in Vietnam was the massacre at My Lai. In 1968, soldiers under the command of Lieutenant William Calley killed about 350 civilians in the village of My Lai. News of the massacre only surfaced in 1969. Calley was put on trial and was found guilty of murder. Calley's superiors said that he had not been acting under orders and he became the scapegoat for the massacre. He was sentenced to twenty years' hard labour. During the trial the American public heard the evidence of several soldiers who had been present at My Lai.

We huddled the villagers up. We made them squat down... I poured about four clips into the group... The mothers was hugging their children... Well, we kept on firing.

An extract from the evidence of Paul Meadlo, who was a soldier at My Lai.

Women and children shot dead by American soldiers lie in the road at the village of My Lai, 1968

The American public could see that it was becoming hard to defend American involvement in Vietnam.

6 Look at Source B and the photographs on that page.
   i What can you learn about Ho Chi Minh's determination?
   ii How did this determination influence his followers?
7 Look at Sources D and E. Explain why Johnson and Fulbright adopted these positions about the conflict in Vietnam.
8 What role did television play in forming public opinion about the War?
9 What was the importance of the Tet Offensive?
10 What was the significance of the My Lai massacre?

The ending of the War

Rising casualties, the Tet Offensive, demonstrations at home, increasing costs, and a fall in popularity forced President Johnson to reconsider the American position.

After the Tet Offensive, General Westmoreland and the Joint Chiefs of Staff asked for another 200,000 troops. However, Johnson refused the request. In April 1968, President Johnson said that he would limit the bombing of North Vietnam and he then called on the leaders of North Vietnam to begin negotiations for an end to the fighting. Preliminary peace talks began in the following month in Paris. Johnson then shocked the American people when he declared that he would not stand as presidential candidate in the forthcoming elections.

The Vietnam War became one of the major issues of the presidential election. Richard Nixon, the Republican candidate, promised to end the War 'honourably'. Nixon won the election and began to carry out his plan to end the War. The policy became known as 'Vietnamisation' – South Vietnamese soldiers were to be trained and equipped to replace the American forces and this would allow American soldiers to return home. In the three years after 1969, more than 400,000 American soldiers were withdrawn from Vietnam. But the war did not come to an end.

▶

South Vietnamese soldiers with American supplied equipment

The Paris peace talks had produced few results. The opposing sides were reluctant to make any compromises and Nixon decided to try to force the North Vietnamese into making concessions. Nixon ordered the bombing of Vietcong bases and supply routes which were situated in North Vietnam and the neighbouring countries of Cambodia and Laos. More than 110,000 tons of bombs were dropped but they failed to produce any results. The American public were not told of the secret American bombing of countries bordering Vietnam – the pilots were ordered to keep quiet and their flight logs were altered to hide it. Nixon continued the escalation of the War by sending troops into Cambodia in April 1970. This time, however, he informed the American people on television. There were many protests and students across America demonstrated. At Kent State University, four students were shot dead by the National Guard.

One of the four Kent State University students shot dead by the National Guard in 1970 whilst he was protesting against the Vietnam War

In October 1972, peace talks re-opened and by now both sides were ready to make concessions. Nixon was keen to have some diplomatic success before the 1972 presidential elections and in November, his chief negotiator, Henry Kissinger, announced that 'Peace is at hand'. This turned out to be rather premature because President Thieu of South Vietnam refused to sign the agreement – he was only too aware that his fate had been sealed. The North Vietnamese would soon overrun the South because the peace agreement allowed them to keep their forces in the South. There was a stalemate. Nixon resorted to brute force to bring the North Vietnamese to the peace table again. On 18th December 1972 American bombers attacked Hanoi and Haiphong for twelve days. It was the heaviest series of raids in history – more than 100,000 bombs were dropped. Thousands of civilians were killed and massive numbers of homes, hospitals, schools, and factories were destroyed.

Newspapers across the world condemned the bombing – *The New York Times* called it 'Diplomacy through terror'. The North Vietnamese returned to the negotiating table and an agreement was signed. It was the same as the one reached in the previous October. However, President Thieu's fears were lessened when the USA promised to grant South Vietnam $1 billion of military equipment.

The USA pulled their last troops out of South Vietnam in March 1973. The ceasefire soon collapsed, however, and within two years the South Vietnamese had surrendered to the North.

11 Use the words below to explain why the Americans were unable to win the War.

Guerrilla warfare

Tet Offensive

American military tactics

Public opinion

My Lai

Consequences of the Vietnam War

The human cost of the War is still being counted. The death toll was horrific.

2 million Vietnamese killed
58,000 Americans killed
300,000 Americans injured
(Figures for those killed and injured in Laos and Cambodia cannot even be estimated with any accuracy – some estimates are as high as 10% of the population.)

More than three million American servicemen served in the Vietnam War and more than 58,000 have committed suicide since they came home.

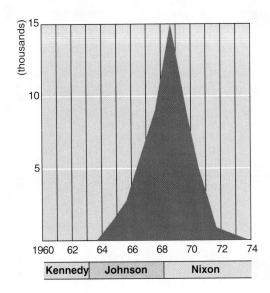

US dead in Vietnam

A disabled Vietnam veteran looks for the names of dead friends on the Vietnam memorial wall in Washington DC

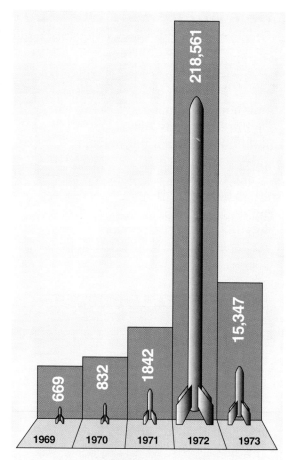

The weight of bombs dropped on North Vietnam by the USA in the Vietnam War. Bombs were also dropped on South Vietnam, Cambodia and Laos.

1969	1970	1971	1972	1973
669	832	1842	218,561	15,347

The people of Vietnam and South-East Asia have paid a great price for the conflict. More than eight million tons of bombs were dropped by the US Air Force. The impact on the land was devastating. Millions of gallons of defoliants such as 'Agent Orange' were dropped on the rainforest and it has not been able to recover. Humans who were exposed to the defoliants have produced malformed children. Landmines and booby traps planted during the war are still killing and injuring many Vietnamese each year.

A shell shocked American soldier awaits transportation away from the front line in 1968

The effects of defoliants like Agent Orange on the Vietnamese rainforest in 1970. These defoliants were used to destroy the vegetation to stop the Vietcong hiding and ambushing American soldiers.

Since the dumping of 11 million gallons of Agent Orange there has been a huge increase in the frequency of genetic malfunctions. Children have been born without eyes, with twisted, mangled limbs, even without brains. In the main hospital in Tay Ninh, a quarter of all births are miscarriages.

Bob Muller, a US veteran, describing his visit to a hospital in Ho Chi Minh City (formerly Saigon).

After the fall of South Vietnam, more than half a million refugees fled the country. About half of these left by boat - earning the name 'boat-people'. The 'boat-people' used any kind of vessel and many died as a result of starvation. Some managed to reach Hong Kong but here, as in other places, they were immediately put in refugee camps in preparation for repatriation.

The Vietnam War showed that a superpower could be defeated; and a similar defeat was to be repeated by Afghanistan over the USSR in the 1980s. The paradox of the War was also clear for many to see. The USA had been trying to prevent the spread of Communism, yet by the end of the conflict not only was Vietnam Communist, but Laos and Cambodia were too. The War has also left a great scar on the minds of the American people – the huge monument in Washington DC to those killed in Vietnam is testimony to this.

12 Explain the meanings of the following terms: Vietnamisation, Diplomacy through terror, Agent Orange.
13 Make a timeline from 1954 to 1975. Use one centimetre for each year. Mark onto this timeline the key events of the Vietnam conflict.
14 Why do you think that President Nixon reduced the number of soldiers in Vietnam?
15 Why do you think that Nixon ordered the secret bombing of Laos and Cambodia?
16 Do think that 'diplomacy through terror' was a successful policy? Explain your answer carefully.
17 Draw a spidergram to show the consequences of the conflict in Vietnam.

Further work: There are many books and films about the Vietnam War which you can watch and read to get more information about what the War was like. For example, films like *The Deer Hunter*, *Platoon*, and *Full Metal Jacket*. Some former soldiers have also written about their experiences in Vietnam, e.g. Tim O'Brien *If I die in the combat zone*, and *The things they carried with them*. War reporters, too, have written books about their experiences such as, Neil Sheehan *A bright shining lie* and Michael Herr *Despatches*.

13 The role of the United Nations Organisation

The United Nations (UN) came into existence in June 1945 after a conference held in San Francisco. The 51 countries who signed the Charter of the United Nations agreed to '...employ international machinery for the promotion of the economic and social advancement of all people.'

The road to San Francisco had been a long one. Churchill and Roosevelt had signed the Atlantic Charter in 1941 when both men had stated their aims for the postwar world. The two men were conscious that the League of Nations had been a failure and were keen to ensure that any new organisation had the support of all nations. The Atlantic Charter re-affirmed the idea of self-determination and also indicated that a new world peace organisation would be set up after the end of the War. The Atlantic Charter was confirmed by the signing of the United Nations Declaration in January 1942, and at meetings in 1943 at Teheran and Moscow it was decided to set up 'a general organisation' before the end of hostilities.

The conference which drew up the structure of the United Nations was held in August 1944 at Dumbarton Oaks near Washington DC. Diplomats from Great Britain, the USA, the USSR, and China decided that there would be a General Assembly and a Security Council. The latter would have permanent representatives and others who would serve for a specific term. There were disagreements about how voting would take place but these were resolved at the Yalta Conference in early 1945.

At Yalta it was agreed that the Big Four (Great Britain, the USA, the USSR, and China) would be permitted a veto in the Security Council. The veto meant that one of these four could block a Security Council decision simply by voting 'no'. At San Francisco, the aims of the United Nations were made clear (see Source A).

A

- To maintain international peace and security.
- To develop friendly relations among nations
- To achieve international co-operation in solving international problems ...and in encouraging respect for human rights and for fundamental freedoms without distinction as to race, sex, language
- To be a centre for harmonising the actions of nations in the attainment of these common ends.

An extract from the UN Charter

The diagram opposite shows the main organs of the United Nations. The structure has similarities with the League of Nations but several differences were introduced to give the UN greater powers.

The organisation of the United Nations

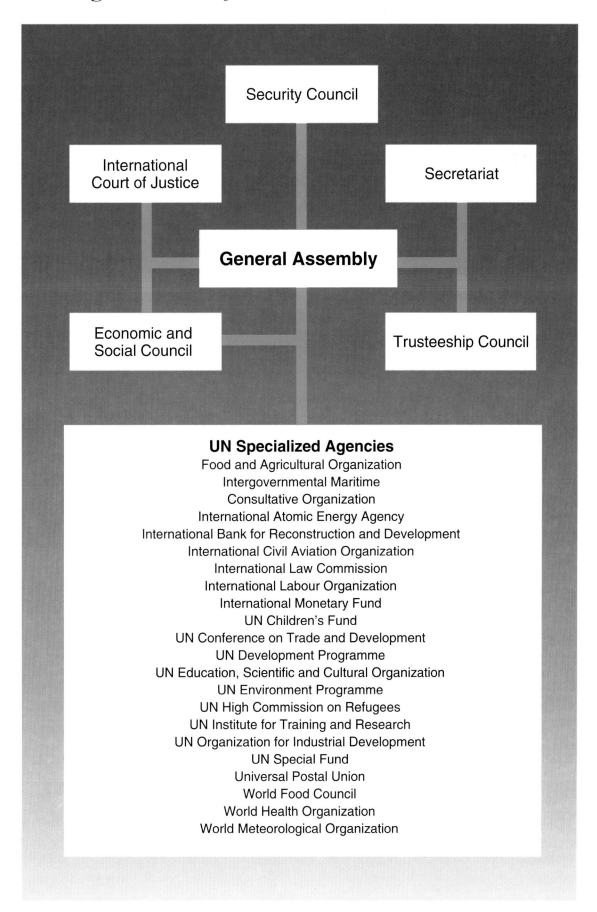

Security Council

International Court of Justice

Secretariat

General Assembly

Economic and Social Council

Trusteeship Council

UN Specialized Agencies
Food and Agricultural Organization
Intergovernmental Maritime
Consultative Organization
International Atomic Energy Agency
International Bank for Reconstruction and Development
International Civil Aviation Organization
International Law Commission
International Labour Organization
International Monetary Fund
UN Children's Fund
UN Conference on Trade and Development
UN Development Programme
UN Education, Scientific and Cultural Organization
UN Environment Programme
UN High Commission on Refugees
UN Institute for Training and Research
UN Organization for Industrial Development
UN Special Fund
Universal Postal Union
World Food Council
World Health Organization
World Meteorological Organization

The UN General
Assembly in session

The General Assembly

The General Assembly consists of all members and each country has one vote irrespective of its size. It meets once a year in September but can also meet in times of crisis. The General Assembly debates and makes recommendations about international problems, the budget of the UN, and membership of the Security Council and the Economic and Social Council. The decisions can be arrived at by a majority vote or when the issue is important then there has to be a two-thirds majority. The decisions are not binding on members.

The Security Council

There are now 15 members of the Security Council, five of whom are permanent – Great Britain, France, the USA, the USSR, and China. (Originally, China was represented by the Nationalists. However, after the success of the Communists under Mao Zedong in 1949, Communist China eventually replaced the Nationalists in 1971.) There are 10 non-permanent members each elected for a term of two years.

If a decision is to be binding then there must be 9 of the 15 in favour and all five permanent members must be in agreement. The five may use their power of veto to block a decision. If one of the five abstains, it is not seen as using the veto. On occasions the Security Council has been overruled by the General Assembly. This first happened in 1950, at the time of the Korean War. The General Assembly introduced the 'Uniting for peace' resolution which allowed the Assembly to meet within 24 hours of a blocked motion and vote whether to override the veto. The Assembly would have to be a two-thirds majority in favour of the original motion.

The Secretariat

Members of the Secretariat look after the administration of the UN. They are drawn from different member countries and there is a broad cross-section of nationalities. The Secretariat is headed by the Secretary-General, who is elected by the General Assembly on the recommendation of the Security Council. The Secretary-General is elected for a term of five years.

There have been only six Secretary-Generals since the UN was founded:
- Trygve Lie (Norway) 1946–53
- Dag Hammarskjold (Sweden) 1953–61
- U Thant (Burma) 1961–71
- Kurt Waldheim (Austria) 1971–81
- Perez de Cuellar (Peru) 1981–91
- Boutros Boutros-Ghali (Egypt) 1991 to the present

Trygve Lie

Dag Hammarskjold

Perez de Cuellar

The International Court of Justice

This is based at the Hague in the Netherlands. There are fifteen judges from different countries and they are elected by the General Assembly and Security Council jointly. The judges serve for a term of three years.

The Trusteeship Council

This body was set up to oversee those territories called mandates after the end of the First World War. The mandates were to be known as 'trust territories'. The most troublesome problem for this Council was South West Africa which was administered by South Africa. South Africa was unwilling to allow this territory independence and did so only in 1989 with the help of the UN Transition Assistance Group.

The Economic and Social Council

This Council has 27 members and is concerned with promoting economic and social progress in the world. The Council is also responsible through its commissions with addressing such major world problems as – drugs, the status of women, health, education, and human rights. The subsidiary organisations of the Council can be seen on the diagram of the UN's structure on page 169.

Membership of the United Nations

Unlike the League of Nations, the UN has always been a body that has members from the whole world. When the European members began to decolonise, membership of the UN increased rapidly. With this increase of African and Asian members, the two superpowers found that they could no longer expect to control the voting. By the late 1960s, the developing nations were often able to determine the outcome of votes in the General Assembly.

1 Explain what is meant by the following terms:
   Atlantic Charter, self-determination, veto, UN Charter, Secretary-General, Trust territories
2 Why do you think that the major powers were granted a veto in the Security Council?
3 Look at the text and Source A. Can you suggest reasons why the UN was set up?
4 What were the main aims of the UN?
5 How is the General Assembly able to overturn a decision of the Security Council?

The growth in membership and composition of the United Nations

▼

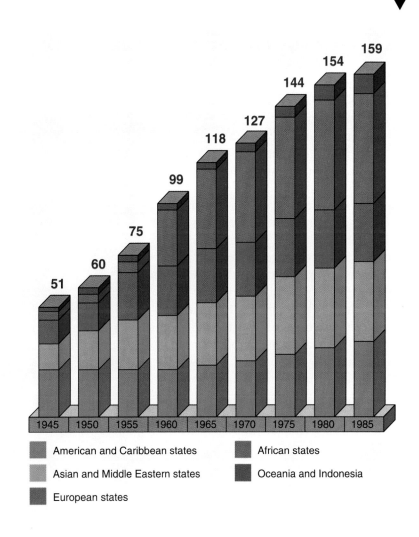

American and Caribbean states
African states
Asian and Middle Eastern states
Oceania and Indonesia
European states

Peacekeeping and the UN

The UN was set up at a time when there was optimism about the future. The use of the atomic bomb at Hiroshima and Nagasaki had made many people realise that there had to be greater co-operation in the world. It had been decided that the UN would have an international peace keeping force which the Security Council would control. However, the rapidly deteriorating relationship between the USA and the USSR meant that no agreement was reached about such a force. The UN could impose sanctions but the idea of its own armed force seemed out of the question in the context of the developing Cold War in the early years after 1945.

However, the UN became involved in several conflicts in the four years after the end of the Second World War.

a   Greece – A special UN monitoring committee was set up to examine Greek claims that Communist rebels were being given assistance by Albania, Bulgaria and Yugoslavia. UN attempts to bring the countries to the peace table failed.

b   Iran – The Iranian government complained to the UN about the continued Soviet occupation of part of its northern territory. The USSR eventually withdrew its troops.

c   Dutch East Indies – After 1945, nationalists in this area fought the Dutch and proclaimed the new state of Indonesia. The UN stepped in and called for a ceasefire and eventually Indonesia was granted independence in 1949.

d   Palestine – This mandate had been under the control of Great Britain but by 1947 Britain was unable to maintain law and order. The UN was asked to devise a plan which would satisfy the Jews and the Arabs. It was decided to partition Palestine but the plan was rejected by the Arabs. In 1948, when Britain withdrew (see Chapter 14), war between the Jews and Arabs began. The UN tried to mediate but was unsuccessful. The saddest part for the UN was the murder of its chief negotiator, Count Bernadotte.

e   Kashmir – After Britain had granted independence to the Indian sub-continent, India and Pakistan argued over ownership of Kashmir and went to war. The UN arranged a ceasefire and a plebiscite which led in effect to Kashmir being partitioned. This did not solve the problem and India and Pakistan fought two wars over this territory in 1965 and 1971.

Korea

The Korean War was the first time that UN forces were sent into a country to restore peace and security in an area. The details of the War can be found in Chapter 8. The Security Council passed a resolution calling for the North Koreans to withdraw their troops from the South. The Soviet Union was absent from the Security Council when the vote was taken because it was protesting against the refusal to allow Communist China into the UN. Therefore, it was unable to use its veto to stop the resolution being passed. Sixteen countries sent troops to assist South Korea, although the vast majority of forces were either from the USA or South Korea itself.

British infantry of the Middlesex Regiment move up to the front line in Korea accompanied by tanks in 1951

American troops take a break during a lull in the fighting in 1952

The war solved little. Korea was not reunited and still remains a divided country today. UN involvement in the Korean conflict resulted in the passing of the 'uniting for peace' resolution (see p.170). The Soviet Union did not accept the legality of this decision. Soviet leaders accused Trygve Lie of having exceeded his powers and said that he had been biased towards the USA. The Soviet diplomats refused to deal with Lie and his position became impossible. He resigned early and was succeeded by Dag Hammarskjold.

1956 – Suez and Hungary

There were two major incidents in 1956 which showed the UN at its strongest and also at its weakest. In 1956, British and French forces invaded Egypt to secure the Suez Canal (see Chapter 11). The Security Council condemned the invasion and so Britain and France vetoed the resolution. However, The UN was able to use the 'uniting for peace' procedure and planned to send a force of UN troops to secure the Suez Canal. The fighting eventually stopped because of pressure from the USA and the USSR, but the world condemnation via the UN was most important. UN peacekeeping troops remained in Egypt for eleven years. However, they were not able to prevent the Arab-Israeli war of 1967 (see Chapter 14).

The UN proved unable to help in the Hungarian crisis of 1956 (see Chapter 9). This happened at the same time as Suez. There was an attempt in Hungary to break free of Soviet control and the Soviet response was to send in thousands of troops. The Hungarian government appealed to the UN and a Security Council resolution calling for the withdrawal of Soviet troops was vetoed by the Soviet Union. The General Assembly passed the resolution but the Soviets refused to comply and refused to have anything to do with the UN committee set up to investigate the issue.

The Soviet Union was safe behind the 'iron curtain', and, unlike Britain and France, would not give in to world pressure. Rather like the League of Nations, the UN could only be successful if all member states accepted the decisions of the majority.

The Congo, 1960

Within days of being granted independence by Belgium in 1960, there was chaos and turmoil in the Congo. Belgium sent in troops to protect its nationals who had remained in the country. However, the Belgian action was illegal and the Congolese Prime Minister, Patrice Lumumba, appealed to the UN for assistance. The situation worsened when Katanga, a copper rich province, broke away from the Congo and declared itself an independent state.

Secretary-General Dag Hammarskjold was able to present a resolution to the Security Council creating a special force which would intervene in the Congo and restore peace and unity. However, the great powers of the UN each had very different views about UN interference. As usual, the USA and the USSR saw the area as a place to gain influence, and Britain and France were concerned that UN intervention in the Congo might mean future problems for them in their own colonies.

A wounded UN soldier is lifted out of a UN vehicle in the Congo

The UN provided more than 4,000 troops and they were drawn from five African countries, although eventually troops from Europe and the Indian sub-continent were also sent. Hammarskjold did not wish to involve UN troops in the internal affairs of the Congo and hoped that Katanga would end her separation. Lumumba was disappointed at the UN decision and appealed directly to the Soviet Union for help against Katanga. The situation grew worse and the President of the Congo, Kasavubu, had Lumumba arrested and killed. The Congo was breaking into three groups – the followers of Kasavubu, Lumumba, and Tshombe (leader of Katanga). In the summer of 1961, the UN changed its approach to the Congo. It ordered all non-UN troops out of the Congo, i.e. the mercenaries who had helped Tshombe to remain in power. UN soldiers fought against the mercenaries in September but were unable to defeat them. Tragedy struck shortly after this when Hammarskjold was killed in a plane crash on his way to meet Tshombe.

U Thant, the new Secretary-General, ordered UN troops to move into Katanga and end the secession (breakaway). By the end of 1962, Katanga was re-united with the Congo and Tshombe fled. UN forces were withdrawn in 1964 and shortly after this trouble flared once more. Order was restored when Colonel Mobutu and the army took over.

It is difficult to measure the success of the UN in the Congo. Thousands of people were killed and military rule was introduced in 1964. However, the UN could point to:
a   the removal of illegal Belgian troops
b   the prevention of foreign intervention
c   reuniting the Congo
d   maintaining the economy and administration

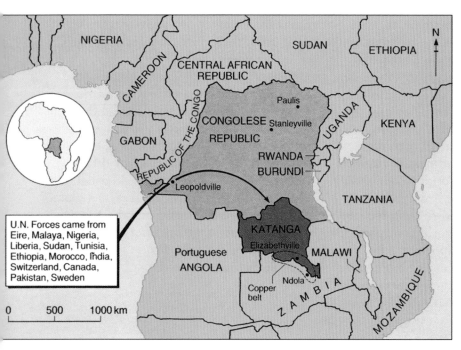

U.N. Forces came from Eire, Malaya, Nigeria, Liberia, Sudan, Tunisia, Ethiopia, Morocco, India, Switzerland, Canada, Pakistan, Sweden

Cyprus, 1964 and 1974

War broke out between Greek and Turkish Cypriots in 1964 and the UN was able to arrange a peacekeeping force which prevented an invasion of the island by Turkey. The UN brought stability but was unable to solve the underlying Greek-Turkish dispute. When Turkey did eventually invade in 1974, UN forces could only stand by and watch. The UN did organise a ceasefire in a now divided island. The ceasefire has held since then. By the middle of the 1960s, the UN could argue that it had had some successes. It had almost 120 member states and had been able to bring some crises to satisfactory conclusions. However, the development of the Cold War and the sour relations between the USA and the USSR meant that the UN sometimes became an observer when there were international crises. The map on page 176 shows those places where the UN was powerless to intervene and was reduced to passing resolutions and making gestures.

More recently, the UN was able to approve of 'all necessary means to restore international peace and security' in the Middle East after Saddam Hussein's invasion of Kuwait. However, there were no UN troops and all forces were under the command of the USA.

The UN has had rather mixed fortunes in the chaos of the former state of Yugoslavia. Despite a large peacekeeping presence (UN Protective Forces – UNPROFOR) the conflict dragged on and two hundred and fifty thousand civilians were killed. Despite the many criticisms of the UN, its peacekeeping activities in world troublespots have continued. See the chart on page 177.

6 To answer the following question, you will have to use the information from this chapter, other relevant chapters in this book and any other sources that you are able to find. 'Was the UN successful in its intervention in Korea and the Congo?'

Canadian UN troops man a checkpoint near the airport in Cyprus as part of the peacekeeping force

Some of the failures of the United Nations to prevent crisis and conflict

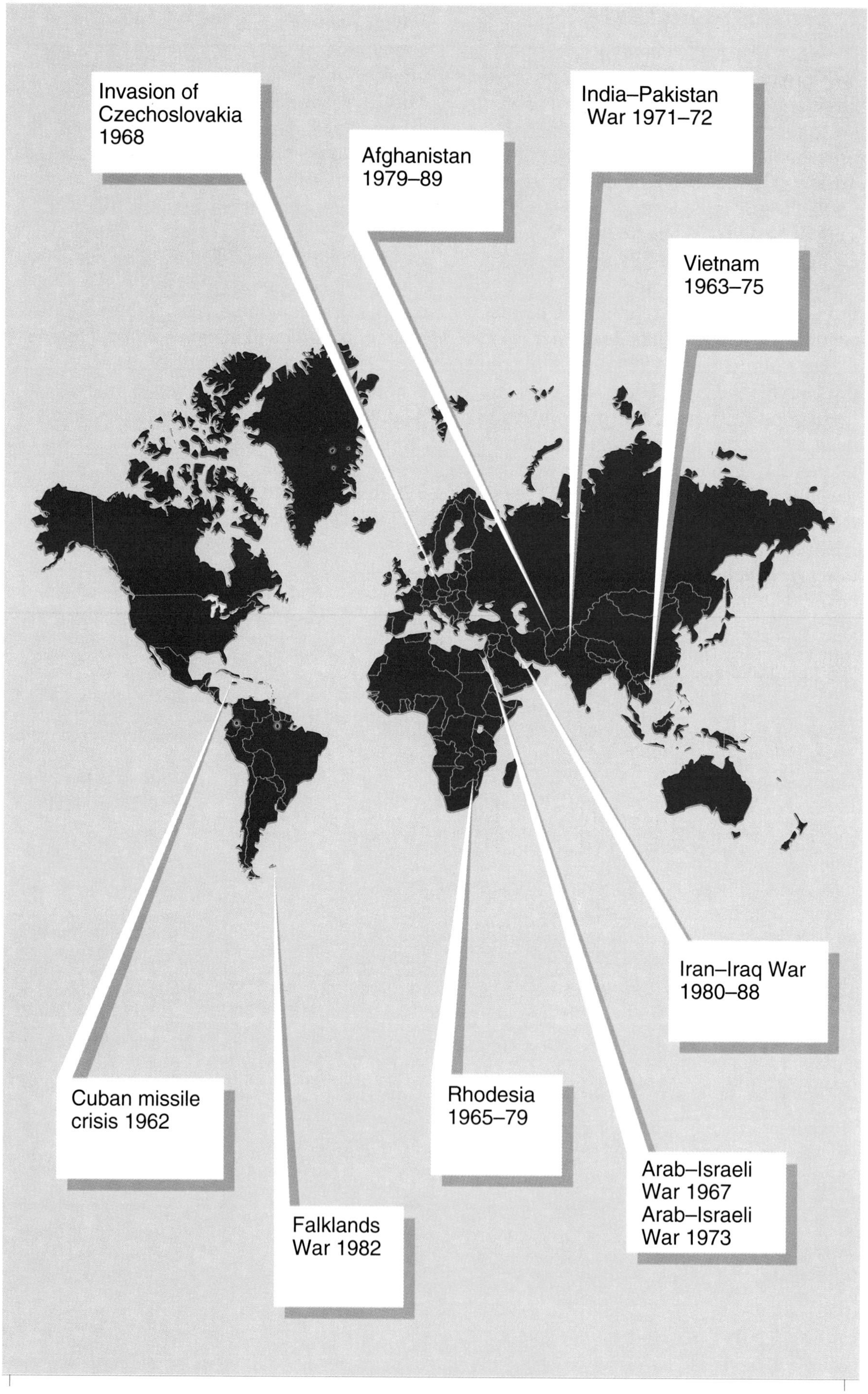

Invasion of Czechoslovakia 1968

Afghanistan 1979–89

India–Pakistan War 1971–72

Vietnam 1963–75

Iran–Iraq War 1980–88

Cuban missile crisis 1962

Rhodesia 1965–79

Arab–Israeli War 1967 Arab–Israeli War 1973

Falklands War 1982

French UN forces provide an escort for a humanitarian convoy in Bosnia in 1992

Date	Name and place	Abbreviation
1948	UN Truce Supervision Organization (Middle East)	UNTSO
1949	UN Military Observer Group in India and Pakistan	UNMOGIP
1964	UN Force in Cyprus	UNFICYP
1974	UN Disengagement Observer (Syria)	UNDOF
1978	UN Interim Force in Lebanon	UNIFIL
1989	UN Angola Verification Mission I	UNAVEMI
1991	UN Mission for the Referendum in Western Sahara	MINURSO
1991	UN Iraq-Kuwait Observation Mission	UNIKOM
1991	UN Observer Mission in El Salvador	ONUSAL
1992	UN Protective Forces (former Yugoslavia, mainly Bosnia)	UNPROFOR
1992	UN Operation in Mozambique	OUNMOZ
1993	UN Mission in Haiti	UNMIH
1993	UN Mission in Somalia II	UNOSOM II
1993	UN Observer Mission in Georgia	UNOMIG
1993	UN Mission in Uganda-Rwanda	UNOMUR
1993	US Assistance Mission in Rwanda	UNAMIR

Current UN peacekeeping operations

The UN and apartheid

There were many occasions when the United Nations condemned apartheid and in 1960, a resolution was passed stating that 'South Africa's policies have led to international friction and if continued, might endanger international peace and security.'

The UN continued to pass resolutions against apartheid and was unhappy with the establishment of the Bantu homelands in 1976. Attempts to introduce sanctions and expel South Africa from the UN failed. Britain, France and the USA voted against these proposals. When change did come, it came from within South Africa itself, not from UN pressure.

The work of the UN's agencies

UN Educational, Scientific and Cultural Organisation. Promotes education, science and culture worldwide

UN Relief and Rehabilitation Administration UNRRA and UNRWA – Relief and Works Agency. Assists in refugee problems eg WWII; Middle East; Africa

UN International Children's Emergency Fund – UNICEF. To assist children worldwide, raises awareness of problems; 1979 was The Year of the Child

Economic & Social Council

International Labour Organization. Tries to secure minimum standards of employment, training, management and safety standards

Food and Agriculture Organization. Designed to help farmers of the developing world to improve agricultural production

International Monetary Fund. Provides loans to nations in financial difficulty

World Health Organization. Raises health standards. Aims to eradicate epidemics and diseases. Promotes health education, child care etc.

▲ Doctors working for the World Health Organisation vaccinate villagers in the Congo to protect them against a smallpox epidemic

Whose UN is it?

In the first thirty years of the United Nations, the nations of the west and the Communist bloc dominated. The Cold War was often played out in the Security Council and sometimes the superpowers simply ignored the United Nations altogether. As decolonisation took place the African and Asian countries began to hold the key to any majority in the General Assembly.

There were even claims that some of the UN's agencies were moving away from their purpose and were becoming politically biased. The USA and Great Britain withdrew from UNESCO and the USA from ILO as a result of what they saw as political interference.

During the last ten years, the UN has experienced budgetary problems which have meant that certain programmes of work have been cancelled.

7 Make a list of the successes and failures of the United Nations since its foundation.

8 Divide into groups of 3 or 4. Prepare a case for
a the continued existence of the UN
b the break up of the UN.

14. *The Middle East 1948–1995*

Background to the conflict

Conflict in the Middle East has been a constant feature of twentieth-century history. The Prime Minister of Israel, Yitzhak Rabin, was assassinated in December 1995, and there were three suicide bomb attacks on Israeli citizens at the beginning of 1996. Hopes for a lasting peace between the Palestinian Arabs and Israel were dented by these events. Nevertheless, the events of the 1990s were so astonishing that many felt that the conflict between Israel and her neighbours was coming to a close.

In 1897, the first Zionist conference in Switzerland declared its aim to set up a separate state for the Jewish people in Palestine. The Jews had been expelled from Palestine in AD70 and since then had not had a national land of their own. However, it was decisions taken during the First World War that sowed the seeds of eventual conflict in Palestine.

At the time of the War, Palestine was part of the Ottoman (Turkish) Empire, and Britain was at war with Turkey after 1915. The British wanted the help of the Arabs and promised independence after the War, if help was given.

However, there were also secret Franco-British talks which revolved around the partition of the Turkish Empire in the event of an Allied victory. These talks led to the Sykes-Picot Agreement in 1916 and the promises made by McMahon (see below) were broken.

▼ **A**

Subject to modifications, Great Britain is prepared to recognise and support the independence of the Arabs in all regions... I am convinced that this declaration will assure beyond all possible doubt of the sympathy of Great Britain towards the aspirations of her friends the Arabs and will result in a firm and lasting alliance...

Sir Henry McMahon, British High Commissioner for Egypt to a leading Arab nationalist, March 1916.

However, the situation was complicated in 1917, when the British Foreign Secretary, Balfour, wrote to a leading Zionist leader.

 B

His Majesty's Government view with favour the establishment in Palestine of a national home for the Jewish people... it being clearly understood that nothing shall be done which may prejudice the civil and religious rights of existing non-Jewish communities in Palestine.

Arthur Balfour to Lord Rothschild, 1917.

1 Study Sources A and B. Why were the ideas contained in them likely to cause problems between the Arabs and the Jews?

Britain's policies paid off because the Arabs of the Ottoman Empire did rebel against the Turks and the Zionists across the world, especially in the USA, offered support for Britain. At the end of the War very little of the Ottoman Empire was granted independence and much of the Middle East became mandated territory under the control of either Britain or France. (A mandate meant that land belonging to Turkey would be looked after by Britain or France with the expectation that independence would be granted to it in the near future.) The Arabs in Palestine felt let down by the settlement, especially when Jewish immigration into Palestine began to increase rapidly in the 1920s and 1930s.

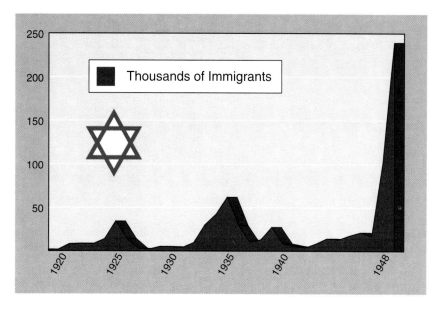

Thousands of Immigrants

Jewish immigration into Palestine, 1918–1948

Tension between Jews and Arabs grew in the 1920s and there were several clashes which resulted in many deaths. The Jews set up their own defence group, called the 'Haganah', because they felt that the British were unable to keep order. Jewish immigration increased after 1933 and the Arabs could see that one day they would be outnumbered. The Arab Revolt of 1936-39 was a product of this fear and, during the Revolt, almost 2,000 people were killed. Arab action caused the Jews to develop another 'security' group called Irgun Zvai Leumi (National Military Organisation).

Britain found it difficult to police Palestine and in 1937 suggested that the mandate be partitioned. There would be a Jewish and an Arab state with a section controlled by Britain. The plan was dropped and further ideas were discussed in 1939, but the situation was changed when war broke out in September of that year.

When the world became aware of the full extent of the 'Holocaust' (the mass extermination of 6 million Jews in the Nazi concentration camps) sympathy for the Jewish cause grew. There were many Jewish survivors whose ideas were changed by their experiences of the War.

Some of the Jewish victims of the Holocaust who died or were murdered in the Nazi concentration camps before they were liberated by the allies

The number of Jewish refugees wishing to go to Palestine after 1945, increased and pressure was put on Britain by the USA to allow 100,000 settlers immediately. Britain refused because here was a fear that there would be bloodshed between the Jews and the Arabs. Britain was careful not to offend member states of the Arab League because of the importance not only of the Suez Canal but also oil.

Jewish terrorist groups began actively to campaign for an independent Jewish state and their actions became increasingly violent. The British army headquarters at the King David Hotel were blown up in 1946, killing more than 70 British people (see page 147). Soldiers were killed, roads were mined and letter bombs were sent. 338 British people were killed by terrorist activities in the three years after the Second World War. The Jewish group Irgun and also the Stern Gang were responsible for these deaths.

Despite these terrorist activities, Britain was unable to win the propaganda war. There were occasions when Britain was seen to be turning away Jewish refugees seeking a home in Palestine. The best example of this was when Britain turned away a ship called 'Exodus' carrying several thousand refugees, forcing it to return to Germany. Britain was cast in the role of villain. For Britain the Palestine Mandate was becoming a nightmare. It was costing £40 million per year and ten percent of its army was stationed there.

In 1947, Britain referred the problem to the newly formed United Nations which put forward a plan of partition. The plan was accepted by the Jews but rejected by the Arabs. Nevertheless, the UN approved the plan and Palestine was to be partitioned.

It was then that tension between Jew and Arab began to increase and there were

Two ships full of Jewish refugees are boarded by British troops in Palestine

The proposed UN partition plan for Palestine

many incidents which resulted in communal deaths. The worst incident was at Deir Yassin where several hundred Arabs were murdered by Jewish forces.

Britain eventually pulled out of Palestine on 14th May 1948. There was immediate fighting between the Jews and the surrounding Arab states. The Jews proclaimed their new state of Israel, but the future looked bleak because they were being attacked by Iraq, Lebanon, Transjordan, Egypt, and Syria.

David Ben-Gurion proclaims the independence of the state of Israel in 14th May 1948. He became Israel's first Prime Minister and Defence Minister.

The Israelis were able to repel their attackers and, despite being outnumbered, defeated them. Their only setbacks were that they were unable to secure the West Bank and parts of the city of Jerusalem. Nevertheless, they had gained more land than the UN partition offered.
The Israelis had won a famous victory because they had had the determination to succeed. They were literally fighting for their lives. Their enemies were divided and their equipment was not as modern as the Israelis' because large amounts of money had been raised by American Jews and this had been spent on modern Czech armaments.

However, there was a sting in the tail of victory for the Israelis. After the war, about one million Palestinian Arabs fled their homeland to live in neighbouring Arab

states. These people were housed in refugee camps and became stateless citizens. The refugee camps became the breeding grounds for the Palestinian freedom fighters who would create tremendous havoc for Israel in their own struggle for a homeland in Palestine.

2 Why did Britain need help from the Arabs in the First World War?

3 Look at Balfour's statement (Source B). How does this contradict McMahon's statement (Source A)?

4 Look again at Balfour's statement. In what ways could this be interpreted differently by both the Jews and the Arabs?

5 Why did Jewish immigration increase after 1933? Think of what was happening in Europe at this time.

6 Explain what is meant by the terms:
i mandated territory
ii Holocaust.

7 Look at the words in the box and use them to explain why the Jews were able to gain their independence.

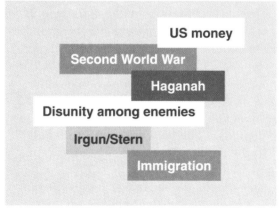

US money
Second World War
Haganah
Disunity among enemies
Irgun/Stern
Immigration

The Suez Crisis, 1956

The creation of a Jewish state and the defeat of its neighbours did not bring Israel security. The Arab states had suffered humiliating defeat and revenge was high on their agenda. There were constant reminders of defeat for the Arab states in the form of one million Palestinian refugees who were living in shabby camps. War broke out once more in 1956, but this time it showed that the Middle East was a cauldron of international intrigue. The Suez crisis involved not only the Arab state of Egypt, and Israel, but also Britain, France, the USA, and the USSR. Even the newly formed United Nations was unable to prevent open conflict.

One of the consequences of the Arab-Israeli war of 1948-9 was a military takeover in Egypt. The new leader, Colonel Nasser, was determined to take revenge on Israel and make his country the leading Arab state in the Middle East. Nasser developed closer links with the USSR and in 1955 bought 80 Mig 15 fighters and 45 Ilyushin 28 bombers. Soviet experts were also to be invited to Egypt to help train Nasser's armed forces. Moreover, he organised groups of Palestinians into bands to attack Israeli settlements. These bands were called 'fedayeen' (self sacrificers). Nasser's squeeze on Israel was taken further when the Israeli port of Eilat was blockaded at the Gulf of Aqaba. Nasser was surprised that his actions were interpreted by the Americans as allowing the Russians to move into the Middle East, and therefore, a promised American loan to build the Aswan Dam was stopped.

A group of Palestinian 'fedayeen' commandos – some little more than boys

Nasser kept the pressure on by nationalising the Suez Canal Company and insisting that he would complete the Aswan Dam with the revenue from the Canal. The majority shareholders of the company were Britain and France, and they thought that if Egypt were allowed to control the Canal, then oil supplies could be cut off at will.

The nationalisation of the Canal is...of the widest international importance...Any failure on the part of the Western Powers to take the necessary steps to regain control over the Canal would have disastrous consequences for the economic life of the Western Powers and for their influence in the Middle East.

Sir Anthony Eden, British Prime Minister, July 1956.

There then followed secret negotiations between Britain, France and Israel at Sevres near Paris. The three agreed to create a situation whereby Israel would invade Egypt allowing Britain and France to intervene. The end results would be the retaking of the Suez Canal by Britain and France and the destruction of fedayeen bases by the Israelis. Nasser would be humiliated and his future as leader of the Arab states would be in doubt. However, the scheme did not go according to plan. The Israeli invasion of Egypt (29th October) was swift and successful and within days they had captured the Sinai Peninsula, but British and French intervention was slow. Their forces landed around the canal on 5th November, and soon world opinion began to swing against them. The USA opposed the action because they feared that the Arabs would see the invasion as old style imperialist policy and as such it might mean that the Soviet Union could exploit this and increase their own influence in the Middle East. The Soviets even threatened military action against Britain, although at the time the Soviet

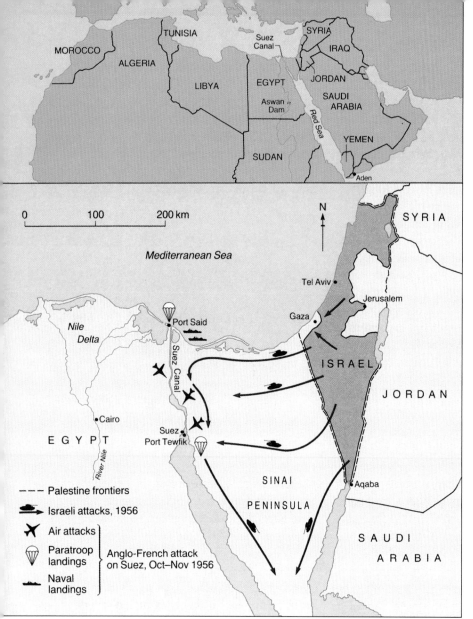

The Suez crisis, 1956

disgraced because there was clear evidence that it had made secret plans with Israel to invade a sovereign state – details of this did not emerge until several years after the affair but hints at it were enough to bring discredit.

Nasser emerged from the crisis with his reputation enhanced. Although his forces had suffered defeats again at the hands of Israel, he could point to the humiliation of Britain and France and show that he would stand up to Western powers.

E

> Instead of opening the Canal, it was blocked; instead of saving British lives and property, they had been put at Nasser's mercy; instead of toppling Nasser, he was enthroned; instead of keeping the oil flowing, it was soon to be rationed; instead of winning friends, we had lost them... the expedition had achieved the exact opposite of the Government's declared intention

Michael Foot, Labour M.P. in 1956, writing in 1975.

For Israel, the crisis did achieve their aims, the fedayeen bases were destroyed and the border raids stopped. The United Nations Emergency Force was sent into the Sinai to try to keep peace between Egypt and Israel.

Union was keen to deflect attention away from her invasion of Hungary (see Chapter 9). Faced with international disapproval and economic chaos (Britain experienced a run on the pound and there was a loss of 15% of its gold and dollar reserves, see Chapter 11 for further details) Britain and France agreed to halt their action and pull out.

Results of the Suez crisis

The Middle East had become the focus of world attention and the area became yet another playground for the two superpowers. Britain suffered humiliation and was made to realise that it was no longer a world power and could not take unilateral action. Britain was also

8 Explain what is meant by the term fedayeen.

9 Look at the words in the box below and then use them to explain why the Suez crisis can be considered more than just a clash between Egypt and Israel.

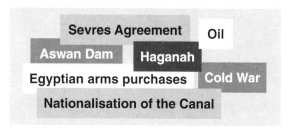

10 How reliable do you think Foot's comment is for someone studying the Suez crisis? Explain your answer carefully.

The Six Day War, 1967

Peace was not long lasting after Suez. There were continued border skirmishes carried out by the Palestinian group 'El Fatah' and the newly formed Palestinian Liberation Organisation. Both sides built up their armed forces. Israel was supplied by the USA, Britain, France, and West Germany; and the Arab states by the USSR. Though the Arab states were not really united after 1956, they did have access to large funds from oil revenue. The Arab border raids and Israeli retaliatory raids worsened in 1966-67 and it did seem that war could break out at any time.

 This Lebanese cartoon from May 1967 shows Israel squeezed between the military forces of her Arab neighbours

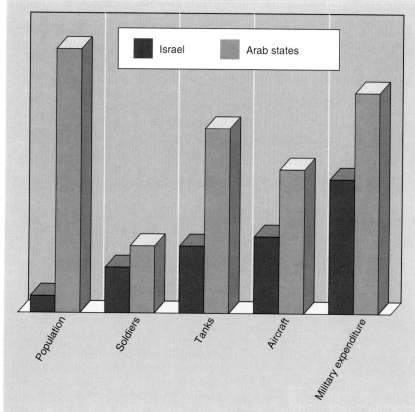

The balance of military power between Israel and the four Arab states of Egypt, Jordan, Syria and Iraq in 1967

In May 1967, Nasser ordered the UNEF to withdraw from the Sinai and he then closed the Gulf of Aqaba to Israel, thus blockading her port, Eilat. There were also troop movements near Israel's borders with Lebanon, Syria, and Jordan, whose forces were supplemented by Iraqi, Saudi Arabian, and Algerian troops. The table above shows the build up of forces of Israel's neighbours.

Without waiting to be attacked, the Israelis launched a pre-emptive strike against their enemies. The fighting was over in six days, after which Israel had maintained her borders and had greater security than ever. Employing blitzkrieg tactics, the Israelis were able to destroy their enemies' air forces on the ground – they lost only 26 planes compared with 400 enemy aircraft. The Egyptians were pushed back through the Sinai desert and large numbers of tanks were destroyed at the Mitla Pass. The Israelis then secured their southern border by occupying the Gaza strip. In the north, the Syrians were also defeated and the Israelis captured the strategic Golan Heights. It was just the same in the fighting against Jordan, where the West Bank of the River Jordan was captured. But above all for the Israelis, the eastern part of Jerusalem was at last captured. The victory was stunning and comprehensive. Not only were Israel's borders secure, but the Egyptian forces had been destroyed and Nasser's allies were not in any position to threaten Israel. Moreover, the victory was so quick that there had been no chance for world opinion to have any impact on the conflict.

Consequences of the Six Day War

The Israeli victory meant that there was another surge of Arab refugees who left the occupied territories to swell the refugee camps. There were now about 1.5 million refugees. However, although they were at the height of their success, the Israelis were to discover that the Palestinian Arabs refused to accept defeat.

▲ Yasser Arafat, head of the Palestine Liberation Organisation (PLO)

Yasser Arafat and the Palestine Liberation Organisation became more violent and terrorist raids on Israeli settlements were stepped up. However, the PLO, based in Jordan was like a state within a state, and King Hussein of Jordan was worried at its growing strength and power. He decided to expel the PLO from Jordan and was able to do so only after bitter fighting. The PLO then established itself in the Lebanon. The Popular Front for the Liberation of Palestine (PFLP) also emerged and was more radical in its approach to the problems. The PFLP became involved in the hijacking of aeroplanes; the most famous of which led to the destruction of three planes at Dawson's Field, Jordan, in 1970. There was also a terrible massacre at Lydda Airport where 30 people were shot and more than 70 were injured. Many Israelis began to feel that there was no security for them. The most striking terrorist attack came at the Munich

Olympic Games in 1972. Here, another Palestinian group, Black September, murdered several Israeli athletes. The event happened in front of the world's media and highlighted the plight of the Palestinian Arabs. However, the Israelis, as expected, became more determined after such events and were unwilling to discuss matters with the Palestinians. Moreover, the Israelis were unwilling to consider Resolution 242 which the United Nations had passed in November 1967 shortly after the Six Day War.

 F

i Withdrawal of Israel from the occupied territories
ii Acknowledgement of the sovereignty and territorial integrity and political independence of every state in the Middle East
iii A just settlement to the refugee problem.

United Nations Resolution 242, 1967.

President Sadat, who became leader of Egypt on Nasser's death in 1970, was just as keen to see Israel defeated and it seemed that there could be no peace in the Middle East when he issued statements such as Source D.

 G

We have had enough of words... we know our goal and we are determined to reach it... the liberation of our territory is the fundamental task before us...

Anwar Sadat

11 'Victory in 1967 did not bring Israel the security that was expected.' Do you think that this is an accurate verdict on the Six Day War? You must explain your answer carefully.
12 'Israel was successful in the wars of 1948-9, 1956, and 1967 because her enemies were disunited.' Study all the sources and use them to explain whether you agree.
13 Draw up a balance sheet which justifies and condemns the actions of the PLO, PFLP and Black September.

The Yom Kippur War, 1973

Peace was a fragile commodity after 1967 and within six years it was once again shattered. However, this war was different. On 6th October 1973 Egyptian forces crossed the Suez Canal and captured territory in the Sinai desert. Simultaneously the Syrians attacked Israel at the Golan Heights. The two countries had made a secret plan to invade and had attacked on one of Israel's most sacred days – the religious festival of Yom Kippur. This was a national holiday for Israel and they were taken completely by surprise. The startled Israelis were unable to gain air superiority as in 1967 because the Egyptians were able to use the advanced technology of the USSR with surface to air missiles (SAMs). The SAMs were based on the west side of the canal and acted as a shield for the Egyptian forces. There were even portable SAMs which increased the power and confidence of the Egyptians. The Israelis decided to hold off the Egyptians and they concentrated on pushing back the Syrians. By 12th October the Golan Heights had been retaken and the Israelis were able to move forces from the north to the Sinai front. The Egyptians had pushed inland and in doing so moved out of the cover that their SAMs offered. At this point the Israelis were able to crush the Egyptian forces at the Mitla Pass and pushed them back to the Canal. The Israelis then made a most daring counter-attack. They crossed the Suez Canal, captured some of the SAM bases and began to move on Cairo. The Egyptian forces were stranded on the Sinai side of the Canal.

During the fighting, both the USA and the USSR supplied the two sides with arms and military material – once again showing the complex nature of the Middle East conflict. But the Yom Kippur War turned out to be vastly different from previous wars. The difference this time was oil. The

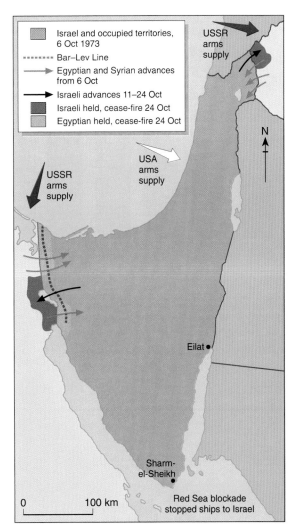

The Yom Kippur War, 1973

Map legend:
- Israel and occupied territories, 6 Oct 1973
- Bar–Lev Line
- Egyptian and Syrian advances from 6 Oct
- Israeli advances 11–24 Oct
- Israeli held, cease-fire 24 Oct
- Egyptian held, cease-fire 24 Oct

USSR arms supply
USSR arms supply
USA arms supply
N
Eilat
Sharm-el-Sheikh
0   100 km
Red Sea blockade stopped ships to Israel

oil producing states of the Arab Gulf were members of OPEC (Organisation of Petroleum Exporting Countries) and they now decided to use oil as an economic weapon against Israel and her western allies. The price of oil was raised by 70% and Saudi Arabia cut her production by 10%. No oil was to be exported to the USA. The threat to the oil supplies of the west made the western politicians realise the enormity of the situation. The economies of western Europe and the USA would be severely disrupted if the War was to last for a long time. Intense diplomacy therefore began in October.

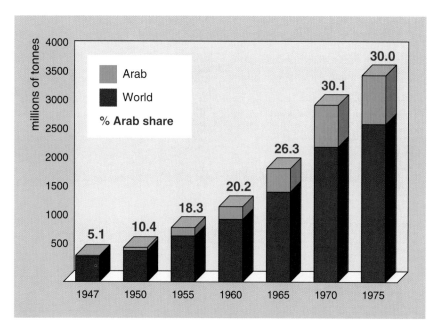

World oil production figures, showing the growing influence of the Middle East

The USA, the USSR and the UN each put pressure on the combatants and a ceasefire was reached on 24th October. It was difficult to see who had won. It was certain that the world would never be the same again.

The rise in oil prices had helped to create inflation and world wide recession, hitting not only the industrialised nations but the developing ones. The war had shown that the Israelis were not invincible and the Arab armies had regained their lost pride. The Israelis could point to some successes because they had pushed both the Syrians and the Egyptians back after their initial advances. Both Israel and Egypt now seemed to realise that there could never be a lasting peace unless each was prepared to make concessions. Within five years these concessions had been made.

14 What were SAMs?
15 Explain how SAMs made a difference to the Yom Kippur War.
16 Divide into groups, each choosing one of the following: USA, USSR, UN, ISRAEL, EGYPT and her ALLIES, WESTERN EUROPE. For each one explain how and why they were involved in the Yom Kippur War and how the War affected them. When you meet to discuss your findings, you should then be able to answer the next question – Was Yom Kippur a war between the Arabs and Israelis?
17 What do you think is meant by the phrase 'the world would never be the same again'?

Ölgespräche
Oil talks   1973

The Arab states use the power of oil to influence the USA and western Europe

The quest for peace

The world was stunned in 1979, when Egypt and Israel signed peace treaties which ended 30 years of hostility. How had such enemies become friends?

After the Yom Kippur War the USA tried hard to re-establish good relations with the Arab world in order to buy Middle Eastern oil again. The US Secretary of State, Henry Kissinger, was able to bring the two sides together and by 1975, Egypt took control of the Suez Canal and permitted Israel to use it. This was quite a breakthrough. However, the main reason behind the two sides coming together in 1977 was economics. Both Israel and Egypt were having to spend huge amounts of money on defence and this diverted cash away from other more needy areas of the nation's life.

President Sadat made the first momentous move when he visited Israel and addressed the Israeli parliament in Jerusalem. Prime Minister Begin addressed the Egyptian parliament the following month. Peace talks began between the two countries in 1978 and when they ran into difficulties, President Carter of the USA offered to act as mediator and invited Sadat and Begin to his holiday retreat at Camp David. Carter expressed his sympathy for the Palestinian Arabs and at the same time was able to express his support for Israel's independence and security. At Camp David, Carter was able to persuade the two sides to agree to a basis for peace:

i A framework for peace in the Middle East – this would give the West Bank and the Gaza Strip full self-government
ii An Israeli-Egyptian peace – Israel would make a phased withdrawal of the Sinai over three years.

The agreements also meant that Egypt would recognise Israel's right to exist. Begin and Sadat won the Nobel Prize for Peace in 1978.

Although the two countries could now exist side by side, the two leaders had to face much internal opposition over Camp David. The Israeli army had to evict forcibly the Jewish settlers in the Sinai and the more right-wing Israelis were opposed to any surrender of territory. Sadat was accused of betraying the Arab cause and many of his allies refused to have anything to do with him. In 1981, Sadat was assassinated by Muslim extremists. It seemed that peace was unattainable.

President Carter of the USA flanked by President Sadat of Egypt and Prime Minister Begin of Israel at Camp David in 1978

A cartoon from the Saudi Arabian newspaper *Al-Riyadh* in 1980

Lebanon – the conflict takes on another dimension

Just as peace was secured in the south, Israel faced problems on her northern borders. The PLO had established its headquarters in the Lebanon and carried out terrorist activities against Israel from there. In 1978, Israel invaded southern Lebanon in order to secure the border. Israeli troops went as far as the Litani river but withdrew when UN forces were called in to keep the peace. The situation did not improve and a second invasion followed in 1982, planned by Minister of Defence, Ariel Sharon.

My intention is to push back the terrorists to a distance of 40 kilometres to the north so that all our civilians in the region of Galilee will be set free of the permanent threat on their lives.

Prime Minister Begin in 1982.

The 40km target was soon reached but the Israeli forces kept on pressing north. They were determined to crush the PLO once and for all. The Israeli tactics meant that Syrian aircraft were shot down and civilians in the Lebanon were bombed. The major cities of Tyre and Sidon were left in ruins and the Lebanese capital, Beirut, was besieged. For ten weeks the Israelis shelled Beirut killing not only members of the PLO but ordinary innocent citizens of Beirut. The world watched the devastation on television every day. Sympathy for Israel began to diminish. The Israelis used phosphorous shells which were outlawed by the UN.

Dr Shamaa found that the two five day old twins had already died. But they were still on fire. 'I had to take the babies and put them in buckets of water to put out the flames', she said. 'When I took them to the mortuary they smouldered for hours.

An extract from an article in *The Times* by Robert Fisk written in July 1982.

Eventually a ceasefire was made and an international force (American, French and Italian) took the PLO survivors and the shattered remnants were sent to surrounding Arab states. Worse was to come when some of the Lebanese Christian Militia (allies of Israel) massacred 1,000 Palestinians in the refugee camps of Sabra and Chatila.

...the victims were men, women, and children of all ages, from the very old to the very young, even babies in arms. They were killed in every possible way. The lucky ones were shot, singly or in groups. Others were strangled or had their throats slit. They were mutilated, before or after death; genitals and breasts were sliced off...

Michael Jansen a war journalist, writing in 1982 about the massacre.

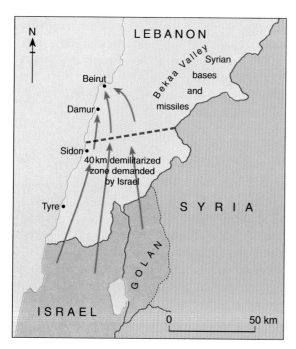

The actions of the Israelis had lost them a great deal of support and there was a growing acceptance around the world that the Palestinians had a right to a homeland which could be carved out of the West Bank and perhaps the Gaza Strip. Israel continued to resist these international pressures.

The Israeli invasion of Lebanon in 1982

The Intifada

Even within the territories that they controlled, the Israelis found that 'control' was not always possible. In 1988, many young Palestinians in the Gaza Strip and the West Bank began to defy Israeli authority. They demanded the withdrawal of Israeli troops from Arab cities and refugee camps and wanted free elections. Civil disobedience spread and the defiance of the Palestinians took on a special name – the Intifada. There was no cooperation with the Israelis and demonstrations usually ended with the Israelis using extreme force against the demonstrators. As usual the actions were caught on television cameras and the Israelis lost the propaganda war.

An Israeli soldier fires on stone throwing Palestinian youths in the Gaza Strip during the Intifada

In 1992, Yitzhak Rabin became the Prime Minister of Israel and he was determined to secure lasting peace and tranquillity. He had been a hardliner but realised that there must come a time when a compromise must be struck. In a changing world after the Gulf War, and when the mighty Soviet Union had disintegrated, Rabin and some of his advisers felt that they could make the compromise.

Arafat himself needed to produce results. There was much internal squabbling in the PLO and Arafat's position as leader was in question. The USA did much to bring the two sides together after the Gulf War and Secretary of State, Warren Christopher, made several visits to the Middle East. Against this background, there were secret talks held in Norway between Israel and the PLO. Remarkable progress was made and both sides made concessions. The PLO recognised Israel. Israel granted two Palestinian cities self-rule: Gaza and Jericho. By May 1994, the Israelis had pulled out of these two cities and the first step toward a Palestinian state had been made. There are now moves to give the Palestinians control over other parts of the West Bank, which means ending further

Israeli settlement there. This also naturally means that existing Israeli settlements will have to be destroyed and the right-wingers in Israel do not want this.

The general peace process gathered momentum in 1994, and in October, Jordan and Israel signed a peace treaty ending more than 40 years of hostility. Negotiations then began between Syria and Israel to try and solve the issue of the Golan Heights, but this has proved more difficult to solve. The peace accord was hailed in many quarters as astonishing yet there are still many who oppose it. Arafat has had to face extreme criticism for 'selling out' and Hamas (Islamic Resistance Movement) and Hezbollah (a Fundamentalist Islamic group) have been most forthright in their rejection of the accord. They have continued to wage a

▲ The wreckage of an Israeli bus destroyed by a Palestinian suicide bomber in February 1996

▲ President Clinton of the USA watches the signing of the historic Middle East Peace Accord between Yasser Arafat of the PLO and Yitzhak Rabin of Israel. Behind them stand King Hussein of Jordan and President Mubarek of Egypt.

guerrilla war against Israel and in early 1996 used the tactic of suicide bombers against civilians. Hamas even boycotted the Palestinian elections held in 1996.

Israel has continued to respond to guerrilla activities in her customary way – swift retaliatory attacks. Leaders of Hamas have been murdered by Israeli agents. Israeli helicopter gunships even attacked Hezbollah bases in Beirut in early 1996.

▲ The funeral of Yitzhak Rabin

▲ Israeli Cobra helicopters attack Hezbollah bases in the Lebanon in revenge for terrorist attacks like the one on the left

Within Israel opposition has taken an extreme form. Prime Minister Rabin was assassinated by Yigal Amir a right-wing opponent of the peace accord. There are still many in Israel who believe that there should never be any dealings with the PLO and the peace accord has sharpened divisions in Israeli society.

It is difficult to make predictions about the Middle East. World history has been so unpredictable in the 1980s and 1990s – the collapse of the Soviet Union, the reunification of Germany, and the ending of Apartheid in South Africa are events that few people could have forseen. The peace accord between Israel and the PLO was equally unexpected but the peace is very fragile. The extremists in Israel and among the Arabs could cause problems in the future.

18 Explain how Egypt and Israel made peace in 1979.
19 How could Israel justify the invasions of Lebanon in 1978 and 1982?
20 Look again at the section on the invasion of Lebanon. Explain why the Israelis lost international support after 1982.
21 What is meant by the term 'Intifada'?
22 Why had circumstances changed so much for both Israel and the PLO in the early 1990s?
23 Make a list to show why i Arafat's enemies opposed the peace accord ii Israeli right-wingers did not wish to compromise with the PLO.
24 Find out more about Hamas and Hezbollah.
25 How did the assassination of Rabin affect Israel and the peace process?

15 The impact of the two world wars on Britain

It may seem strange to have a chapter about the ways in which the two world wars affected a country, but it is important to understand how international relations could affect the lives of ordinary people. This chapter is a special case study of Britain at war.

Britain and the First World War

When Britain declared war on Germany on 4th August 1914 there was a tremendous rush by thousands of young men to enlist in the British army. There was a general feeling that the War would be a 'lark' and would be over by Christmas. Many young men saw the War as an opportunity to go abroad and see something of the world, and for some it was the chance to secure paid employment. There was no real understanding of the seriousness of the conflict - most people relied on the local newspapers for information and the local press did not have the means to cover international events.

Recruitment

Look at Sources A and B which show the number of men who were recruited into the army during the War.

1914	1.18 million
1915	1.28 million
1916	1.19 million
1917	0.82 million
1918	0.49 million

August 1914	298,923
September	462,901
October	136,811
November	169,862
December	117,860
January 1915	156,290
February	87,896
March	113,907
April	119,087
May	135,263
June	114,679
July	95,413
August	95,980
September	71,617
October	113,285
November	121,793
December	55,152
Total	**2,446,719**
January 1916–November 1918	2,504,183
August 1914–November 1918	4,970,902
Strength of British Army, Territorials and reserves, August 1918	733,514
Total serving in British army, 1914–18	**5,704,416**

As the Sources show, there were large numbers enlisting at the beginning of the War. As mentioned above, this was understandable but there were other reasons why recruitment figures were high. War was given a high status in the public schools - for instance, Winchester School sent no students to Oxford University in 1915. In the years before 1914, Germany had been portrayed in the press and novels as a potential enemy because it challenged Britain's industrial, imperial, and naval supremacy. Moreover, the stories emerging from Belgium in the early days of the War -

of Germans killing babies, assaulting nurses, and torturing soldiers - helped to feed the hatred towards the 'barbaric Hun'. However, recruitment did slow down and the momentum had to be maintained by a campaign of posters.

A British cartoon called 'The Evil Hun'

In 1916 Britain introduced conscription when the *Military Services Act* was passed. Firstly, all single men between the ages of 18-41 were to be called up and then in May all married men between those ages were conscripted. Conscription was introduced because there was a shortage of volunteers and in some cases those who did volunteer were skilled workers who could not be replaced. One historian, Arthur Marwick, writing about conscription has said that 'It marked the lowering of the remaining barriers of prejudice to the full scale employment of women.'

Conscription was not universally welcomed. A No Conscription Fellowship had been in existence since December 1914 and several Liberal and Labour MPs voted against the *Military Services Act*. There were many pacifists in Britain during the War, and they challenged the idea of compulsory military service. These men were called conscientious objectors. They were allowed exemption from combat service provided that they did such work as ambulance driving or stretcher bearing. The conscientious objectors were nicknamed 'conchies', which was a term of abuse, and they had to appear before a tribunal (a special court) which would decide if their case was valid.

There were about 16,000 conchies in the War and most did some kind of non-combatant service. Those who refused to have anything at all to do with the War were imprisoned. These were the 'absolutists'. About 6,000 went to prison and some eventually did some kind of war work. There were about 1,500 absolutists who refused to deviate from their principles and they endured terrible conditions in prison. 71 conchies died in prison and 31 went mad.

We were placed in handcuffs and locked in the cells and tied up for two hours in the afternoon. We were tied up by the wrists to horizontal ropes about five feet off the ground with our arms outstretched and our feet tied together. Then we were confined to cells for three days on 'punishment diet'- four biscuits a day and water... Rats were frequent visitors to the cells. There were twelve prisoners in a cell which measured 11' 9" by 11' 3".

This is part of an account of the treatment of Howard Martin, a conchie, in jail.

1   Explain what is meant by: recruitment, conscription, conchie, *Military Services Act*, absolutist, tribunal.
2   Why did young British men rush to join the army in 1914?
3   What can you learn from Sources A and B about recruitment in the First World War?
4   There were only 16,000 conscientious objectors. Can you explain why the Government treated them so badly?

Government methods of control

Within days of the outbreak of the War, the Government passed the *Defence of the Realm Act*. This became known as DORA and several were enacted during the years 1914-1918.

[the Cabinet can] issue regulations as to the powers and duties of the Admiralty and Army Council, and other persons acting on their behalf, for securing the public safety and defence of the realm.

An extract from the first DORA in 1914.

One of the most well-known actions of DORA was the introduction of limited opening times for public houses. DORA restricted pub opening times to 2.5 hours in the middle of the day and 2 or 3 hours in the evening. The alcohol content of beer was also gradually reduced during the War.

We are fighting Germany, Austria, and Drink, and, as far as I can see, the greatest of these deadly foes is Drink.

Lloyd George speaking in the spring of 1915.

DORA meant that the Government had very wide powers, and by 1918 it controlled the coal mines, and the railways. There was censorship of the press, propaganda, and rationing, ensuring that the lives of all citizens were at some time touched by the Government.

Censorship and propaganda

In the first few months of the War there was no need for the Government to use propaganda. The initial mood of patriotism meant that the local and national press were able to write many human interest stories. The national press also printed rumours and stories of atrocities, and, when the Cunard liner *Lusitania* was sunk with the loss of 1201 men, women and children, the press highlighted the savagery of the Germans. The fact that the *Lusitania* was carrying shells and cartridges was never made known to the British public. As the war progressed and the expectations of an early end to it died away, the press was censored. DORA permitted this.

Eventually, all Government propaganda was controlled by a Department of Information (this became a Ministry in 1918). The cinema division of the department became very important because large numbers of British civilians visited the 3000 cinemas each week. After 1916, the need to win the support of the people became more crucial. By controlling the press and films, the Government was able to control what people thought and was, therefore, able to minimise public criticism of their handling of the War.

An official film of the Battle of the Somme could devote loving detail to the massive artillery bombardment, the awesome mine explosion at Beaumont Hamel, and the seemingly inexhaustible build-up of supplies which preceded the offensive, but told little of the hideous cost of the fighting. Corpses, in this case, were conspicuous by their absence.

From *British Society 1914-45* by J Stevenson.

Official reports, press coverage and film material always tended to play up the optimistic side of the War and to hide as much as possible of its true horror.

From *British Society 1914-45* by J Stevenson.

5   What is meant by: DORA, censorship, propaganda?
6   Why did the Government consider it necessary to restrict the opening times of public houses?
7   Can you suggest reasons why the British Government did not publish the details of the *Lusitania*'s cargo?
8   Study Sources G and H. Why was it necessary to control the flow of news to the public?
9   Do you think that a Government has the right to restrict the flow of information to its people?

Total war - the impact on British civilians

The First World War became a total war which means that all people were affected by it. In December 1914, three German cruisers shelled Scarborough, Whitby and Hartlepool. There were 19 people killed and 80 wounded at Scarborough during a forty-five minute attack. It was said at the time that the attack led to a great surge of volunteers joining the army.

Civilians came under further attacks from German Zeppelins (airships) and later bombers. The Zeppelin raids were unco-ordinated and in June 1917, raids in London killed 162 and injured 432. When further raids occurred in the autumn of that year, Londoners sheltered in the Underground and some even moved to Bath and Brighton.

This is one of the houses in Scarborough shelled by German ships. Five people died in this house.

This drawing was used on the front cover of *The Sphere* in June 1917. It shows injured children being taken from a London school which had been bombed, and was designed to provoke outrage in the reader. In the Second World War, scenes such as this were censored by the Government (see page 211).

(see page 211).

January 1915–April 1918
(51 Zeppelin raids) 1,913 casualties
December 1914–June 1918
(57 aeroplane raids) 2,907 casualties
Total civilian casualties in the war
5,611 (1,570 dead of which 1,413 were killed in air attacks).

The town which suffered greatest from aerial attacks was Dover. However, the bombing raids never really depressed the population, indeed, they led to a demand for more energetic retaliation from the Government.

Food shortages and rationing

If the War was brought to the mainland by the aeroplane, then the naval conflict brought it to the meal table. Britain needed to import large amounts of food to sustain its population. By the autumn of 1916, German U-boats (submarines) were beginning to sink large numbers of British merchant vessels and in April 1917 sank 866,000 tons. This represented one quarter of the merchant shipping left at Britain's disposal. These April losses meant that Britain had only four days' supply of sugar and 9 weeks' supply of wheat remaining.

The U-boat problem was eventually solved when the convoy system was adopted. Using a convoy meant that the merchant vessels would be protected by accompanying destroyers which would act as a screen for torpedoes and would also engage in anti-submarine warfare. Convoys protected 24,604 vessels in 1917 and only 147 were sunk. (During this same period, the Germans lost 65 out of 139 operational U-boats.)

Lloyd George, the Prime Minister, tried to solve the problem of food shortages by creating the job of Food Controller and he encouraged the Board of Agriculture to introduce methods to increase domestic food production. By 1918, wheat production had risen by 1million tons and potatoes by 1.5million tons. (Agriculture had already been helped by the introduction of British summertime in 1916. This meant that all British clocks were advanced by one hour during the summer, thus giving longer and lighter evenings for farmers.) There was voluntary rationing but there was also some hoarding of food which still resulted in food shortages. In early 1918 the Government introduced compulsory rationing on essential foodstuffs such as: meat, tea, sugar, and butter.

10 What is meant by: total war, Zeppelin, convoy system?
11 Can you suggest reasons why the German attack on Scarborough led to a rise in British recruits?
12 What methods did the British Government use to combat food shortages?

The role of women in the First World War

The First World War was the first war that involved huge numbers of British civilians and its impact on women was especially great. By the end of the War, women had been granted the vote (albeit on a restricted basis) and the number in employment had increased by 50% to almost 5million.

Female employment 1914–18

	July 1914	July 1918
Metal industries	170,000	+424,000
Chemicals	40,000	+64,000
Textiles	863,000	-36,000
Clothing trades	612,000	-44,000
Food/drink/tobacco	196,000	+39,000
Government	2,000	+233,000
Agriculture	80,000	+33,000
Transport	18,200	+99,000
Banking/commerce	505,500	+429,000
Civil service	66,000	+168,000
Local government	196,200	+30,000

There were many women in employment before 1914, but they had the lowest paid jobs and they did not receive equal pay. When the War began, many female domestic workers were sacked and female workers in luxury jobs, such as dressmaking and jewellery, were laid off. Trade unions feared that, in the absence of the men who were volunteering for the armed forces, the employment of women would lead to reduced wages and diminished job security. Therefore many unions were unwilling to see women replace men and it was only after special talks with the Government in 1915 that unions began to accept women. It was agreed that returning soldiers would be given their jobs back at the end of the War.

There were strict limits not to what women were capable of, but to what trade unions and employers would tolerate. By the end of the War, five-sixths of women were probably doing 'women's' work.

From *Women and the women's movement* by M Pugh.

The attitude of most male workers to their female colleagues was quite hostile. The opposition to female employment and involvement in the War can be gauged by the famous suffragette march in July 1915, when 20,000 led by the Pankhursts demanded the right to work in the war industries. It was the munitions crisis and the introduction of conscription which brought about the widescale employment of women.

Women workers making artillery shells in a munitions factory.

Not only did women work in industry and agriculture (although there were only 33,000 extra female agricultural workers by 1918), but they were also able to work as nurses and join branches of the armed forces. The Women's Army Auxiliary Corps was formed in January 1917, the Women's Royal Naval Service in November 1917 and the Women's Royal Air Force in April 1918. Most of the jobs in these services were of a clerical and domestic nature although some women did become drivers and fitters. There were the usual disparaging comments about women in uniform - the WRAFs were called the 'penguins' because they did not fly.

Two of the additional women workers who worked in agriculture during the First World War.

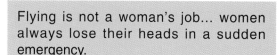

Flying is not a woman's job... women always lose their heads in a sudden emergency.

From the *Daily Express*, June 1918.

For many women the war was an enjoyable experience. They took pride in their work and were able to show that they could easily develop the skills that were said to be the preserve of men. The war also brought better wages for many:

- Industrial jobs in 1914 earnt 63p per week
- Industrial jobs in 1918 earnt £1.25 per week
- Munitions jobs in 1918 earnt £2 per week.
  (On average, women were paid half the rate of men during the War.)

Women over the age of thirty were given the vote in 1918 and many people felt that they had won greater equality. It was said that women had won the War, but it had been noticeable in some newspapers in 1918 that attitudes to women were becoming increasingly negative. There were many articles which began to praise the traditional role of women as the mother and housewife. The number of women workers fell in 1919, particularly in the munitions industry, and many were forced to seek jobs in domestic service.

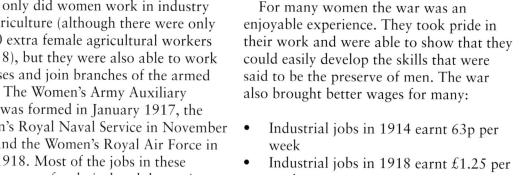

The aftermath of the First World War saw only a minimal expansion in the range of work open to women. It saw the reassertion of traditional values and also the continued use of women as a reserve of labour in low paid jobs.

From *War and society in Britain* by R Pope.

The War did bring some changes for women, but most were short-lived and it took another world war and then several Acts of Parliament before women could begin to claim that they had equal status with men.

13 Essay: Study Sources I, J and K. Use the evidence of these sources, the information contained in this section and your own knowledge to explain whether the First World War brought lasting changes in the role played by women in British society.

When the First World War finished, the people of Britain praised the Prime Minister, Lloyd George, as the man who had steered the nation to victory. He had solved the munitions crisis, tackled the food shortages, and promised 'homes fit for heroes' for the returning soldiers. Unfortunately, the promises were not kept. Almost every family in Britain had been touched by the War. Britain suffered 750,000 soldiers killed, and villages, towns and cities soon began to erect war memorials to their dead. In 1918, the politicians and the people looked to the past and not to the future as they did in 1945.

Lloyd George's wartime Cabinet. Lloyd George himself is the fourth from the right in the front row.

Britain and the Second World War

It had been hoped that the war of 1914-1918 would be the 'war to end wars'. It was not. Britain found herself at war with Germany again in 1939, and the memory of the 'Great War' was still fresh in everyone's mind. There were hopes that a negotiated peace could be made, but this time there were no wild optimistic claims that the War would be over by Christmas. The Second World War was another total war and, because of the advances in military technology, it was difficult for anyone to escape its effects. Fortunately, the combined death toll of British armed forces and civilians was lower than in the First World War but the impact on Britain and her people was perhaps greater. Millions of women and children were evacuated to rural areas, hundreds of thousands of homes were destroyed, and rationing began as early as January 1940 and continued on some items into the 1950s. In order to win the War, the Government had to build on the experiences of 1914-18 and adapt to changing methods of warfare.

Evacuation

One of the most important features of the Second World War for British people was evacuation. Politicians and military experts in the 1930s expected the bomber to play a significant part in any future war. The bombing of Guernica in the Spanish Civil War and the attack on Shanghai by Japan seemed to confirm these expectations. The British experts estimated that in any

European war, Britain could anticipate at least 600,000 deaths from air-raids in about 60 days. It was thought that such a death toll would lead to chaos and immediate surrender. Therefore, plans for evacuating children were made and as the crisis of August 1939 developed, they were carried out. About 3.5 million people were moved to 'safe' areas during the period from late June to early September 1939.

L ▼

The fear of poison gas bombing attacks by the Germans, led the British Government to issue gas masks to the entire civilian population at the start of the War

▼

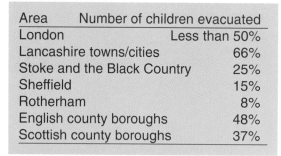

Area	Number of children evacuated
London	Less than 50%
Lancashire towns/cities	66%
Stoke and the Black Country	25%
Sheffield	15%
Rotherham	8%
English county boroughs	48%
Scottish county boroughs	37%

▲ Children who were evacuated from the cities had labels attached to them to say who they were

However, there were still many children left in urban areas by the end of September as many parents did not wish to let their children go. Also, the organisation of evacuation had in some cases been poor. There were problems with transport, and methods of billeting (placing the children with 'new' families) were inadequate and there was often social mis-matching. Many of the people receiving the children (and their mothers) were astonished to discover that they had lice, fleas, scabies, and impetigo. Moreover, they were disgusted at their manners, their coarse speech, and their eating and toilet habits. The Government had to give thousands of pounds to local authorities to ensure that the very poorest of children were clothed adequately.

By the beginning of 1940, nearly 700,000 evacuees had returned home, for a variety of reasons. There had been no air-raids, the children suffered from homesickness, there was dissatisfaction with the foster homes, and parents found it difficult to send money to the foster homes to support their children.

Many evacuee stories are heart-rending, ranging from homesickness, protracted coldness or indifference towards vulnerable little children by those who reluctantly took them in, to downright physical or mental cruelty and even child-abuse.

From *Never again* by P Hennessy, 1992.

There were some children, many from homes and orphanages, who were said to be impossible to place, and special hostels were created for them.

...they were unbilletable because they were socially unacceptable - bed-wetters, potential criminals or medical liabilities with severe eczema, severe asthma.

From *No time to say goodbye* by B Wicks, 1988.

There was a second wave of evacuation in mid-1940 when 100,000 children were moved from London - some for the second time. By mid-July 1940 half of the population of East Anglia's coast towns and about 40% of Kentish coast towns had left for 'safer parts' of Britain. (The evacuation of children to the Dominions such as Canada was stopped when the *SS City of Benares* was sunk with 73 children on board.)

There were many evacuees who enjoyed their time during the war. However, there were as many who said that evacuation scarred them for life (see Sources O and P).

I trace my own lifelong interest in the environment, natural history, hill-walking and outdoor activities to the initial shock of total immersion in a rural environment. It is the only part of my childhood that I remember with any clarity.

From *No time to say goodbye* by B Wicks, 1988.

I'm still searching for my sister who was evacuated with me over 40 years ago. I have not seen her since. I am now a mother and grandmother and shudder when I think of my evacuation. I thank God none of my children will have to go through what I went through. How I survived to tell this tale I shall never know.

From *No time to say goodbye* by B Wicks, 1988.

Evacuation revealed to the Government and the middle classes that there was still great poverty in Britain. The glaring inequalities in society which evacuation showed made large numbers of politicians determined to rid Britain of poverty when the War was over.

I never knew that such conditions existed, and I feel ashamed of having been so ignorant of my neighbours. For the rest of my life I mean to make amends by helping such people to cleaner and healthier lives.

Prime Minister Neville Chamberlain, writing in September 1939. This was from a politician who had been Minister of Health from 1924-29.

14 What is meant by evacuation and billeting?
15 Why were women and children evacuated at the beginning of the War.
16 What can you learn about evacuation from Source L.
17 What is meant by social mis-matching?
18 Why did many evacuees return home by mid-1940?
19 Study all of the sources. Using the evidence of these sources and your own knowledge, explain whether the Government should have carried out the policy of evacuation.

If evacuation was the first major impact on the civilian population before the fighting began in earnest, then **rationing** was perhaps the second. There was the experience of the First World War and the Government was determined to ensure that there would be a fair provision for all. Rationing began in January 1940 and Lord Woolton, as Minister of Food, was to supervise the rationing system. With the Ministry of Agriculture, there was a tremendous propaganda campaign to encourage people to save food, cook wisely and save kitchen waste for pigs and chickens. There was a 'Dig for Victory' campaign which wanted people to turn their lawns and any spare ground into vegetable gardens. Some councils even dug up grass verges and grew vegetables!

Rationing was thought of as a necessary restriction during the War, and people happily turned the queue into a national institution. Memories of wartime shortages in the First World War were associated with unfair distribution and with profiteering. The Second World War was not to be like that.

Quoted in *Never again* by P Hennessy, 1993.

The moat of the Tower of London was turned into a vegetable garden during the War

There was still a 'black market' (illegal trade in rationed goods) for some items, but on the whole a sense of fairness existed throughout the War.

20 What is meant by: rationing, black market, and Dig for Victory?
21 Look at the photograph of the grounds of the Tower of London. In what ways could this photograph been used for propaganda purposes?

The Blitz

These white rings are being painted onto a lamp post to help drivers during the 'blackout'

Evacuation was designed to minimise the expected huge civilian casualties when the bombing raids began. Other plans included the use of the 'blackout' which banned the use of any lights that enemy aeroplanes might be able to see and thus use as targets. The 'blackout' meant that car and street lights were not used and houses had to ensure that all windows did not allow light to escape. The 'blackout' remained in operation until late 1944. The Air Raid Precautions organisation was set up to co-ordinate the emergency services in an attack and to ensure that the 'blackout' was maintained. Air-raid shelters were built and the Government provided more than 2,250,000 Anderson shelters for construction in people's backyards. Most cities did have anti-aircraft guns, but these rarely shot down night bombers although they did create a feeling that there was some defence.

Britain experienced devastating air-raids which killed more than 60,000 civilians. This was far fewer than had been expected. German bombers did not attack British cities until 7 September 1940 when London suffered its first raid. London was then bombed for 76 consecutive days. It was May 1941 before the 'Blitz' on British cities came to a temporary halt.

A badly damaged building in London collapses during an air raid

By mid-1941, more than 2million houses had been damaged or destroyed, 60% of them in London. Fatalities amongst civilians amounted to almost 43,000. (It is interesting to note that it was 1942 before the number of soldiers killed exceeded the number of civilians.) The raids on Britain's industrial cities and ports began on 14th November 1940 and one city which was subjected to a most intense attack was Coventry. In one ten hour raid, 554 people were killed, 865 were injured and 33% of the city's homes were destroyed.

There were more signs of hysteria and terror observed than during the whole of the previous two months together in all areas. Women were seen to cry, to scream, to tremble all over, to faint in the street, to attack a fireman and so on. The overwhelmingly dominant feeling on the Friday was that of utter helplessness. The tremendous impact of the previous night had left people practically speechless in many cases... This helplessness accelerated depression. On Friday evening there were signs of panic as darkness approached. If there had been another attack, the effects in terms of human behaviour would have been more striking and terrible.

From *Living through the Blitz* by T Harisson. This is taken from the mass observation studies and is describing Coventry the day after the raid mentioned in the text.

The civilian population in some cases felt let down by the Government for failing to provide adequate defences. There was anger and sometimes hysteria and in Portsmouth there was even looting. The people of London sought shelter in the Underground but at first this was not allowed. On most nights in the London 'Blitz' there could be as many as 200,000 people sheltering in the tube.

▲ Londoners sheltering in the Underground from an air raid during the Blitz

People would rush to get to the tubes, almost knock you over to get to the escalator... We lived like rats underground... People spread newspapers on the floor or left bundles to show where it was their territory... Sometimes you'd get people squaring up, and fights.

From *Blitz the civilian war* by J Waller and M Vaughan-Rees, 1990.

In any office such as ours, besides the day's work we would go on fire-watching at night... five or six people, and then doss down in great discomfort in one of the offices... And then the visible signs of any kind of difference in class disappeared.

Quoted in *Now the War is over* by P Addison, 1985.

People... met in the air-raid shelters, in the tubes at night or they queued for spam or whatever it was they could get hold of, one egg a week. Everybody lost their inhibitions about talking to their next door neighbours. When the raids were over they used to celebrate in the early morning and this was the spirit that I think a lot of people hoped would continue after the War.

Quoted in *Now the War is over* by P Addison, 1985.

There was an air-raid somewhere almost every night of the War. In 1942, the raids changed somewhat. The Germans set out to destroy those cities which were amongst the oldest and most beautiful in Britain such as Bath, Norwich, Exeter, York, and Canterbury. Many people in these cities copied what had happened in other places - they would leave the city in late afternoon and return early next morning. This had become known as 'trekking'.

The final phase of the aerial assault on Britain came in 1944 and lasted until March 1945. For many the raids during this period were even worse than the 'Blitz'. The raids were carried out by V1s (flying bombs or doodlebugs or pilotless planes) and later V2s (rockets). London again took the brunt of the 8,000 V1s and 1,000 V2s. These attacks killed about 9,000 and injured almost 35,000.

This poster is encouraging women to take an active role in the Air Raid Precautions (ARP) service

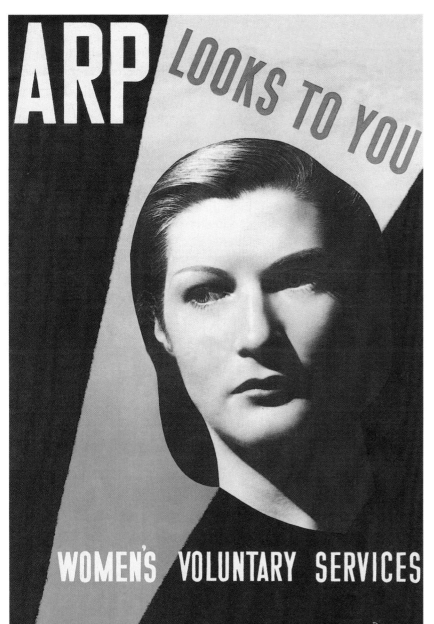

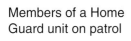

A V1 flying bomb about to land on London in 1944

The Home Guard

In a radio broadcast made on 14th May 1940, Anthony Eden, Foreign Secretary, asked for males between the ages of 15 and 65 who were not involved in military activity to enlist in a new defence force, the Local Defence Volunteers. Within 24 hours, more than a quarter of a million men had offered their services and within six weeks the number had risen to 1.5 million. The LDV was renamed the Home Guard in July and was often jokingly referred to as 'Dad's army'. (The BBC TV comedy series is testimony to this.)

The Home Guard was to help defend Britain against invasion, but at first it would have been unable to repel any invader. In the early days, the uniform was an armband. As the War went on, they were not only better equipped but better trained and would have been able to support the regular forces. The Home Guard patrolled the coast and watched for any aerial invasion. They also secured strategic locations such as telephone exchanges and bridges. Moreover, they allowed the regular army to concentrate on more important issues.

22 What is meant by : Blitz, Anderson shelter, blackout, and trekking?

23 Study all of the sources. The writer of Source V believed that the Blitz created a spirit of unity and friendliness. Use these sources and your own knowledge to explain whether you agree with this view about the Blitz.

24 Find out if there is a video of a 'Dad's army' programme in school. Do you think that such a programme is of any use to anyone who is studying the Home Guard?

Members of a Home Guard unit on patrol

The role of women in the Second World War

> How astonishing it is, when the country is in a muddle, how women are regarded as very important. This is not the first time. I did a man's job in the last war and enjoyed it. Women should get on with the job, do it well, and then ask for the good conditions they are entitled to.

From an article in the *West Ham Gazette* in 1941. It was written by a female member of the Council.

German successes in 1939 and 1940 meant that the Second World War for Britain was rather different than the conflict of 1914-18. The frontline was Britain itself and because of this there was a greater pressure on the part played by women especially in the uniformed services.

Members of the ATS changing a lorry wheel

At the height of the War, there were about 7 million women employed in industry, civil defence and the armed forces. There were, however, still almost 9 million who remained full-time housewives. Many women did not wish to participate in the evacuation schemes, and even if they wanted to work, there were not enough nurseries (for which they had to pay).

At the beginning of 1941, it was estimated that industry needed about 2 million extra workers. Women had volunteered only slowly and it was decided that female conscription would be introduced to meet the shortfall. The Government was rather slow in accepting the fact that many women with children only wanted part-time employment and

Strength of Women's Auxiliary Services in thousands

	Total	Women's Royal Naval Service	Auxiliary Territorial Service	Women's Auxiliary Air Force	Nursing Services
1939 Dec	43.1	3.4	23.9	8.8	7.0
1940 Dec	75.1	10.0	36.4	20.5	8.2
1941 Dec	216.0	21.6	85.1	98.4	10.9
1942 Dec	400.6	39.3	180.7	166.0	14.6
1943 Dec	467.5	64.8	207.5	176.8	18.4
1944 Dec	457.1	73.4	196.4	166.2	21.1
1945 June	437.2	72.0	190.8	153.0	21.4

Female employment 1939–1945

	1939	1943
Transport	5%	20%
Local government	17%	46%
Metal manufacturing	6%	22%
Engineering	10%	34%

1.5 million more women were working in industry in 1943 than in 1939

this was why many had been reluctant to offer themselves for jobs.

Married women found the strains of war rather difficult to bear - raising children whose fathers were in the army, the air-raids, rationing, and general disruptions all served to lead to stress. The Government's propaganda machine targetted women remorselessly. There were countless posters aimed at women to evacuate children, save fuel and ensure that food was not only used wisely but sparingly.

A Government propaganda poster

MOTHERS
Send them out of London

Give them a chance of greater safety and health

I'm going home to do an evening's cleaning. First I've got to do my shopping on the way home. I have to queue for it. My little boys are in school all day. They have their dinners there. I call for them at six o'clock. But I have to get the meal ready, and there's always some washing and mending to do every night.

A woman speaking in 1941 describes her evening routine at home after working in a factory all day.

Food is a weapon of war, don't waste it. You women at home are winning the War as much as your menfolk in the services. You have withstood the Blitz, economised and saved; now here is one more way to help and it's up to you. We must eat more potatoes. The Government has grown large crops specially because potatoes are a healthy food and because they save shipping space.

From a leaflet produced by the Ministry of Food in 1941.

...it was in fact the ordinary housewife who was decisive. She could have lost the War in any week. Struggling to feed and clothe her family amid rations and coupons - if she had once revolted the whole system would have become unworkable.

From a history text book written in the 1970s.

Female employment did fall after the end of the War and many women were happy to give up their jobs, but more did survive in the workforce than after 1918. Surveys in the War did actually show that most women wanted to return to or embark on domestic life when hostilities ceased.

25 Study Source X. In what ways does Source X help you understand the problems faced by women during the Second World War?

26 Study all of the sources. Source Z states that women's most important role was that of housewife in the War. Use the sources and your own knowledge to explain whether you agree with this view.

Censorship and propaganda

Just as in the First World War, the Government was concerned that no information should be published which might affect the war effort and which also might be of use to the enemy. The Ministry of Information played an important role in this and relations between the press and the Government were nearly always harmonious. News of air-raids was generally printed on the second day - only when it had become certain that the Germans knew where they had hit.

However, this war was rather different for the British people because of technological developments in communications. During the War, the wireless (radio) and the cinema came into their own.

	radio licences	population able to listen
1937	8.48 million	68.5%
1942	9.02 million	not available
1946	10.77 million	not available

38 pupils were killed when their school in South London was bombed in 1943. This photograph of the children wrapped up in body bags, was censored by the Government during the War, as it was felt to be demoralising.

As you have seen from posters earlier in the chapter, the Government knew the power of political advertising and there were posters everywhere. The posters covered every conceivable aspect of the war effort and to some degree the messages did get through.

The people were kept informed of the events in the War by the radio and the news readers of the time became quite famous - Alvar Lidell, Frank Phillips, and Wilfred Pickles (Pickles caused something of a stir because of his broad Yorkshire accent). Above all, the Prime Minister, Winston Churchill, used the radio to speak to the nation in order to maintain and foster the patriotic spirit. There were many radio programmes which kept spirits high, the most famous of which was ITMA (It's that man again).

People in a pub in 1941 gather round the radio to hear one of Churchill's radio broadcasts to the nation

Despite the War, people also continued to visit the cinema in increasing numbers. It was estimated that most people under 40 saw at least 50 feature films per year during the War. There were many documentaries which tended to be rather propagandistic. One of the best documentaries was *Fires were started*, which looked at the Blitz. Some feature films were made at the instigation of the Government, e.g. *Millions like us* which was about women working in the munitions industry. One of the most famous films made during the War was *Henry V* which was released in 1944 and it can be seen as a stirring patriotic film. Many people saw it at the time of the D-day invasion.

Cinema attendances	millions
1938	987
1942	1494
1946	1635

27 Essay:
Explain why the radio and the cinema were important to the British Government during the Second World War.

Winston Churchill

The hero of the First World War was Lloyd George. There can be little doubt that the hero of the Second World War was Winston Churchill. Much has been written about this man and you can complete your own research about him as war leader. He took over as Prime Minister on 10th May 1940 at a time of crisis just as Hitler's forces were smashing their way through the Low Countries. Initially, he was not liked by his own party, the Conservatives, but more importantly he was liked by the British people. His speeches and radio addresses (though not all were made by him) helped to unite the country in the dark years of 1940-1942. Churchill became the symbol of the person who would not surrender and this spirit was passed to the people.

He chose wisely when selecting his ministers (from both major parties) and was eventually able to build a Grand Alliance against Hitler.

This Ministry of Information propaganda poster uses the personal influence of Churchill to unite the British people

Published in 1940, this cartoon is entitled 'All behind you Winston'

Glossary

Abdicate: To give up the Throne, or other position of leadership.

Alliance: One or more countries joined together for defence purposes.

Allies: The members of an alliance.

Anschluss: A German word for 'union.' Specifically, union between Austria and Germany.

Appease: To make concessions in order to prevent conflict.

Armistice: An end to fighting. A cease fire before a peace treaty has been signed.

Balkans: The area of land in South Eastern Europe which is nowadays made up of the countries of Albania, Bosnia, Croatia, Montenegro, Greece and Serbia.

BENELUX: A grouping of Belgium, the Netherlands and Luxembourg.

Blitzkrieg: 'Lightening War.' Tactics used by Germany during the Second World War.

Blockade: When a country in blocked in, or surrounded, usually by ships, preventing supplies getting in.

Bolshevik: Early name of the Russian Communist Party.

Bombardment: A large scale bombing or shelling operation.

Capitalism: A system of running an economy which relies on private business and 'Free Enterprise.'

Collective Security: The principal by which countries join together in an alliance or organisation to provide for each others' security from attack by another.

Colonies: Land or countries which belongs to a 'mother' country.

Commonwealth: The group of countries which had been the British Empire and which chose to carry on their ties with Britain in the form of membership of a free association of countries, called a Commonwealth.

Communism: A system of running a country based upon the rule of a Communist Party and the idea of State ownership of agriculture and industry.

Conciliation: A way of resolving disagreement through talking and making concessions.

Conscientious Objector: A person who refused military service on the grounds of their beliefs.

Conscription: When people are made to join the armed forces of their country.

Convoy: A line of (usually) ships travelling together for safety.

Coup d'etat: Armed rising and take over of the government of a country, usually resulting in a change of leader.

Democracy: A system of running a country's government which relies on involving the ordinary people, eg by holding elections.

Détente: An easing of tensions between two or more countries and a move towards better relations.

Diplomat: An official representative of one country to another.

Diplomatic: A way of trying to solve a problem by use of the correct procedures and without making it worse.

Economy: The way a country earns or creates wealth.

Empire: Land and people taken over by one country and ruled over by it.

Enlist: To join the armed forces, the airforce, army or navy.

Fascist: The right wing extremist party of Mussolini in Italy, but also applied to other extremist parties of the right such as the Nazis.

Free Elections: Elections which give the people real choice of candidate and party, in which voting is secret, there is no intimidation and the results are not 'fixed'.

Free Enterprise: See Capitalist.

Front: A military term for an area of fighting, ie Western Front; Russian Front.

Great Depression: A period of high unemployment and falling standards of living that affected many areas of the world following the Wall Street Crash in the USA in 1929.

Guerrilla: Literally 'small war.' Usually used to describe the tactics used by irregular 'peoples' armies' against more powerful opposition, (ambush, hit and run, raids, etc.) For example, the methods used by Tito against the Germans in the Second World War and by the Vietnamese against the French and American troops in Vietnam.

Holocaust: Literally, death and destruction from fire. Usually applied to the destruction of the Jews in Nazi Germany.

Imperial: Any thing of or about an Empire, eg 'Imperial forces' are the forces of the Empire.

Independence: The right of a nation to rule itself and to be responsible for all its own affairs.

Intifada: Resistance of Palestinian Muslims to Israel's occupation of the Gaza Strip and West Bank.

Isolation: Alone. Outside of an alliance, conflict or group.

Lebensraum: 'Living space', specifically this refers to Hitler's aim to expand Germany eastward into Czechoslovakia, Poland and the USSR.

Left wing: In politics; Socialists and Communists.

Lend-Lease: System by which the USA aided Great Britain and the USSR during the Second World War.

Liberal: Political attitude which is in favour of personal freedoms, elections, etc.

Nationality: The ethnic, religious and cultural identity which makes a group of people feel like a nation.

Nazi: The National Socialist Party of Germany led by Adolf Hitler.

Negotiated peace: When the countries involved in a conflict or war, come together to decide the terms of peace.

Offensive: Military term for a large scale attack.

Pacifist: A person who believes in peace and non-violent methods of resolving disagreements.

Pact: An agreement made between each country.

Plebiscite: When a decision is put directly to the people for them to choose. They would usually do this by voting for or against. Eg the 'referendum' held in Britain in 1975 to decide whether Britain should remain inside the EEC.

Post: After, eg 'Post War', after the war.

Propaganda: Deliberate use of publicity campaign to get people to believe a particular interpretation.

Refugees: People who have lost their homes and their homeland, usually due to war or natural disaster.

Reparations: Payments made by one country to another after a war, to compensate for damage done during the war.

Right wing: In politics; Conservatives, Christian Democrats and (at the extreme) Fascists.

Sanctions: Measures which can be used to influence or to punish.

Satellite: Politically; when one country is dominated by a larger, more powerful near neighbour.

Treaty: An official agreement signed by a number of countries, detailing agreements they have made. It may come at the end of a war (eg the Treaty of Versailles, 1919) or it may begin a movement or association of countries (eg the Treaty of Rome, 1957, which began the EEC.)

Territorial Adjustments: Changes in borders between countries, often made in a Treaty after a war.

Unanimous: A decision made in which everybody has agreed.

Veto: When one vote against can stop something from happening.

Western Powers: The western democracies, especially the USA, Britain and France after the Second World War.

*I*ndex